DATE DUE			

Folger Documents of Tudor and Stuart Civilization

THE EXECUTION OF JUSTICE IN ENGLAND

❦

A TRUE, SINCERE, AND MODEST DEFENSE OF ENGLISH CATHOLICS

FOLGER DOCUMENTS

OF TUDOR AND STUART CIVILIZATION

This volume is one of a series of publications of Tudor and Stuart documents that the Folger Library proposes to bring out. These documents will consist of hitherto unprinted manuscripts as well as reprints of rare books in the Folger Library. An effort will be made to choose significant items that will throw light on the social and intellectual background of the period from 1485 to 1715. In response to almost unanimous requests of interested historians, the spelling, punctuation, and capitalization will be modernized in printed texts. In some cases, where the original printing is clear and easily read, texts may be photographically reproduced. The Folger Library is prepared to supply microfilm of original texts to scholars who require a facsimile.

The Execution *of* Justice *in* England

BY WILLIAM CECIL

AND

A True, Sincere, *and* Modest Defense *of* English Catholics

BY WILLIAM ALLEN

EDITED BY

Robert M. Kingdon

PUBLISHED FOR

The Folger Shakespeare Library

BY

CORNELL UNIVERSITY PRESS

Ithaca, New York

CORNELL UNIVERSITY PRESS

First published 1965

Library of Congress Catalog Card Number: 65-17623

PRINTED IN THE UNITED STATES OF AMERICA
BY VAIL-BALLOU PRESS, INC.

PREFACE

THIS edition is based upon copies of *The Execution of Justice in England* and the *Defense of English Catholics* in the collection of the Folger Shakespeare Library. It follows the editorial rules adopted for this entire series of Folger reprints. The particular copy of *The Execution of Justice in England* which I have used is Folger Copy I of STC 4903. It is of the second English edition of this pamphlet and includes in the same binding the *Declaration of the Favorable Dealing of Her Majesty's Commissioners.* I have used the second edition in preference to the first because it is clearly the one which Allen used in preparing his *Defense.* Allen refers both to the appended *Declaration* (see p. 70 below) and to facts which are not contained in the first edition (e.g., pp. 109–110 below). I have, however, collated this copy with one of the first edition, Folger Copy I of STC 4902. Some of the results of the collation are indicated in my text. Passages and words which can be found only in the second edition are enclosed in brackets. Minor differences which appear from the collation, like changes in tense of verbs or of number in nouns, are not indicated in my text. Later reprintings of both original editions are widely available. Copies of the second edition are included in the *Somers Tracts, The Harleian Miscellany,* and Holinshed's *Chronicles,* with the appended *Declaration* included in the former two.[1] A

[1] *A Collection of Scarce and Valuable Tracts . . . in . . . Libraries, Particularly That of the Late Lord Somers,* ed. by Walter Scott, I (2nd ed., London, 1809), 189–212; *The Harleian Miscellany,* I (London: Robert

facsimile reprint of the first edition, with an introduction by Franklin Baumer, was printed in New York in 1938. None of these later printings contains much annotation.

The particular copy of the *Defense of English Catholics* which I have used is the Folger copy, STC 373. It once belonged to the great seventeenth-century English antiquary Roger Twysden and on its title page bears his signature and the date 1647. It also contains the beginnings of a hand-written index, on extra sheets of paper which precede the title page in this binding. Its printed text is frequently underlined and is occasionally accompanied by ink marks in the margins. These margins also contain a large number of printed running comments on the text. Most of these printed marginalia merely summarize the contents of the paragraphs to which they are adjacent, and these I have omitted in this edition. Others provide additional information or indicate the sources of Allen's references, and these I have included, in brackets, in my footnotes. Errors indicated by the *Defense*'s own printed table of errata have been corrected. The Table of Contents has been rearranged slightly and incorporated in the general table for this volume rather than being left in the back of the book, its location in the original edition. There is a modernized reprinting of the *Defense*, published in two volumes in *The Catholic Library* (London, 1914). It was obviously prepared in haste, however, and contains some inaccuracies in transcription and almost no annotation.

My footnotes to both works normally do not give sources for general information which can be obtained easily and reliably from such obvious and widely available works of reference as the *Dictionary of National Biography*, the *Encyclopaedia Britannica*, the *Catholic Encyclopedia*, and the Cambridge Medieval and Modern Histories. Neither do they give sources for information on the Catholic missionaries to England which can easily be

---

Dutton, 1808), 489–517; *Holinshed's Chronicles of England, Scotland, and Ireland*, IV (London, 1808), 515–533.

obtained from the J. H. Pollen edition of Richard Challoner's *Memoirs of Missionary Priests,* and from Joseph Gillow's *Bibliographical Dictionary of the English Catholics.* Gillow's work I have used sparingly, however, since, as all experts on this subject are aware, it contains frequent errors of fact.

For the sake of uniformity, I have used the 1611 Authorized (King James) Version of the Bible for all biblical allusions identified in my footnotes. This has required occasional departures from Allen's practice in the numbering of verses and in the spelling of proper names. In translating Allen's quotations from the Latin Vulgate Bible, I have always provided the wording of the Authorized Version rather than fresh translations.

In identifying allusions to the Church Fathers and to such other widely republished works as Foxe's *Book of Martyrs* and Bodin's *Republic,* I have limited my references to book and chapter and have not specified page numbers, which vary from edition to edition. In cases in which there are differences among editions in the numbering of works by the Church Fathers, as in the numberings of their letters, I have followed the order adopted in the Migne *Patrologiae.* These are, of course, the most complete and most useful editions of the Fathers, even if they are not always the best. Most of the allusions made by both Allen and Cecil can also be found in the conveniently abridged and translated editions of the Fathers directed by Schaff and Wace.

As in all editions in this series, spelling, punctuation, and capitalization have been modernized. This has necessarily introduced a few minor ambiguities into my transcriptions which may displease purists, but it should make the edition much more widely useful, particularly to students and those who are not specialists. My general guide for spelling and definition of words was the unabridged version of Webster's Third New International Dictionary. Where it did not supply enough information on meanings, I used the Oxford English Dictionary.

Acknowledgments

My first and greatest debt is to the late Garrett Mattingly. From him I received most of my graduate training in historical research, and from him I absorbed much of whatever grace or wisdom in the interpretation of history I possess. He also first called to my attention the importance of the career of William Allen and of his *Defense of English Catholics*. Shortly before his sudden death, he suggested that I edit this work, along with *The Execution of Justice in England.*

That his suggestion bore fruit is due in large part to the Folger Shakespeare Library, its staff, and its Fellows. I am grateful to them all for the relaxed, stimulating, and profitable summer I spent at the Folger in 1963, working on this edition. And I am particularly grateful to Dr. Louis B. Wright, director of the Library, for inviting me to include this edition in the Folger Documents Series, to Virginia A. LaMar, for reading through my entire typescript and making many valuable suggestions for its improvement, and to Dorothy E. Mason, for help in unraveling some of my problems in identifying sources.

This edition and I also owe a good deal to graduate students in history at the State University of Iowa. James R. King, as my research assistant, prepared a modernized draft of the *Defense of English Catholics,* and Francis E. Fowler, his successor as my research assistant, prepared a typed copy of the entire edition. Mary T. Anglim, my current research assistant, has helped in correcting proofs and compiling the index. Students in one of my graduate seminars, Jack Allen, J. Wayne Baker, Weldon S. Crowley, Thomas J. Goss, and James R. King, gathered much of the material needed for annotation of the edition. I have checked over all this material personally, however, and all blame for any remaining omissions or errors must be mine.

ROBERT M. KINGDON

Iowa City, Iowa

CONTENTS

INTRODUCTION

THE two short books reprinted in this volume illustrate a problem which has bedeviled western civilization throughout its history, that of dual allegiance. It is the problem, to paraphrase Holy Scripture, of what one owes to God and of what one owes to Caesar. It is the problem, to state it in modern terms, of what one owes to the society of which one is a part and of what one owes to those forces in life which transcend any particular period or place. This problem was forced, in a peculiarly painful way, upon many of the English subjects of Queen Elizabeth I by that great revolution in sixteenth-century society, the Reformation. Because of the Reformation, men in every part of Europe had to choose between rival ways of explaining and organizing the Christian religion. That choice often also forced secondary choices, between rival forms of society and between rival rulers of government.

In Elizabethan England, this critical decision took the shape of a choice between Rome and Westminster—between, on the one hand, a church and international society presided over by the Bishop of Rome, the Pope, the lineal descendant, according to Catholic tradition, of the Apostle Peter; and, on the other hand, a church and national society presided over by the Queen, the only "Supreme Governor" under Christ of the Church in England, according to act of Parliament. This choice forced fusions of loyalties that earlier had been separate. It tore apart other loyalties that had long been fused. The result, inevitably, was considerable personal anguish and a social turmoil which mixed together politics and religion in all sorts of ways. Many Englishmen did not believe it possible to remain loyal to both the Pope and the Queen. Many devout Roman Catholics became absolutely convinced that the true worship of Christ, under the direction of his only true vicar on earth, the Pope, could never be restored in England without the overthrow of the heretical government of Elizabeth I, by armed force if necessary. And many loyal subjects of the Queen felt that the government of England and the valuable way of life which it maintained would never be secure until every trace of this international subversive conspiracy, the Roman Catholic Church, directed by a malicious foreign prince, the Pope, was wiped out of England.

Emotions did not reach this intensity immediately upon the accession of Elizabeth I. When she had become Queen in 1558 upon the death of her older sister, Mary, the nation had slipped with relative ease and peacefulness from the militant Catholicism chosen for it by Mary to the bland Protestantism favored by Elizabeth. Englishmen in all walks of life, including many in the clergy, who had become Anglo-Catholics during the reign of Henry VIII, had turned militant Protestants under Edward VI, and returned to militant Catholicism under Mary, found it relatively simple to make one more switch. The change involved a few complications, to be sure, particularly for members of the clergy. Those in the Marian church hierarchy who had been most enthusiastically in favor of the return to Rome and the industrious persecution of all who remained Protestant could not with decency make yet another switch. Most of them resigned their influential and lucrative appointments and retired to their country estates. Many of them lived out their lives in more or less elegant house arrest. But there was very little attempt in these early years to prevent the development of a Protestant religious settlement. And there was consequently very little need on the part of the government to treat domestic Catholics with the rigor which was the common treatment governments applied to their subjects of another religion in that period.

All this changed midway through the reign of Elizabeth I. It changed because of the rising tide of religious enthusiasm known as the Catholic Counter Reformation. This movement, while it can be traced back to impulses toward reform which preceded the Protestant Reformation, had really taken shape in the 1530's and 1540's among certain idealistic young churchmen in and about Rome. It had won control of the administrative apparatus of the Roman Catholic Church during the pontificate of Pope Paul III. It had elaborated a program of belief and action for the entire Roman Catholic Church during the long and arduous sessions of the ecumenical Council of Trent, which concluded eighteen years of periodic deliberations in 1563. It had created new orders of dedicated and determined religious, the most famous of which was the Society of Jesus. During the 1560's and 1570's this militant new reform movement spread throughout Europe. It even penetrated Protestant England. Particularly at Oxford University, the older of the two great nurseries of the English elite, idealistic students heard whispers of the exciting new ideas spreading from Rome. Some among them were so fired with curiosity that they traveled to the Catholic Continent to learn more. Their interest and their yearning for action were soon channeled into a number of new educational institutions created precisely for this purpose. Pre-eminent among these institutions was the seminary at Douai, in the Spanish Netherlands, only a short distance from the narrow channel which separates England from the Continent. At Douai these students found a leader fully capable of developing and guiding their enthusiasm. He was Dr. William Allen, later appointed Cardinal of England.

William Allen had originally come of a modestly comfortable family in Lancashire. He had received his early education at Oxford during the reigns of Edward and Mary and had moved to the Continent soon after the accession of Elizabeth. But he had returned to England at least once and had kept in close touch with developments in his native country. And he turned out to be an ideal choice for the job of directing the new Douai seminary. For William Allen possessed many of the traits which characterized great leaders during the age of the Reformation. He was a formidable scholar, particularly in biblical studies, and was in important ways responsible for the Douai-Reims translation of the Bible into English, a translation still widely used by Catholics of the English-speaking world. He was a brilliant and effective polemicist, whose cutting prose, perhaps at its best in the book edited for this volume, could infuriate his enemies and delight his followers. He was a skillful and resourceful intriguer, who knew how to gain access to the great movers of the world of his day—the Pope, the King of Spain, the Dukes of Guise in France—and how to enlist their support for his projects. He usually had the good sense to avoid the more inflammatory sorts of polemic and the more harebrained kinds of intrigue favored by activists of that period, which often did more harm than good to whatever cause they were supposed to advance. And he was a natural leader of men. He had the intensity and enthusiasm to gather men around him and he possessed the tact and patience to persuade them to work together. In many ways he reminds one in temperament and impact of certain Protestant leaders of his century whose very memory he despised, for example, John Calvin.

The great practical purpose for which William Allen created the Douai seminary was to launch a Mission to England. Hundreds of the eager young exiles from England were to be fully educated as priests. The ablest among them were to be sent to Rome for more advanced training, and many of these were to be inducted into the Society of Jesus. When training was complete they were to be smuggled back into England, where their very presence was illegal. There they were to nourish the Roman Catholic faith in those scattered pockets where it had been able to survive and to persuade the uncertain masses who conformed to the requirements of the Church of England that sure salvation could be found only in communion with Rome. It was hoped that ultimately they could usher England back to the bosom of the Mother Church.

A first group of these missionaries to England, headed by the Jesuits Robert Parsons and Edmund Campion, were smuggled into their native country in the summer of 1580. Their arrival suddenly made the problem of dual allegiance acute. The leaders of the Elizabethan government were certain that the missionary priests came as spies and traitors, determined to overthrow the government by force. Allen and the others who sent them insisted that they came only for religious purposes—to celebrate the sacraments and to reconcile Englishmen peacefully to the only true Church of Christ. These two sharply opposing points of view were developed publicly, forcefully, and authoritatively in the two books which make up this volume.

The claim that the Mission to England was in fact treasonous is advanced by *The Execution of Justice in England.* This book, although slight in size and crabbed in style, was of great importance. It was widely circulated and possessed an official character. Evidence of its wide circulation is provided by its publication history. A first edition was published, according to its own title page, on December 17, 1583. A second, slightly expanded and revised, with *A Declaration of the Favorable Dealing of Her Majesty's Commissioners* appended to it, was published, again according to its title page, in January, 1583, Old Style (1584, New Style). Neither edition bears the name of a printer, but both carry the mark and use the type of Christopher Barker, an official printer to the Queen.[1] A translation into Latin was published,

[1] Barker is also apparently identified as the printer in a passage in *A Transcript of the Registers of the Company of Stationers of London, 1554–1640 A.D.*, ed. by Edward Arber (5 vols., London and Birmingham,

according to its title page, by Thomas Vautrollerius of London, in March, 1584. Further translations, into French and Dutch, were published in 1584. An Italian translation was published in 1589.[2] Yet other translations may have been published. Father Parsons, writing in 1584, speaks not only of the English, Latin, and French versions but also of ones in German and Italian as having already appeared.[3]

Evidence of the official character of *The Execution of Justice in England* is provided by the identity of its author. While none of the many editions of the book bears any indication of its writer, we can be quite certain that it was William Cecil, Lord Burghley, the most important single person in the government of Elizabeth I throughout the early decades of her reign. Contemporaries, including a diplomat in the service of the English government, W. Herle, and a usually well-informed opponent, Father Parsons, identify Cecil as the author.[4] A historian writing soon after the period, John Strype, reported seeing a draft of the entire *Execution* in Cecil's own hand.[5] A modern historian, Conyers Read,

---

1875–1894), II, 429: "2 January [1584]. Master Barker. Received of him for a book printed by commandment touching the state &c. . . . vj*d*." For other entries in these registers, which do not mention the printer but do indicate titles and dates of the several editions, see V, Index, nos. 2930, 2931, 3043, 3125.

[2] These four translations carry STC nos. 4904–4907.

[3] Parsons to Aquaviva, July 23, 1584, in Robert Parsons, *Letters and Memorials of Father Robert Persons, S.J.* (hereafter cited as Parsons, *Letters*), ed. by L. Hicks, S.J., I (London, 1942), 220, 223. Purists may prefer the spelling "Persons," but "Parsons" seems to be used more widely.

[4] W. Herle to the Queen, July 22 [1584], in *Calendar of State Papers* (hereafter cited as *CSP*), *Foreign, 1583–1584,* p. 628; Parsons to Agazzari, December 13, 1584, in Parsons, *Letters,* I, 266–268.

[5] John Strype, *Annals of the Reformation and Establishment of Religion, and Other Various Occurrences in the Church of England, during Queen Elizabeth's Happy Reign* (hereafter cited as Strype, *Annals*) (Oxford, 1824), III, pt. I, 706; cited by Conyers Read, "William Cecil and Elizabethan Public Relations" (hereafter cited as Read, "Public Relations"), in *Elizabethan Government and Society: Essays Presented to Sir John Neale,* ed. by S. T. Bindoff, J. Hurstfield, and C. H. Williams (London, 1961), p. 37.

could not find this complete draft but did find many parts of a draft by Cecil scattered through the Domestic State Papers in the Public Record Office.[6]

Opinion is somewhat less unanimous about the authorship of the *Declaration* which is appended to *The Execution of Justice.* Read believes that it is not the work of Cecil but rather of Thomas Norton, a Puritan pamphleteer whose attacks on Catholicism were occasionally sponsored by the government.[7] His argument is based in part, however, on the claim that the two were not combined until the publication of the Latin edition in March, 1584. In fact they were combined in the second English edition of January, 1584.

The argument of *The Execution of Justice* begins with a reminder of two recent armed revolts against the government of Elizabeth I. One was the Rising in the North, directed by the Earls of Westmorland and Northumberland in 1569. The other was the invasion of Ireland by a group of English Catholic exiles in 1579. Both had been easily stamped out by troops loyal to the Queen. But both revolts, Cecil insists, had been instigated by the Pope. The northern earls had revolted after secret consultations with a special papal agent who had been smuggled into England; their revolt had been accompanied by the formal promulgation in Rome of a papal bull, *Regnans in excelsis,* which declared Elizabeth to be excommunicate and absolved all English subjects from their allegiance to her. The invaders of Ireland had been gathered and were partially financed by the papal state in Italy; they carried the Pope's battle flags as they stormed ashore on the Irish coast; they were accompanied by a specially appointed papal nuncio, the incendiary polemicist Nicholas Sanders. All of

[6] Read, "Public Relations," p. 37; Conyers Read, *Lord Burghley and Queen Elizabeth* (hereafter cited as Read, *Burghley*) (London [1960]), p. 566, n. 76.

[7] Read, "Public Relations," p. 37; Read, *Burghley,* pp. 251 and 566, n. 75.

these facts were widely known and easy to demonstrate. Cecil does not dwell upon them at length.

What he does dwell upon is the connection, crucial to his argument, between these bloody revolts against the government and the Mission to England. He insists that the missionary priests trained by Allen and led into England by Parsons and Campion were in fact engaged upon a military errand. He quotes Sanders to the effect that the earlier revolts had failed only because the great number of loyal Catholics still residing in England had not known that the Pope had excommunicated the Queen and absolved them from all allegiance to her government. Cecil claims the Mission to England was organized primarily to remedy this earlier mistake, to make sure that the Catholics of England all knew that Elizabeth had been deposed by the Pope and that they were under religious obligation to rise in revolt against her at the earliest feasible moment. In short, the missionary priests had been sent to England as advance agents for an invading army. While they were not, to be sure, clad in armor, carrying battle flags, or swinging battle-axes, they were as truly a part of an invading army as the saboteurs who would open its way or the scouts who would direct its movements. The priests' function was as covert and as pernicious as that of these other auxiliaries of an army. It was to recruit fighting men within England and to give them the signal when the time actually came for revolt to begin.

When it came to providing hard evidence for this central claim, however, Cecil had to scratch a bit. He quotes part of the papal bull of deposition issued back in 1570. He rehearses the story of the promulgation in London of the bull by a rash young zealot who posted a copy upon the door of the Bishop of London's palace and was quickly seized and executed for this temerity. He quotes the "faculties" granted to Parsons and Campion by the reigning Pope shortly before the Mission was launched, which temporarily suspended the application of the bull among English Catholics—apparently evidence, to Cecil, that they had been sent to inform the English about the bull and prepare the way for its eventual implementation. But above all Cecil relies upon evidence extracted under torture from Campion and certain members of his party who had been seized and imprisoned by the government shortly after their clandestine arrival in England. This evidence had been made public in a show treason trial which had ended predictably in the gruesome public execution of Campion and most of his associates. It consisted of a series of evasive answers to a series of "bloody" questions, some of them hypothetical, forcing the prisoners to state choices between allegiance to the Queen and allegiance to the Pope in a variety of actual or possible situations.[8]

Some of this part of Cecil's argument boils down to an attack upon the papal power of deposing rulers. Like practically all convinced Protestants, he did not really believe that any important general ecclesiastical power should be vested in the Bishop of Rome. Even if the Pope might lay some claim to spiritual powers, Cecil felt certain that he had no right to temporal powers of a sort which would permit him to intervene in the politics of any Christian nation. This he felt to be demonstrated clearly by the Holy Scriptures, by the medieval history of the Christian Church, and by the advice of such of its great saints as Gregory the Great and Bernard of Clairvaux.

Much of the rest of Cecil's argument is designed to counter criticism of the severity his government had displayed in its persecution of these missionary priests. He insists at several points that they had not been punished for their religious beliefs. In support of this contention, he supplies a list of the many distinguished Marian prelates who had simply been permitted to retire without punishment at the accession of Elizabeth, many of

[8] See *Cobbett's Complete Collection of State Trials,* I (London, 1809), cols. 1049–1084, for a complete record of the Campion trial. The "bloody" questions and the prisoners' answers are printed in cols. 1078–1084. A record of the confession and execution of John Felton, who posted the papal bull of 1570 in London, is added in cols. 1085–1088.

whom were still living in relatively peaceful seclusion, in spite of their obstinate devotion to Catholic dogma and their illegal refusal to accept the Queen as governor of the Church in England.

Cecil insists further that the Catholic missionaries who had been arrested upon their recent return to England had been treated with the greatest possible leniency. He contrasts the slow and circumspect procedures of his own government with the quick and wholesale execution of batches of Protestants by the preceding government of Mary. To make the point vivid he recalls, with almost indecent relish, gory details of some of the more striking atrocities perpetrated by that government. The most striking is the story of a pregnant young woman who, while tied to the stake and being burnt for heresy, gave birth, and whose baby was sadistically thrown back into the very flames which were consuming its mother.

In the *Declaration* appended to *The Execution of Justice* this argument of leniency is developed one step farther, to a point, in fact, where it begins to strain credulity. Its author argues that the torture used on Campion and certain of his fellow prisoners was unusually mild. He goes into substantial detail upon the reasons torture had to be used and the care with which the decision to use it was reached. He dwells further upon the slowness, the reluctance, and the relative gentleness with which Campion and others were stretched on the rack or otherwise mutilated. All of this, I should suppose, must seem a bit forced to most modern readers.

The Execution of Justice in England, and its official claim that the Mission to England was treasonous, was countered directly and quickly by the second work which makes up this volume, *A True, Sincere, and Modest Defense of English Catholics.* This formal retort is much longer than Cecil's work. In style and erudition it is quite an improvement upon his book. It is written trenchantly and vigorously, with occasional flights of eloquence. Study of its references makes clear that its author's command of relevant examples from Holy Scripture and ecclesiastical history is much more precise and detailed than Cecil's. Yet its real importance stems again from the fact that it was widely circulated and possessed an official character of a sort. No direct evidence of this comes from the book itself, since it was printed without any indication of author, date, place of publication, or printer. But such evidence can be found in the collected correspondence of Father Parsons and Dr. Allen, corroborated by reports to the English government from one of its diplomats on the Continent. These sources make it clear that the author of the book was William Allen.[9] Since it was thus the work of the most responsible leader produced by the English Catholic community in exile, it obviously represents, in an important way, the official view of that community. The book was first published in English, early in August, 1584, and copies were quickly smuggled into England—one of the first going to Mary, Queen of Scots, the Catholic candidate for the throne of England should Elizabeth's reign end soon, then under house arrest.[10] A translation into Latin was ready within months, probably by the beginning of December, 1584,[11] and a translation into Italian was projected.[12] Copies of the Latin version were quickly presented to prominent church officials, notably the papal nuncio in Paris, who forwarded one

[9] *The Letters and Memorials of William Cardinal Allen (1532–1594)* (hereafter cited as Allen, *Letters*), ed. by Fathers of the Congregation of the London Oratory (London, 1882), pp. 14, 239–240, 243–244, 424; Stafford to Walsingham, August 24, 1584, and Stafford to Burghley, September 18, 1584, *CSP, Foreign, 1584–1585*, pp. 33, 68.

[10] Mary Stuart to William Allen, October 30, 1584, in Allen, *Letters*, pp. 243–244, acknowledges receipt of a copy mailed to her on August 14.

[11] Parsons to Agazzari, November 12, 1584, in Parsons, *Letters*, p. 259, expresses regret that the printing, evidently of the Latin edition, had not as yet been completed. Parsons to Agazzari, December 13, 1584, in *ibid.*, pp. 266–268, states that copies of the Latin translation had been sent to Agazzari.

[12] See Parsons to Aquaviva, July 23, 1584, in Parsons, *Letters*, pp. 220, 223.

to Rome for the perusal of the Pope.[13] The precise place at which this book was published remains somewhat mysterious. The best guess seems to be that it was run off by Father Parsons' press in Rouen, a good spot for the preparation and export of clandestine books to England. Father Parsons' letters reveal that he followed the preparation and the printing of the *Defense of English Catholics* quite carefully. My examination of its typography, particularly of the large illuminated letters, convinces me that it was printed by the same press which produced Father Parsons' *Christian Directory* of 1585. My examination of other books attributed to Father Parsons' press by bibliographers, however, makes me quite certain that they came from some other press or presses.[14] Furthermore, a contemporary English diplomat sent to London a report that the *Defense* had been printed in Reims, where Dr. Allen and the seminary were then temporarily located.[15] To confuse things still further, the same diplomat included in this dispatch a second report, less reliable in his view, that the book had been printed in Germany.

Allen's immediate and explicit purpose in writing his book was

[13] Parsons to Agazzari, December 13, 1584, in Parsons, *Letters,* pp. 266–268; Ragazzoni, nuncio in Paris, to the Cardinal of Como, papal secretary of state, December 11, 1584, in *Girolamo Ragazzoni, évêque de Bergame, nonce en France: Correspondance de sa Nonciature, 1583–1586,* ed. by Pierre Blet (Rome, Paris, 1962), 341–342.

[14] For attributions of the *Defense,* the *Christian Directory,* and other books to Father Parsons' press in Rouen, see A. F. Allison and D. M. Rogers, "A Catalogue of Catholic Books in English Printed Abroad or Secretly in England, 1558–1640," *Biographical Studies* (now *Recusant History*), III, 3 and 4 (Bognor Regis, 1956), item no. 13 (*Defense*); items nos. 619 and 621 (*Christian Directory*), *et al.,* as indicated by index. For the earlier history of this press, see A. C. Southern, *Elizabethan Recusant Prose, 1559–1582* (London and Glasgow [1950]), pp. 353–363. For Parsons' comments on progress in composing the *Defense,* see his *Letters,* pp. 220, 223, 226, 229–230, 236, 255, 259, 266–268. *STC* attributes the *Defense* to a press in Ingolstadt.

[15] Stafford to Walsingham, August 24, 1584, in *CSP, Foreign, 1584–1585,* p. 33. On May 30, however, Stafford had reported to Walsingham that the book was to be printed in Rouen (*ibid., 1583–1584,* p. 522).

to provide a direct, point-by-point refutation of *The Execution of Justice*. Much of the tone and structure of the *Defense of English Catholics* is accordingly determined by this goal. It begins with a direct challenge to Cecil's contention that English Catholics were being put to death for treason alone. Allen cites a number of recent cases in which no political charge was made. He observes that many of the Catholics recently haled into court had been tried under recent laws which expanded the definition of treason in ways which were unprecedented and can fairly be described as unreasonable. It had become treason, for example, to bring into England any copy of a papal bull or dispensation, even if it dealt with some trivial disciplinary matter. It had become treason to "reconcile" or convert any Anglican back to Roman Catholicism. It had been made difficult, and then illegal, to go abroad for advanced study. It had become illegal to bring into England any religious object obtained in Rome—any crucifix, any rosary, any "Agnus Dei" or cake of wax stamped with a figure of a lamb and blessed by the Pope. All of these expanded definitions of treason and sedition surely exceeded the intentions of the drafters of the fourteenth-century statute under which Campion and his fellows had been tried and convicted. They had been adopted by the government to provide objective tests of disloyalty that could be of use to courts and government officials. But it was easy to argue, as Allen does, that they in fact shifted the grounds of persecution from political to religious ones.

If Allen had rested his case at this point, it would have seemed reasonably convincing, particularly to modern readers. But he did not. And he probably could not. To make of his case nothing but a plea for religious toleration would have meant abandoning many of the claims which the sixteenth-century Roman Catholic Church still felt essential to its mission on earth. It would also have meant abandoning many of the specific projects for winning England back for his church to which Allen was already committed.

Allen could not, to begin with, argue for toleration in any general or logical way. For he did not believe in toleration of all religious points of view. He particularly did not believe in toleration of the contemporary Protestant variants of heresy. This he makes quite clear in Chapter III, which compares the persecution of Protestants under Mary to the current persecution of Catholics by Elizabeth. The Marian persecution was fully legal and fully justified, Allen argues, because heresy had generally been illegal for centuries in all Christian countries and was specifically illegal under prevailing English law. Mary's government was simply applying clear and obvious law when it delivered hundreds of obstinate Protestants to the flames. His case basically rests upon this contention, although it does include some rhetorical attacks upon the social standing and character of the Protestant victims Cecil held up for commiseration. In contrast, the Elizabethan government had no legal right to put Catholics to death. Since it wiped all laws against heresy off the books early in the Queen's reign, there was no law proscribing any aberrant form of Christianity. Even if there were English laws against heresy, they could not apply to Catholics, for Christians remaining in full obedience to Rome could not, by definition, be classified as heretics.

Allen could not, furthermore, deny the Pope's right to depose heretic princes. Nor did he wish to do so. He does argue that the 1570 bull deposing Elizabeth was not at that time in effect, for Catholics, so that English Catholics were not then under orders to rise in revolt against her government. But the bull's threat of deposition had only been suspended, not canceled, and it would hang over Elizabeth's head like a sword of Damocles until she could be persuaded to rejoin the only true church. The power to depose, Allen contends, had been granted to the first Pope, St. Peter, according to Holy Scripture. It remains, he insists, inherent in the papal office. This argument is developed at length in a part of Chapter IV and in the bulk of Chapter V. It is there supported by elaborate references not only to Scripture but also to canon law, the ecclesiastical history of antiquity and the Middle Ages, and the reasoning of such great systematic theologians as St. Thomas Aquinas. It is even supported, in a rather surprising excursus toward the end of Chapter IV, by references to a number of prominent Protestant theologians.[16] Allen had gathered a series of carefully selected quotations from the writings of Luther, Zwingli, Calvin, Beza, John Knox, and Christopher Goodman. He uses this evidence to make the point that the occasional right to resist secular government upon religious grounds is claimed by every Christian group that creates an accepted place for itself in established human society. He also uses it to demolish the contention, dear to many of his Anglican opponents, that Protestants make loyal and obedient subjects while Catholics are perverse troublemakers.

This particular part of Allen's argument drew the most fire from his opponents in England. Most prominent among these was Thomas Bilson, the warden of Winchester. He had already been preparing a formal refutation of Allen's *An Apology and True Declaration of the Institution and Endeavors of the Two English Colleges* (STC 369) when two other books in whose making Allen had a part appeared. One was the Reims New Testament (STC 2884), with its detailed glosses on the Scripture text so fundamental to all Protestant argument. The other was the *Defense of English Catholics.* Bilson accordingly decided to expand his volume to include refutation of all three. The result is a tome, massive for a polemic, titled *The True Difference between Christian Subjection and Unchristian Rebellion,* published in Oxford, 1585, and London, 1586 (STC 3071, 3072). That part of *The True Difference* devoted to refutation of the *Defense of English Catholics* is limited almost entirely to an examination of the last

[16] For further analysis of this excursus, see Robert M. Kingdon, "William Allen's Use of Protestant Political Argument," in the forthcoming volume, *From the Renaissance to the Counter Reformation: Essays in Honor of Garrett Mattingly,* ed. by Charles H. Carter (New York, 1965), pp. 164–178.

part of Chapter IV and the bulk of Chapter V. This limitation was quite deliberate and explicit. Bilson justifies it in his introduction with these words:

Only the Pope's power to deprive princes, which with all his skill, learning, and eloquence he [Allen] seeketh to prove and persuade to the people of this realm (as the chiefest bulwark of their *Defense*, that were condemned, he saith for religion, we say for treason, and indeed the very ground of all their actions), I thought needful to examine, and to let the simple see on what a sandy slime they have built as well their consciences as their colleges, and in how wretched and unrighteous a quarrel they have hazarded their lives in this world and their souls in the next, to enlarge the power and make up the purse of their Rhemish founder. Taking that therefore in hand I have word by word refelled the fifth chapter of their *Defense* which purposely treateth of this matter; and inserted so much of the fourth as tended to this end, the rest being a voluntary pang of their unbridled eloquence.[17]

Bilson lived up to his promise to provide a word-by-word refutation. In his long and laborious third chapter he exposes again and again the relative hastiness, exaggeration, and occasional unfairness of Allen's exegesis of Scripture and history. Bilson's refutation lacked the stylistic flair and the official standing of the writings of Cecil and Allen. But it achieved enough prominence to embarrass later English governments, for it conceded more of a right of resistance than rulers by divine right cared to allow.[18]

To return to the *Defense*, however, it should finally be noted that Allen allows the Pope the right to engage in direct military action against a heretic ruler. This is an argument he develops in Chapter VII. He is careful to distinguish among the kinds of military action in which a Pope may engage. A Pope may, for

[17] From second page of "To the Christian Reader," in front matter of Bilson's *True Difference*.

[18] *Dictionary of National Biography,* "Bilson," V, 43–44. Cecil also tried to arrange for a refutation of the *Defense* by the Puritan pamphleteer John Stubbs. See Strype, *Annals,* II, pt. II, 305–306; III, pt. I, 706–709.

example, form armies and go to war in defense of the states of the Church in central Italy, as one among many Italian princelings. When acting in this capacity, a Pope can lawfully be resisted, and this principle excuses the armed resistance to the Pope undertaken in Italy at various times during the sixteenth century by the King of Spain, the King of France, the Holy Roman Emperor, and other less prominent Catholic sovereigns of Europe. But the Pope may also levy troops and go to war to fulfill his spiritual responsibilities and to enforce certain temporal claims that have accrued to the Popes, not as Italian princes, but as heads of the Church. The recent Irish invasion had been a case in point. Although nominally under the control of England, the vast majority of the Irish had remained loyal to Rome since the beginning of the Reformation. Centuries earlier, furthermore, the Irish had granted to the Pope certain ultimate suzerain rights over their territory. These facts made it right and legal for the Pope to send an actual military force into Ireland if he so decided.

In developing this argument, Allen was parting company with his friend and future colleague in the College of Cardinals, Robert Bellarmine. Bellarmine's theory that the temporal power of the Pope is never rightly exercised directly, but only indirectly, through Catholic princes, had not as yet been published but was being circulated in manuscript and was definitely known to some of the English Catholic exiles. This theory of indirect power soon became an object of controversy within the Roman Curia, with Pope Sixtus V reacting violently against it and threatening to place the book in which it was developed upon the *Index*. When this later controversy developed, Allen was one of several who tried to save Bellarmine from disgrace.[19] But on the issue of whether the Pope had direct temporal power or not, Allen clearly

[19] See James Brodrick, *The Life and Work of Blessed Robert Francis Cardinal Bellarmine, S.J., 1542–1621* (London, 1928), I, ch. 12, re Bellarmine's theory of indirect temporal power; ch. 13, re the attempt to proscribe it; *N.B.* p. 272 on Allen's role.

sided with the faction led by Sixtus, at least in Chapter VII of his *Defense*. This fact deserves emphasis. It forces modification of the view advanced by one recent scholar that Allen's political thought is merely an unsophisticated restatement of Bellarmine's.[20] Unsophisticated it may be, but a mere restatement it is not.

The rival arguments about the Mission to England presented in these two books may seem completely incompatible. Yet it should be possible to evaluate them critically. Their differences stem not only from opposing a priori assumptions. They stem also from differing reports of facts and of law. At least some of these latter differences should be resolvable, given our modern advantages of hindsight, of relative detachment, and of the privileged information from both sides made available by recent research. My own evaluation of these arguments convinces me that both were advanced with a certain lack of frankness. In fact, if one wanted to be brutal, one could accuse both authors of dishonesty.

Cecil's claim that his government put no one to death for religion cannot be altogether convincing. Some of its weaknesses Allen was quick to point out. Many Catholics had been put to death or treated very brutally under laws other than the treason statute used against Campion. Many of these other laws proscribed acts and ideas which few would regard simply as fair "definitions" of treason, which were in fact essentially religious, without any clear connection to politics. Many Catholics who had not been put to death were nevertheless harassed and penalized in other ways. It was illegal, even though the penalties were not exceptionally harsh, to attend mass. It was illegal, similarly, not to attend services of the Church of England periodically.[21] A con-

[20] Thomas H. Clancy, *Papist Pamphleteers: The Allen-Persons Party and the Political Thought of the Counter-Reformation in England, 1572–1615* (Chicago, 1964), pp. 52–54.

[21] For a thoughtful and useful summary of these laws and of their application, see Arnold Oskar Meyer, *England and the Catholic Church under Queen Elizabeth* (London, 1916), pp. 145–189.

scientious Catholic necessarily had to violate both of these provisions of law and consequently had to pay continuing fines. Clearly, the government of Elizabeth wanted to drive Catholicism out of England, even though its ultimate reason for doing so was probably political.

Furthermore, Cecil's claim that Campion and the missionaries had been put to death solely for treason will not bear objective study. The statute under which they were charged was not clearly applicable to their activities. There was little or no hard evidence that they were guilty. None of them could be connected in any direct way with the actual revolts that had already occurred—the Rising in the North and the Irish invasion. None of them could be proved to have ever conspired to overthrow the government or even to have talked much of politics. At most they could be convicted only of being "potential" traitors, who might turn against the Elizabethan government in certain hypothetical circumstances. But such a charge had as little standing then as it has now in any Anglo-Saxon court. It is hard to believe that any rigorously impartial court would have found them guilty. Obviously Cecil and his assistants had them "railroaded."

This, however, leaves open the question of why they did so. Why could Cecil not admit that the missionaries were being put to death for their religion?

There are, to begin with, several fairly obvious prudential reasons for Cecil's decision to prosecute these men for treason rather than for their religion. He could not forget that Englishmen of all persuasions had reacted with hostility against the executions of Protestants on charges of religious deviation alone during the reign of Mary. He had himself profited from this revulsion to rise to power under Elizabeth. The fact was that religious persecution was not particularly popular in England. Cecil could not forget, in addition, that an important group of Englishmen, including such powerful aristocrats as members of the Howard family, remained loyal to Catholicism and would particularly resent violence done to their spiritual leaders. How large or resolute this segment of public opinion within England actually was, Cecil could not know. It tended to remain quiescent and inarticulate, partly because the laws which Cecil had secured made expression of its views dangerous if not illegal. But that this segment was substantial Cecil could not afford to doubt. And he did not want to goad it to desperation and violence by a policy which seemed designed to wipe out Catholic clergy simply because they were Catholic clergy. Cecil also had to keep considerations of foreign policy in mind. England's great rivals in the European-wide game of politics were all Catholic. Some of them were militantly Catholic. If the English government could persuade the King of Spain and the King of France and the Holy Roman Emperor that it persecuted Catholics only on grounds of sedition or treason, it might reasonably hope to escape any threat of foreign intervention. But if these militantly Catholic foreign monarchs got the idea that England was resolved to crush Catholicism at any cost, the country faced the very real possibility of massive intervention, even of armed invasion.[22] And the physical power of these Continental monarchs was such that if any one of them had really set his mind to crushing England, England would have been crushed. This fear of foreign hostility is clearly suggested by the exceptionally wide distribution given to *The Execution of Justice in England.* It explains the many translations of that tract into Continental languages. It explains the fact that English diplomats of the period were supplied with copies for presentation to the governments to which they were accredited.[23] Altogether, such

[22] Cecil may also have wanted to avoid upsetting negotiations to arrange a marriage alliance beween Elizabeth I and the French Duke of Alençon, which had entered a critical stage during the very months he was preparing *The Execution of Justice.* See Read, *Burghley,* pp. 269–271, on these negotiations.

[23] Stafford to Walsingham, March 18, 1584 (N.S.), in *CSP, Foreign, 1583–1584,* p. 418, reports a presentation to the King of France; Herle to the Queen, July 22, 1584, in *ibid.,* p. 628, reports presentations to the Archbishop of Cologne and others. Both report favorable reactions.

prudential considerations create reasons enough to explain why Cecil might not want to be completely straightforward.

But Cecil had further reasons for his deviousness. In fact, he had good reason to believe that there was a kernel of truth in his charges of treason, even if he could not prove them under existing laws or could not bring to the bar those Catholics who were most obviously guilty. In some ways, Cecil's dilemma was like that of the twentieth-century statesman who is trying to frustrate a Communist conspiracy. He knows that his enemy is out to "bury" him. He knows that it has laid explicit plans for the burial. But he cannot connect this general intention and these plans to any overt acts or statements by Communists within his jurisdiction. So he trumps up charges, creates peculiar new laws, and engages in a general campaign of harassment. For Cecil did have hard evidence, which was not of a kind he could submit to any court, of a Catholic hostility to his government which reached the brink of treason and went beyond.

This brings us to Allen's lack of frankness. For he also had withheld an important part of the truth from his statements. It is a fact, made increasingly clear by archival studies conducted over the last century, that Allen had been engaged personally in a number of international plots to invade England and overthrow the government of Elizabeth. From 1575 to 1578, even before the Mission to England had begun, he had plotted with Spain and the Vatican to send Don John of Austria, the Spanish regent in the Netherlands, across the channel to England with an invading army which would rescue Mary Stuart and impose a Catholic government under her direction.[24] From mid-1582 to mid-1583, Allen had plotted with Spain, the Vatican, and the Dukes of Guise in France to send the Scottish Duke of Lennox south into

[24] Albert J. Loomie, *The Spanish Elizabethans: The English Exiles at the Court of Philip II* (New York, 1963), pp. 22–24; P. O. de Törne, *Don Juan d'Autriche et les projets de conquête de l'Angleterre, 1568–1578*, II (Åbo, 1928), 76–95, and corroborating documents published in his appendixes.

England, while a Continental army crossed the channel, again to rescue Mary Stuart and impose a Catholic regime. At a late stage in this plot, it was even decided to hire an assassin to murder Queen Elizabeth, and prize money was obtained from the Dukes of Guise to pay for one. From mid-1583 through 1584, when Cecil was drafting his *Execution of Justice* and Allen was writing his *Defense of English Catholics,* the doctor was again plotting with Spain, the Vatican, and the Guises to launch an invasion of England, either directly or by way of Scotland, that would overthrow Elizabeth and re-establish Catholicism.[25] In later years, Allen was to plot with the Vatican and Philip II, King of Spain, to invade England with crack detachments of Europe's best troops, borne in a mighty Armada launched from Iberian ports hundreds of miles away from the English coast.[26] This last plot was the one which came nearest to success, although it, as history of course knows, ended in 1588 with disastrous failure. But many of the earlier plots also came close to fruition. Several times very precise plans were drawn for the size and equipment of an invading army. Funds were actually raised to finance invasions. Arrangements were made for the first steps that would follow invasion in re-establishing Catholicism. If an invading army had entered England from the North, for example, Allen himself would have followed its first conquests by speeding home to assume the post of Bishop of Durham, by papal appointment.[27]

In all of this plotting, Allen was in continual touch with the Vatican. He had visited Rome personally early in 1576 to help

[25] Allen's role in these plots is described and documented in detail by T. F. Knox in his introduction to Allen, *Letters,* pp. xxxii–lxxi. See also Johannes Kretzschmar, *Die Invasionsprojekte der Katholischen Mächte gegen England zur Zeit Elisabeths* (Leipzig, 1892), hereafter cited as Kretzschmar. Both ignore the earlier plot centering on Don John.

[26] Garrett Mattingly, *The Armada* (Boston, 1959), ch. 6 and *passim.*

[27] This appointment was recommended by the papal nuncio to France in a letter to the papal secretary of state, May 22, 1582, published in Kretzschmar, p. 132; Allen, *Letters,* pp. xli and below.

mount the first of his plots. After his return to northern Europe, he kept in constant touch with the papal nuncio to France and maintained frequent correspondence with the papal secretary of state. From at least 1582 on, his regular English companion in the plotting was Father Robert Parsons, head of the English province of the Jesuit order and the actual leader only two years earlier of the first big detachment of missionaries to England. At nearly every step in these plots Allen received substantial encouragement from the Vatican. If most of them did not come to fruition it was largely because one or another of the Catholic princes who were expected to supply most of the troops failed to co-operate.

The English government was aware of many of these plots. Thanks in large part to Sir Francis Walsingham, who normally worked very closely with Cecil in matters of high policy, England had developed a superb diplomatic service. Its efficient spies, operating at the courts of Spain and France, sneaking themselves under false pretenses into Allen's seminaries, occasionally even smuggling themselves into Rome itself, sent back to Cecil and Walsingham reports of suspicious meetings between the leaders of international Catholicism and of the English exiles and surmises about the plots which were in fact discussed at these meetings.[28] The English government naturally connected all this Continental intrigue with the Mission to England, even when it had no precise evidence of the connection. After all, both Mission and plotting were directed by one man, William Allen.

Apologists for Allen, then and since, have argued that he kept these two activities sharply separate.[29] They have argued that the men trained for the Mission to England were given no political instruction of any sort, were warned never to discuss politics, were never informed of their leaders' hopes to win England for

[28] For a detailed analysis of Walsingham's spy system, both at home and abroad, see Conyers Read, *Mr. Secretary Walsingham and the Policy of Queen Elizabeth* (Oxford, 1925), II, 318–339.

[29] E.g., Philip Hughes, *The Reformation in England,* III (London, 1954), 345.

Catholicism by armed invasion. Allen himself claims, in the *Defense of English Catholics,* that the routine of studies in the Continental seminaries included none of the usual public disputations on the temporal powers of the Pope and the use of those powers to depose heretical rulers such as Elizabeth (pp. 121–122). It omitted these disputations precisely because Allen did not want to put bad ideas into students' heads, did not want to distract them from a mission which was to be purely religious.

Much of this claim can be accepted. Certainly Father Campion and most of the other missionaries in England were remarkably circumspect. If they ever did talk politics, the strenuously vigilant priest-hunters hired by the government could not find hard evidence of it. It also stands to reason that Allen and Parsons would not have discussed plots of invasion with anyone who did not need to know of them, particularly when they were still in preliminary stages.

But some of this claim must be rejected. As a reading of the *Defense of English Catholics* will make clear, the very book which claims that none of Allen's students ever discussed the papal right to depose rulers presents an eloquent defense of that right. Perhaps most students, then as now, did not read their professors' books, but surely a few did. Further damaging evidence can be found in some of the letters which record details of the plots in which Allen was engaged. In 1582, for example, as the Lennox plot was being developed, the papal nuncio in Paris reported to the papal secretary of state the general details of the new plan. It included the provision that, once the invasion was launched, "the principal Catholics in England will be advised in time through their priests," [30] and will thus be able to rise in support of the general attempt to overthrow Elizabeth. Finally, in 1585, Allen presented to Pope Sixtus V a memorial only recently reprinted

[30] "Al tempo saranno avvisati li principali catholici in Inghilterra de la cosa per via de sacerdoti," in Kretzschmar, p. 133; Allen, *Letters,* p. xli and below.

and attributed to him, in which he reported that "we have now (although many have been recently deported) almost three hundred priests in the households of noblemen and men of substance, and we are daily sending others, who will direct the consciences and actions of the Catholics in this affair when the time comes."[31] The "time" coming was quite clearly the one of invasion. It would consequently appear that, no matter what the missionary priests were themselves informed, their leaders intended to use them for a subversive political purpose at the appropriate time.

In a way, then, the Catholic Mission to England was engaged in treason, potentially if not actually, in intention if not in deed. This should not really surprise us. Militant minorities have proposed revolt against intolerant governments in many other times and places, as the histories, among others, of sixteenth-century Calvinism, of eighteenth-century Jacobinism, and of twentieth-century Communism make clear. Revolt and repression are likely to result whenever the conflict between allegiances becomes too intense, whenever any allegiance is absolutized and all others are rejected. They are likely to result, to be brief, whenever men become fanatics.

[31] Edited and attributed to Allen by Garrett Mattingly in "William Allen and Catholic Propaganda in England," *Aspects de la propagande religieuse,* ed. by E. Droz (Geneva, 1957), pp. 325–339, an article which presents in detail the argument summarized in this paragraph. See pp. 328, 336–337 for this particular quotation.

The Execution of Justice in England for maintenance of public and Christian peace, against certain stirrers of sedition, and adherents to the traitors and enemies of the realm, without any persecution of them for questions of religion, as is falsely reported and published by the fautors and fosterers of their treasons

Secondly
Imprinted at London mense Jan. 1583.*
An. Reg. Eliz. 26. With some small alterations of things mistaken or omitted in the transcript of the first original

* 1584, New Style

IT HATH been in all ages and in all countries a common usage of all offenders for the most part, both great and small, to make defense of their lewd[1] and unlawful facts by untruths and by coloring and covering their deeds (were they never so vile) with pretenses of some other causes of contrary operations or effects, to the intent not only to avoid punishment or shame but to continue, uphold, and prosecute their wicked attempts to the full satisfaction of their disordered and malicious appetites. And though such hath been the use of all offenders, yet of none with more danger than of rebels and traitors to their lawful princes, kings, and countries. Of which sort of late years are specially to be noted certain persons, naturally born subjects in the realm of England and Ireland, who, having for some good time professed outwardly their obedience to their sovereign lady, Queen Elizabeth, have nevertheless afterward been stirred up and seduced by wicked spirits, first in England sundry years past, and secondly and of later time in Ireland, to enter into open rebellion, taking arms and coming into the field against Her Majesty and her lieutenants, with their forces under banners displayed, inducing by notable untruths many simple people to follow and assist them in their traitorous actions. And though it is very well known that both their intentions and manifest actions were bent to have deposed the Queen's Majesty from her crown and to have traitorously set in her place some other whom they liked, whereby if they had not been speedily resisted they would have committed

[1] Base, evil, wicked.

great bloodsheds and slaughters of Her Majesty's faithful subjects and ruined their native country; yet by God's power given unto Her Majesty they were so speedily vanquished as some few of them suffered by order of law according to their deserts, many and the greatest part upon confession of their faults were pardoned, the rest (but they not many) of the principal escaped into foreign countries; and there, because in none or few places rebels and traitors to their natural princes and countries dare for their treasons challenge at their first muster open comfort or succor, these notable traitors and rebels have falsely informed many kings, princes, and states, and specially the Bishop of Rome, commonly called the Pope (from whom they all had secretly their first comfort to rebel), that the cause of their fleeing from their countries was for the religion of Rome and for maintenance of the said Pope's authority. Whereas divers of them before their rebellion lived so notoriously the most part of their lives out of all good rule, either for honest manners or for any sense in religion, as they might have been rather familiar with Catiline [2] or favorers to Sardanapalus [3] than accounted good subjects under any Christian princes. As, for some examples of the heads of these rebellions, out of England fled Charles Neville, Earl of Westmorland,[4] a person utterly wasted by looseness of life, and by God's punishment even in the time of his rebellion bereaved of his children that should have succeeded him in the earldom, and his body now eaten with ulcers of lewd causes, as his companions do say, that no enemy he hath can wish him a viler punishment [; a pitiful loss to the realm of so noble a house never before in any age attainted for disloyalty]. And out of Ireland ran away

[2] A Roman who conspired against his country in 63 B.C., a prototype of a conspirator.

[3] A Greek form of Assur-bani-pal, King of Assyria, a prototype of luxurious effeminacy.

[4] Charles Neville (1543–1601), leader of the 1569 Rising in the North, shortly after its collapse took refuge in the Spanish Netherlands.

one Thomas Stukely,[5] a defamed person almost through all Christendom and a faithless beast rather than a man, fleeing first out of England for notable piracies and out of Ireland for treacheries not pardonable, which two were the first ringleaders of the rest of the rebels, the one for England, the other for Ireland.

But notwithstanding the notorious evil and wicked lives of these and others their confederates, void of all Christian religion, it liked the Bishop of Rome, as in favor of their treasons, not to color their offenses, as themselves openly pretend to do, for avoiding of common shame of the world, but flatly to animate them to continue their former wicked purposes, that is, to take arms against their lawful queen, to invade her realm with foreign forces, to pursue all her good subjects and their native countries with fire and sword; for maintenance whereof there had some years before at sundry times proceeded, in a thundering sort, bulls, excommunications, and other public writings denouncing Her Majesty, being the lawful Queen and God's anointed servant, not to be the queen of the realm; charging and, upon pains of excommunication, commanding all her subjects to depart from their natural allegiances whereto by birth and by oath they were bound; provoking also and authorizing all persons of all degrees within both the realms to rebel; and upon this anti-Christian warrant, being contrary to all the laws of God and man and nothing agreeable to a pastoral officer, not only all the rabble of the foresaid traitors that were before fled, but also all other persons that had forsaken their native countries, being of divers conditions and qualities, some not able to live at home but in beggary, some discontented for lack of preferments, which they gaped for unworthily in universities and other places, some bankrupt merchants, some in a sort learned to contentions, being not contented to learn to obey the laws of the land, have many years, running up and down from country to country, practiced some in

[5] Thomas Stukely fled Ireland for Spain in 1570, hoping to return with an invading army, but was killed in Morocco in 1578.

one corner, some in another, some with seeking to gather forces and money for forces, some with instigation of princes by untruths to make war upon their natural country, some with inward practices to murder the GREATEST, some with seditious writings, and very many of late with public infamous libels, full of despiteful vile terms and poisoned lies, altogether to uphold the foresaid anti-Christian and tyrannous warrant of the Pope's bull.[6] And yet also by some other means, to further these intentions, because they could not readily prevail by way of force, finding foreign princes of better consideration and not readily inclined to their wicked purposes, it was devised to erect by certain schools which they called seminaries,[7] to nourish and bring up persons disposed naturally to sedition, to continue their race and trade and to become seedmen in their tillage of sedition, and them to send secretly into these the Queen's Majesty's realms of England and Ireland under secret masks, some of priesthood, some of other inferior orders, with titles of seminaries for some of the meaner sort and of Jesuits for the stagers [8] and ranker sort and suchlike; but yet so warily they crept into the land as none brought the marks of their priesthood with them; but in divers corners of Her Majesty's dominions these seminaries, or seedmen, and Jesuits, bringing with them certain Romish trash, as of their hallowed wax, their *Agnus Dei,*[9] [their grains, and] many kind of beads, and suchlike, have as tillage men labored secretly to persuade the people to allow of the Pope's foresaid bulls and warrants and of his absolute authority over all princes and countries, and striking many with pricks of conscience to obey the same; whereby in process of small time, if this wicked and dangerous,

[6] The bull excommunicating Elizabeth is titled *Regnans in excelsis* and dated February 25, 1570. See below, pp. 15–17.

[7] In Douai, founded in 1568, moved to Reims in 1578; and in Rome, founded in 1579.

[8] Ones with experience, veterans.

[9] A small disk of wax stamped with the figure of a lamb and blessed by the Pope.

traitorous and crafty course had not been by God's goodness espied and stayed, there had followed imminent danger of horrible uproars in the realms and a manifest bloody destruction of great multitudes of Christians. For it cannot be denied but that so many as should have been induced and thoroughly persuaded to have obeyed that wicked warrant of the Pope's and the contents thereof should have been forthwith in their hearts and consciences secret traitors, and for to be indeed arrant and open traitors there should have wanted nothing but opportunity to feel their strength and to assemble themselves in such numbers with armor and weapons as they might have presumed to have been the greater part and so by open civil war to have come to their wicked purposes.

But God's goodness, by Whom kings do rule and by Whose blast traitors are commonly wasted and confounded, hath otherwise given to Her Majesty, as to His handmaid and dear servant ruling under Him, the spirit of wisdom and power, whereby she hath caused some of these seditious seedmen and sowers of rebellion to be discovered, for all their secret lurkings, and to be taken and charged with these former points of high treason, not being dealt withal upon questions of religion, but justly [by order of laws, openly] condemned as traitors. At which times, notwithstanding all manner gentle ways of persuasions used to move them to desist from such manifest traitorous courses and opinions, [with offer of mercy,] yet was the canker of their rebellious humors so deeply entered and graven into the hearts of many of them as they would not be removed from their traitorous determinations. And therefore, as manifest traitors in maintaining and adhering to the capital enemy of Her Majesty and her crown (who hath not only been the cause of two rebellions already past in England and Ireland, but in that of Ireland did manifestly wage and maintain his own people, captains and soldiers, under the banner of Rome, against Her Majesty, so as no enemy could do more), these, I say, have justly suffered death, not by force or form of any new laws established, either for religion or against the Pope's supremacy, as the slanderous libelers would have it seem to be, but by the ancient temporal laws of the realm, and namely by the laws of Parliament made in King Edward the Third's time, about the year of Our Lord 1330,[10] which is above two hundred years and more past, when the Bishops of Rome and Popes were suffered to have their authority ecclesiastical in this realm, as they had in many other countries. But yet of this kind of offenders, as many of them as after their condemnations were contented to renounce their former traitorous assertions, so many were spared from execution and do live still at this day; such was the unwillingness in Her Majesty to have any blood spilled without this very urgent, just, and necessary cause, proceeding from themselves. And yet, nevertheless, such of the rest of the traitors as remain in foreign parts, continuing still their rebellious minds and craftily keeping themselves aloof off from dangers, cease not to provoke sundry other inferior seditious persons newly to steal secretly into the realm, to revive the former seditious practices, to the execution of the Pope's foresaid bulls against Her Majesty and the realm; pretending when they are apprehended that they came only into the realm by the commandment of their superiors, the heads of the Jesuits, to whom they are bound (as they say) by oath against either king or country, and here to inform or reform men's consciences from errors in some points of religion, as they shall think meet. But yet, in very truth, the whole scope of their secret labors is manifestly proved to be secretly to win all people with whom they dare deal so to allow of the Pope's said bulls and of his authority without exception as, in obeying thereof, they take themselves fully discharged of their allegiance and obedience to their lawful prince and country; yea, and to be well warranted to take arms to rebel against Her Majesty when they shall be thereunto called, and to be ready secretly to join with any foreign

[10] 25 Edw. III, st. 5, c. 2, 1351, an act defining treason, the legal basis for the indictments of Father Campion *et al.*

force that can be procured to invade the realm, whereof also they have a long time given, and yet do for their advantage, no small comfort of success; and so, consequently, the effect of their labors is to bring the realm not only into a dangerous war against the forces of strangers (from which it hath been free above twenty-three or twenty-four years, a case very memorable and hard to be matched with an example of the like), but into a war domestical and civil, wherein no blood is usually spared nor mercy yielded, and wherein neither the vanqueror [11] nor the vanquished [can] have [just] cause of triumph.

And forasmuch as these are the most evident perils that necessarily should follow, if these kind of vermin were suffered to creep by stealth into the realm and to spread their poison within the same, howsoever, when they are taken, like hypocrites they color and counterfeit the same with profession of devotion in religion, it is of all persons to be yielded in reason that Her Majesty and all her governors and magistrates of justice, having care to maintain the peace of the realm (which God hath given in her time to continue longer than ever in any time of her progenitors), ought of duty to Almighty God, the author of peace, and according to the natural love and charge due to their country, and for avoiding of the floods of blood which in civil wars are seen to run and flow, by all lawful means possible, as well by the sword as by law, in their several seasons to impeach and repel these so manifest and dangerous colorable practices and works of sedition and rebellion. And though there are many subjects known in the realm that differ in some opinions of religion from the Church of England and that do also not forbear to profess the same, yet in that they do also profess loyalty and obedience to Her Majesty and offer readily in Her Majesty's defense to impugn and resist any foreign force, though it should come or be procured from the Pope himself, none of these sort are for their contrary opinions in religion prosecuted or charged with any crimes or

[11] Victor.

pains of treason, nor yet willingly searched in their consciences for their contrary opinions that savor not of treason. And of these sorts there [have been and] are a number of persons, not of such base and vulgar note as those were which of late have been executed, as in particular some by name are well known and not unfit to be remembered.

The first and chiefest by office was Dr. Heath,[12] that was Archbishop of York and Lord Chancellor of England in Queen Mary's time, who at the first coming of Her Majesty to the crown, showing himself a faithful and quiet subject, continued in both the said offices, though in religion then manifestly differing, and yet was he not restrained of his liberty nor deprived of his proper lands and goods, but, leaving willingly both his offices, lived in his own house very discreetly and enjoyed all his purchased lands during all his natural life, until by very age he departed this world and then left his house and living to his friends, an example of gentleness never matched in Queen Mary's time. The like did one Dr. Pole,[13] that had been Bishop of Peterborough, an ancient grave person and a very quiet subject. There were also others that had been bishops and in great estimation, as Dr. Tunstall,[14] Bishop of Durham, a person [of great reputation and] also, [whilst he lived,] of very quiet behavior. There were also other, Dr. White,[15] and Dr. Oglethorpe,[16] one of Winchester, the other of Carlisle, Bishops, [persons of courteous natures, and he of Carlisle so inclined to dutifulness to the Queen's Majesty as he did the office at the consecration and coronation of Her Majesty in the church of Westminster] and Dr. Thirlby[17] and Dr. Watson,[18] yet living, one of Ely, the other of Lincoln, Bishops, [the one of nature affable, the other altogether sour, and yet living. Whereto may be added the Bishop then of Exeter,

[12] Nicholas Heath (1501?–1579).
[13] David Pole (d. 1568).
[14] Cuthbert Tunstall (1474–1559).
[15] John White (1510?–1560).
[16] Owen Oglethorpe (d. 1559).
[17] Thomas Thirlby (1506–1570).
[18] Thomas Watson (1513–1584).

Turberville,[19] an honest gentleman but a simple bishop, who lived at his own liberty to the end of his life. And none of all these] pressed with any capital pain, though they maintained the Pope's authority against the laws of the realm; and some abbots, as Mr. Feckenham,[20] yet living, a person also of quiet and courteous behavior for a great time. Some also were deans, as Dr. Boxall,[21] Dean of Windsor, a person of great modesty[, learning,] and knowledge; Dr. Cole,[22] Dean of Paul's, a person more earnest than discreet; Dr. Reynolds,[23] Dean of Exeter, [not unlearned,] and many such others having borne office and dignities in the Church and that had made profession against the Pope, which they only began in Queen Mary's time to change; yet were these never to this day burdened with capital pains, nor yet deprived of any their goods or proper livelihoods, but only removed from their ecclesiastical offices, which they would not exercise according to the laws. And most of them [, and many other of their sort,] for a great time were retained in bishops' houses in very civil and courteous manner, without charge to themselves or their friends, until the time that the Pope began by his bulls and messages to offer trouble to the realm by stirring of rebellion; about which time only, some of these afore named, being found busier in matters of state tending to stir troubles than was meet for the common quiet of the realm, were removed to other more private places, where such other wanderers as were men known to move sedition might be restrained from common resorting to them to increase trouble, as the Pope's bull gave manifest occasion [to doubt];[24] and yet without charging them in their consciences or otherwise by any inquisition to bring them into danger of any capital law, so as no one was called to any capital or bloody question upon matters of religion, but have all enjoyed

[19] James Turberville (d. 1570?).
[20] John de Feckenham (1518?–1585), last Abbot of Westminster.
[21] John Boxall (d. 1571).
[22] Henry Cole (1500?–1580).
[23] Thomas Reynolds (d. 1559).
[24] Fear.

their life as the course of nature would. And such of them as yet remain may, if they will not be authors or instruments of rebellion or sedition, enjoy the time that God and nature shall yield them without danger of life or member. And yet it is worthy to be well marked that the chiefest of all these and the most of them had in the time of King Henry the Eighth and King Edward the Sixth, either by preaching, writing, reading, or arguing, taught all people to condemn, yea, to abhor the authority of the Pope; for which purpose they had many times given their oaths publicly against the Pope's authority and had also yielded to both the said kings the title of supreme head of the Church of England next under Christ, which title the adversaries do most falsely write and affirm that the Queen's Majesty doth now use; a manifest lie and untruth [, to be seen by the very acts of Parliament[25] and at the beginning of her reign omitted in her style]. And for proof that these foresaid bishops and learned men had so long time disavowed the Pope's authority, many of their books and sermons against the Pope's authority remain printed[, both in English and Latin,] to be seen in these times, to their great shame and reproof to change so often, but specially in persecuting such as themselves had taught and stablished to hold the contrary[; a sin near to the sin against the Holy Ghost].

There were also, and yet be, a great number of others, being laymen of good possessions and lands, men of good credit in their countries, manifestly of late time seduced to hold contrary opinions in religion for the Pope's authority, and yet none of them have been sought hitherto to be impeached in any point or quarrel of treason, or of loss of life, member, or inheritance, so as it may plainly appear that it is not nor hath been for contrarious opinions in religion or for the Pope's authority [alone], as the

[25] I Eliz. I, c. 1, section 9, the oath clause, specifies that the Queen shall be styled "supreme governor of this realm, . . . as well in all spiritual or ecclesiastical things or causes as temporal," an intentional departure from the title "supreme head" adopted by Henry VIII.

adversaries do boldly and falsely publish, that any persons have suffered death since Her Majesty's reign, and yet some of these sort are well known to hold opinion that the Pope ought, by authority of God's word, to be supreme and only head of the Catholic Church [through the whole world] and only to rule in all causes ecclesiastical, and that the Queen's Majesty ought not to be the governor over any her subjects in her realm, being persons ecclesiastical; which opinions are nevertheless in some part by the laws of the realm punishable in other degrees, and yet for none of these points have any persons been prosecuted with the charge of treason or in danger of life.

And if then it be inquired for what cause these others have of late suffered death, it is truly to be answered, as afore is often remembered, that none at all were impeached for treason to the danger of their life but such as did obstinately maintain the contents of the Pope's bull afore mentioned, which do import that Her Majesty is not the lawful Queen of England, the first and highest point of treason; and that all her subjects are discharged of their oaths and obedience, a second high point of treason; and all warranted to disobey her and her laws, a third and a very large point of treason. And thereto is to be added a fourth point most manifest, in that they would not disallow the Pope's hostile proceedings in open wars against Her Majesty in her realm of Ireland, where one of their company, Dr. Sanders,[26] a lewd scholar and subject of England, a fugitive and a principal companion and conspirator with the traitors and rebels at Rome, was, by the Pope's special commission, a commander as in form of a legate, and sometime a bursar or paymaster for those wars, which Dr. Sanders, in his book of his Church Monarchy,[27] did, afore his

[26] Nicholas Sanders (1530?–1581), English Catholic polemicist, was sent as papal nuncio to Ireland, where he incited a rebellion in 1579 and died soon after its collapse.

[27] *De visibili monarchia ecclesiae* (Louvain, 1571), and several later editions.

passing into Ireland, openly by writing gloriously avow the foresaid bull of Pius the Fifth against Her Majesty to be lawful, and affirmeth that by virtue thereof one Dr. Morton,[28] an old English fugitive and conspirator, was sent from Rome into the north parts of England, which was true, to stir up the first rebellion there, whereof Charles Neville, the late Earl of Westmorland, was a head captain.

And thereby it may manifestly appear to all men how this bull was the ground of the rebellions both in England and Ireland, and how for maintenance thereof, and for sowing of sedition by warrant and allowance of the same, these persons were justly condemned of treason and lawfully executed by the ancient laws temporal of the realm, without [charging them for] any other matter than for their practices and conspiracies both abroad and at home against the Queen and the realm, and for maintaining of the Pope's foresaid authority and bull, published to deprive Her Majesty of her crown, and for withdrawing and reconciling of her subjects from their natural allegiance due to Her Majesty and to their country, and for moving them to sedition; and for no other causes or questions of religion were these persons condemned, although true it is that when they were charged and convinced [29] of these points of conspiracies and treasons they would still in their answers colorably pretend their actions to have been for religion; but in deed and truth they were manifest[ed to be] for the procurement and maintenance of the rebellions and wars against Her Majesty and her realm.

And herein is now the manifest diversity to be seen and well considered betwixt the truth of Her Majesty's actions and the falsehood of the blasphemous adversaries: that where the factious party of the Pope, the principal author of the invasions of Her

[28] Nicholas Morton, D.D., a papal agent, who secretly visited England in 1569 and met with leaders of the planned Rising in the North but apparently returned to Rome before the rebellion was crushed.

[29] Convicted.

Majesty's dominions, do falsely allege that a number of persons, whom they term as martyrs, have died for defense of the Catholic religion, the same in very truth may manifestly appear to have died (if they so will have it) as martyrs for the Pope but yet as traitors against their sovereign and queen in adhering to him, being the notable and only open hostile enemy in all actions of war against Her Majesty, her kingdoms, and people. And that this is the meaning of all these that have so obstinately maintained the authority and contents of this bull, the very words of the bull do declare in this sort, as Dr. Sanders reporteth them:

Pius Quintus, Pontifex Maximus, de Apostolicae potestatis plenitudine, declaravit Elizabetham praetenso Regni jure, necnon omni et quocunque dominio, dignitate, privilegioque privatam; itemque proceres, subditos, et populos dicti regni, ac caeteros omnes qui illi quomodocunque juraverunt, a juramento hujusmodi ac omni fidelitatis debito, perpetuo absolutos.

That is to say:

Pius the Fifth, the greatest bishop, of the fullness of the apostolic power, declared Elizabeth to be bereaved or deprived of her pretended right of her kingdom, and also of all and whatsoever dominion, dignity, and privilege; and also the nobles, subjects, and people of the said kingdom, and all others which had sworn to her any manner of ways, to be absolved forever from such oath and from all debt or duty of fealty,[30]

and so forth, with many threatening cursings, to all that durst obey her or her laws. And for execution hereof, to prove that the effect of the Pope's bull and message was a flat rebellion, it is not amiss to hear what the same Dr. Sanders, the Pope's firebrand in Ireland, also writeth in his *Visible Church Monarchy*, which is thus:

[30] For a fuller, but still condensed, English text of this bull and commentary on it, see John Hungerford Pollen, *The English Catholics in the Reign of Queen Elizabeth* (London, 1920), pp. 149–151 and *passim.*

Pius Quintus, Pontifex Maximus, Anno Domini 1569, reverendum praesbyterum Nicolaum Mortonum Anglum in Angliam misit, ut certis illustribus viris auctoritate apostolica denuntiaret, Elizabetham quae tunc rerum potiebatur, haereticam esse; ob eamque causam, omni dominio et potestate excedisse, impuneque ab illis velut ethnicam haberi posse, nec eos illius legibus aut mandatis deinceps obedire cogi.

That is to say:

Pius the Fifth, the greatest bishop, in the year of Our Lord 1569, sent the reverend priest Nicholas Morton, an Englishman, into England that he should denounce or declare by the apostolic authority to certain noblemen, Elizabeth, who then was in possession, to be an heretic and for that cause to have fallen from all dominion and power, and that she may be had or reputed of them as an ethnic,[31] and that they are not to be compelled to obey her laws or commandments, etc.

Thus you see an ambassade of rebellion from the Pope's Holiness, the ambassador an old doting English priest, a fugitive and conspirator, sent, as he saith, to some noblemen, and those were the two Earls of Northumberland [32] and Westmorland, heads of the rebellion.

And after this, he followeth to declare the success thereof, which I dare say he was sorry it was so evil, with these words:

Quae denuntiatione multi nobiles viri adducti sunt, ut de fratribus liberandis cogitare auderent, ac sperabant illi quidem Catholicos omnes summis viribus affuturos esse; verum etsi aliter quam illi expectabant res evenit, quia Catholici omnes nondum probe cognoverant, Elizabetham haereticam esse declaratam, tamen laudanda illorum nobilium consilia erant.

That is:

By which denunciation many noblemen were induced or led that they were boldened to think of the freeing of their brethren, and they hoped

[31] Heathen, pagan.

[32] Thomas Percy (1528–1572), executed for his role in leading the Rising in the North in 1569.

certainly that all the Catholics would have assisted them with all their strength; but although the matter happened otherwise than they hoped for, because all the Catholics knew not that Elizabeth was declared to be an heretic, yet the counsels and intents of those noblemen were to be praised.

A rebellion and a vanquishing of rebels very smoothly described.

This noble fact here mentioned was the rebellion in the North; the noblemen were the Earls of Northumberland and Westmorland; the lack of the event or success was that the traitors were vanquished and the Queen's Majesty and her subjects had, by God's ordinance, the victory; and the cause why the rebels prevailed not was because all the Catholics had not been duly informed that the Queen's Majesty was declared to be (as they term it) an heretic; which want of information, to the intent to make the rebels mightier in number and power, was diligently and cunningly supplied by the sending into the realm of a great multitude of the seminaries and Jesuits, whose special charge was to inform the people thereof, as by their actions hath manifestly appeared[; a supplement to amend the former error].

And though Dr. Sanders hath thus written, yet it may be said by such as favored the two notable Jesuits, one named Robert Parsons [33] (who yet hideth himself in corners to continue his traitorous practice), the other named Edmund Campion [34] (who was found out, being disguised like a roister,[35] and suffered for his treasons), that Dr. Sanders' treason is his proper [36] treason in allowing of the said bull and not to be imputed to Parsons and Campion. Therefore, to make it plain that these two by special authority had charge to execute the sentence of this bull, these acts in writing following shall make manifest, which are not

[33] Robert Parsons or Persons (1546–1610), one of the most active and controversial of the Jesuit polemicists in the Mission to England.

[34] Edmund Campion (1540–1581), the most prominent of the Jesuit missionaries put to death by the Elizabethan government. The standard biography is Richard Simpson, *Edmund Campion* (London, 1867).

[35] Bully, ruffian.

[36] Own, personal.

feigned or imagined but are the very writings taken about one of their complices, immediately after Campion's death[; although Campion before his death would not be known of any such matter, whereby may appear what trust is to be given to the words of such pseudomartyrs].

Facultates concessae pp. Roberto Personio et
Edmundo Campiono, pro Anglia, die 14 Aprilis, 1580.

Petatur a summo Domino nostro, explicatio bullae declaratoriae per Pium Quintum contra Elizabetham et ei adhaerentes, quam Catholici cupiunt intelligi hoc modo, ut obliget semper illam et haereticos, Catholicos vero nullo modo obliget rebus sic stantibus, sed tum demum quando publica ejusdem bullae executio fieri poterit.

Then followed many other petitions of faculties for their further authorities which are not needful for this purpose to be recited, but in the end followeth this sentence as an answer of the Pope's:

Has praedictas gratias concessit summus Pontifex patri Roberto Personio, et Edmundo Campiono in Angliam profecturis, die 14 Aprilis, 1580, Praesente patre Oliverio Manarco assistente.

The English of which Latin sentences is as followeth:

Faculties granted to the two Fathers Robert Parsons
and Edmund Campion, for England, the fourteenth
day of April, 1580.

Let it be asked or required of our most holy Lord the explication or meaning of the bull declaratory made by Pius the Fifth against Elizabeth and such as do adhere or obey her, which bull the Catholics desire to be understood in this manner, that the same bull shall always bind her and the heretics, but the Catholics it shall by no means bind, as matters or things do now stand or be, but hereafter, when the public execution of that bull may be had or made.

Then in the end the conclusion was thus added:

The highest pontiff, or bishop, granted these foresaid graces to Father Robert Parsons and Edmund Campion, who are now to take their journeys into England, the fourteenth day of April, in the year of Our Lord 1580. Being present the Father Oliverius Manarke, assistant.

Hereby it is manifest what authority Campion had to impart the contents of the bull against the Queen's Majesty, howsoever he himself denied the same[; for this was his errand].

And though it be manifest that these two Jesuits, Parsons and Campion, not only required to have the Pope's mind declared for the bull, but also in their own petitions showed how they and other Catholics did desire to have the said bull to be understood against the Queen of England; yet to make the matter more plain how all other Jesuits and seminaries, yea, how all papists naming themselves Catholics, do or are warranted to interpret the said bull against Her Majesty and her good subjects, [howsoever they will disguise it,] you shall see what one of their fellows, named Hart,[37] who was condemned with Campion and yet liveth, did, amongst many other things, declare his knowledge thereof the last of December in the same year, 1580, in these words following:

The bull of Pius the Fifth (forsomuch as it is against the Queen) is holden among the English Catholics for a lawful sentence and a sufficient discharge of her subjects' fidelity and so remaineth in force, but in some points touching the subjects it is altered by the present Pope. For where in that bull all her subjects are commanded not to obey her and, she being excommunicate and disposed, all that do obey her are likewise innodate [38] and accursed, which point is perilous to the Catholics; for if they obey her, they be in the Pope's curse, and they disobey her, they are in the Queen's danger. Therefore the present Pope, to relieve them, hath altered that part of the bull and dispensed with them to obey and serve her without peril of excommunication; which dispensation is to endure but till it please the Pope otherwise to determine.

[37] John Hart, S.J., ordained in Douai in 1578, sent to England in 1580, almost immediately arrested, recanted under pressure, imprisoned, and later banished to the Continent, d. 1586.

[38] Involved in an interdict or anathema.

Wherefore, to make some conclusion of the matters before mentioned, all persons both within the realm and abroad may plainly perceive that all the infamous libels lately published abroad in sundry languages, and the slanderous reports made in other princes' courts of a multitude of persons to have been of late put to torments and death only for profession of the Catholic religion, and not for matters of state against the Queen's Majesty, are false and shameless and published to the maintenance of traitors and rebels. And to make the matter seem more horrible or lamentable they recite the particular names of all the persons, which by their own catalogue exceed not for these twenty-five years' space above the number of threescore, forgetting, or rather with their stony and senseless hearts not regarding, in what cruel sort in the time of Queen Mary, which little exceeded the space of five years, the Queen's Majesty's reign being five times as many, there were by imprisonment, torments, famine, and fire, of men, women, maidens, and children, almost the number of four hundred[, beside such as were secretly murdered in prisons]; and of that number above twenty that had been archbishops, bishops, and principal prelates or officers in the Church, lamentably destroyed, and of women above threescore, and of children above forty, and amongst the women, some great with child, [and one] out of whose body the child by fire was expelled alive, and yet also cruelly burned; examples beyond all heathen cruelty. And most of the youth that then suffered cruel death, both men, women, and children (which is to be noted), were such as had never by the sacrament of baptism or by confirmation, professed, or was ever taught or instructed, or ever had heard of any other kind of religion, but only of that which by their blood and death in the fire they did as true martyrs testify. A matter of another sort to be lamented [in a Christian charity] with simplicity of words and not with puffed eloquence than the execution in this time of a very few traitors, who also in their time, if they exceeded thirty years of age, had in their baptism professed and in their youth had learned the same religion which they now so bitterly oppugned. And beside that, in their opinions they differ much from the martyrs of Queen Mary's time; for though they [which suffered in Queen Mary's time] continued in the profession of the religion wherein they were christened [and as they were perpetually taught], yet they never at their death denied their lawful queen, nor maintained any of her open and foreign enemies, nor procured any rebellion or civil war, nor did sow any sedition in secret corners, nor withdrew any subjects from their obedience, as these sworn servants of the Pope have continually done.

And therefore, all these things well considered, there is no doubt but all good subjects within the realm do manifestly see, and all wavering persons (not being led clean out of the way by the seditious) will hereafter perceive, how they have been abused to go astray. And all strangers, but specially all Christian potentates, as emperors, kings, princes, and suchlike, having their sovereign estates either in succession hereditary or by consent of their people, being acquainted with the very truth of these Her Majesty's late just and necessary actions, only for defense of herself, her crown, and people, against open invaders and for eschewing of civil wars stirred up by rebellion, will allow in their own like cases for a truth and rule (as it is not to be doubted but they will) that it belongeth not to a Bishop of Rome, as successor of St. Peter and therein a pastor spiritual, or if he were the bishop of all Christendom, as by the name of Pope he claimeth, first, by his bulls or excommunications in this sort at his will in favor of traitors and rebels to depose any sovereign princess, being lawfully invested in their crowns by succession in blood or by lawful election, and then to arm subjects against their natural lords to make wars, and to dispense with them for their oaths in so doing, or to excommunicate faithful subjects for obeying of their natural princes, and lastly himself to make open war with his own soldiers against princes moving no force against him.

For if these [high tragical] powers should be permitted to him to exercise, then should no empire, no kingdom, no country, no city or town, be possessed by any lawful title longer than one such only, an earthly man, sitting (as he saith) in St. Peter's chair at Rome, should for his will and appetite (without warrant from God or man) think meet and determine, an authority never challenged by the Lord of Lords, the Son of God, Jesus Christ our only Lord and Savior and the only head of His Church whilst He was in His humanity upon the earth, nor yet delivered by any writing or certain tradition from St. Peter, from whom the Pope pretendeth to derive all his authority, nor yet from St. Paul, the Apostle of the Gentiles. But contrariwise, by all preachings, precepts, and writings contained in the gospel and other scriptures of the apostles, obedience is expressly commanded to all earthly princes, yea, even to kings by special name, and that so generally as no person is excepted from such duty of obedience, as by the sentence of St. Paul even to the Romans appeareth: *Omnis anima sublimioribus potestatibus sit subdita,* that is, "Let every soul be subject to the higher powers"; [39] within the compass of which law or precept, St. Chrysostom, being Bishop of Constantinople, writeth that even apostles, prophets, evangelists, and monks are comprehended.[40] And for proof of St. Peter's mind herein, from whom these Popes claim their authority, it can not be plainlier expressed than when he writeth thus: *Proinde subjecti estote quivis humanae ordinationi, propter Dominum, sive regi, ut qui superemineat, sive presidibus ab eo missis;* that is, "Therefore be you subject to every human ordinance or creature, for the Lord, whether it be to the king, as to him that is supereminent or above the rest, or to his presidents sent by him." [41] By which two principal apostles of Christ these Popes, the pretensed successors, but chiefly by that which Christ the Son of God, the only Master of truth, said to Peter and his fellow apostles: *Reges gentium*

[39] Rom. 13:1. [40] St. John Chrysostom, Homily 23 on Romans (13), ver. 1.
[41] I Pet. 2:13–14.

dominantur, vos autem non sic, that is, "The kings of the Gentiles have rule over them, but you not so," [42] may learn to forsake their arrogant and tyrannous authorities in earthly and temporal causes over kings and princes and exercise their pastoral office, as St. Peter was charged thrice at one time by his Lord and Master: *Pasce oves meas,* "Feed my sheep," [43] and peremptorily forbidden to use a sword, in saying to him: *Converte gladium tuum in locum suum,* or, *Mitte gladium tuum in vaginam,* that is, "Turn thy sword into his place," [44] or, "Put thy sword into the scabbard." [45]

All which precepts of Christ and His apostles were duly followed and observed many hundred years after their death by the faithful and godly Bishops of Rome, that duly followed the doctrine and humility of the apostles and the doctrine of Christ, [and were holy martyrs,] and thereby dilated the limits of Christ's Church and the faith more in the compass of an hundred years than the latter Popes have done with their swords and curses these five hundred years, and so continued until the time of one Pope Hildebrand, otherwise called Gregory the Seventh, about the year of Our Lord 1074, who first began to usurp that kind of tyranny which of late the late Pope called Pius the Fifth and since that time Gregory, now the Thirteenth, hath followed, for some example as it seemeth. That is, where Gregory the Seventh, in the year of Our Lord 1074 of thereabout, presumed to depose Henry the Fourth, a noble emperor then being, Gregory the Thirteenth now at this time would attempt the like against King Henry the Eighth's daughter and heir, Queen Elizabeth, a sovereign [and a maiden] queen, holding her crown immediately of God. And to the end it may appear to princes, or to their good counselors in one example, what was the fortunate success that God gave to this good Christian Emperor Henry against the proud Pope Hildebrand, it is to be noted that when the Pope

[42] Luke 22:25–26. [43] John 21:15–17. [44] Matt. 26:52.
[45] John 18:11.

Gregory attempted to depose this noble Emperor Henry, there was one Rudolf, a nobleman, by some named the Count of Rheinfelden, that by the Pope's procurement usurped the name of the emperor,[46] who was overcome by the said Henry, the lawful emperor, and in fight, having lost his right hand, he, the said Rudolf, lamented his case to certain bishops who, in the Pope's name, had erected him up, and to them he said that the selfsame right hand which he had lost was the same hand wherewith he had before sworn obedience to his lord and master, the Emperor Henry, and that in following their ungodly counsels he had brought upon him God's heavy and just judgments. And so Henry the Emperor, prevailing by God's power, caused Gregory the Pope by a synod in Italy to be deposed,[47] as in like times before him his predecessor Otto the Emperor had deposed one Pope John for many heinous crimes.[48] And so were also within a short time three other Popes, namely, Sylvester, Benedict, and Gregory the Sixth, used by the Emperor Henry the Third, about the year of Our Lord 1047, for their like presumptuous attempts in temporal actions against the said emperors.[49] Many other examples might be showed to the Emperor's Majesty and the princes of the holy empire now being, after the time of Henry the Fourth: as of Henry the Fifth, and after him, of Frederick the First and Frederick the Second, and then of Lewis of Bavaria,[50] all emperors cruelly and tyrannously persecuted by the Popes and by their bulls, curses, and by open wars, and likewise to many other the great kings and monarchs of Christendom of their noble

[46] Rudolf of Rheinfelden, Duke of Swabia, was elected anti-Emperor in 1077 by a diet meeting in Forchheim, with two papal legates in attendance.

[47] At Brixen, in 1080.

[48] Emperor Otto I had Pope John XII deposed in 963.

[49] Popes Gregory VI, Benedict IX, and Sylvester III were deposed by Emperor Henry III in 1046 and replaced by Pope Clement II.

[50] Henry V reigned from 1106 to 1125; Frederick I, Barbarossa, 1152–1190; Frederick II, 1212–1246; Louis IV or V, the Bavarian, 1314–1347.

progenitors, kings of their several dominions; whereby they may see how this kind of tyrannous authority in Popes to make wars upon emperors and kings and to command them to be deprived took hold at the first by Pope Hildebrand, though the same never had any lawful example or warrant from the laws of God of the Old or New Testament; but yet the successes of their tyrannies were, by God's goodness, for the most part made frustrate, as, by God's goodness, there is no doubt but the like will follow to their confusions at all times to come.

And therefore, as there is no doubt but the like violent tyrannous proceedings by any Pope in maintenance of traitors and rebels would be withstood by every sovereign prince in Christendom in defense of their persons and crowns and maintenance of their subjects in peace, so is there at this present a like just cause that the Emperor's Majesty, with the princes of the holy empire and all other sovereign kings and princes in Christendom, should judge the same to be lawful for Her Majesty, being a queen and holding the very place of a king and a prince sovereign over divers kingdoms and nations, she being also most lawfully invested in her crown, and as for good governing of her people with such applause and general allowance loved and obeyed of them, saving a few ragged traitors or rebels or persons discontented, whereof no other realm is free, as continually for these twenty-five years past hath been notably seen and so publicly marked, even by strangers repairing into this realm, as it were no cause of disgrace to any monarchy and king in Christendom to have Her Majesty's felicity compared with any of theirs whatsoever, and it may be there are many kings and princes could be well contented with the fruition of some proportion of her felicity. And though the Popes be now suffered by the Emperor in the lands of his own peculiar patrimony and by the two great monarchs, the French king and the King of Spain, in their dominions and territories (although by [many] other kings not so allowed) to continue his authority in sundry cases and his glorious title to be the universal bishop of the world, which title Gregory the Great, above nine hundred years past, called a profane title full of sacrilege, and a preamble of Antichrist; [51] yet in all their dominions and kingdoms, as also in the realm of England, most notably by many ancient laws, it is well known how many ways the tyrannous power of this, his excessive authority, hath been and still is restrained, checked, and limited by laws and pragmatics,[52] both ancient and new[, both in France and Spain and other dominions]; a very large field for the lawyers of those countries to walk in and discourse. And howsoever the Pope's canonists, being as his bombardiers, do make his excommunications and curses appear fearful to the multitude and simple people, yet all great emperors and kings aforetime, in their own cases, of their rights and royal pre-eminences, though the same concerned but a city or a poor town and sometime but the not allowance of some unworthy person to a bishopric or to an abbey, never refrained to despise all Pope's curses or forces, but attempted always, either by their swords to compel them to desist from their furious actions, or without any fear of themselves, in body, soul, or conscience, stoutly to withstand their curses, and that sometime by force, sometime by ordinances and laws; the ancient histories whereof are too many to be repeated and of none more frequent and effectual than of the Kings of France. [And in the records of England doth appear how stoutly the kings and the baronady of England, from age to age, by extreme penal laws have so repelled the Pope's usurpations as with the very name of praemunires [53] his proctors have been terrified and his clergy have quaked, as of late Cardinal Wolsey [54] did prove.]

[51] Pope Gregory the Great, *Letters,* lib. 7, Letter 33. Cf. also lib. 5, especially Letter 18.

[52] Pragmatic sanctions, or royal ordinances issued as fundamental laws.

[53] Writs ordering the summons of persons accused of prosecuting in foreign courts, especially papal courts, suits cognizable by the law of England.

[54] When Cardinal Wolsey fell from the King's favor in 1529, shortly before his death, he was indicted for violating the law of praemunire.

But leaving those that are ancient, we may remember how in this our own present or late age it hath been manifestly seen how the army of the late noble Emperor Charles the Fifth, father to King Philip that now reigneth, was not afraid of his curses, when in the year of Our Lord 1527 Rome itself was besieged and sacked and the Pope, then called Clement, and his cardinals, to the number of about thirty-three, in his Mount Hadrian, or Castle St. Angelo, taken prisoners and detained seven months or more and after ransomed by Don Ugo de Moncada, a Spaniard,[55] and the Marquis of Guasto,[56] at above four hundred thousand ducats, besides the ransoms of his cardinals, which was much greater, having not long beforetime been also (notwithstanding his curses) besieged in the same castle by the family of the Colonnas [57] and their fautors,[58] his next neighbors, being then imperialists, and forced to yield to all their demands. Neither did King Henry the Second of France, father to Henry now King of France, about the year 1550, fear or regard the Pope or his court of Rome when he made several strait edicts against many parts of the Pope's claims in prejudice of the crown and clergy of France, retracting the authority of the court of Rome, greatly to the hindrance of the Pope's former profits.[59] Neither was the army of King Philip now of Spain, whereof the Duke of Alva was general, stricken with any fear of cursing when it was brought afore Rome against the Pope, in the year of Our Lord 1555,[60] where great destruction was made by the said army and all the delicate buildings, gardens, and orchards next to Rome walls overthrown,

[55] An imperial ambassador, who helped negotiate the terms of Pope Clement VII's release, following the sack of Rome.

[56] Probably Alfonso del Vasto, an imperial army commander.

[57] The powerful Roman family of the Colonna had, with encouragement from Moncada, seized Rome for a short time in 1526.

[58] Patrons, partisans, abettors.

[59] Henry II, edict of "small dates" of June, 1550, regulating the impetration of benefices; edict of September 3, 1551, regulating transfer of funds to Rome.

[60] Actually it was in August of 1557 that Alva's army invested Rome. He soon withdrew.

wherewith His Holiness was more terrified than he was able to remove with any his curses. Neither was Queen Mary, the Queen's Majesty's noble late sister, a person not a little devoted to the Roman religion, so afraid of the Pope's cursings but that both she and her whole council, and that with the assent of all the judges of the realm, according to the ancient laws, in favor of Cardinal Pole her kinsman,[61] did [most straitly] forbid the entry of his bulls and of a cardinal hat at Calais that was sent from the Pope for one Friar Peto,[62] an observant pleasant friar, whom the Pope had assigned to be a cardinal in disgrace of Cardinal Pole. Neither did Cardinal Pole himself at the same time obey the Pope's commandments nor showed himself afraid, being assisted by the Queen, when the Pope did threaten him with pain of [curses and] excommunications, but did still oppose himself against the Pope's commandment for the said pretended Cardinal Peto, who, notwithstanding all the threatenings of the Pope, was forced to go up and down in the streets of London like a begging friar[, without his red hat]; a stout resistance in a queen for a poor cardinal's hat, wherein she followed the example of her grandfather King Henry the Seventh for a matter of alum[63] [, wherein the King used very great severity against the Pope]. So as howsoever the Christian kings for some respects in policy can endure the Pope to command where no harm nor disadvantage groweth to themselves, yet sure it is, and the Popes are not ignorant, but where they shall in any sort attempt to take from

[61] Reginald Pole, Archbishop of Canterbury and principal ecclesiastical adviser to Queen Mary.

[62] William Peto or Peyto, an elderly Franciscan friar, probably in his dotage by this time. He gave old age as a reason for declining both the Queen's nomination as Bishop of Salisbury and the Pope's nomination as legate in place of Pole.

[63] The Renaissance papacy had a near monopoly of alum production in the West and used ecclesiastical censures to prevent purchase of alum from other, usually infidel, sources. This monopoly was occasionally resisted by Henry VII and others. See allusions in A. F. Pollard, *The Reign of Henry VII* (London, 1913–1914), I, xlviii; III, 154n.

Christian princes any part of their dominions, or shall give aid to their enemies, or to any other their rebels, in those cases their bulls, their curses, their excommunications, their sentences and most solemn anathematicals, no, nor their crossed keys or double-edged sword, will serve their turns to compass their intentions.

And now, where the Pope hath manifestly, by his bulls and excommunications, attempted as much as he could to deprive Her Majesty of her kingdoms, to withdraw from her the obedience of her subjects, to procure rebellions in her realms, yea, to make both rebellions and open wars, with his own captains, soldiers, banners, ensigns, and all other things belonging to war; shall this Pope [Gregory], or any other Pope after him, think that a sovereign queen possessed of the two realms of England and Ireland, stablished so many years in her kingdoms as three or four Popes have sit in their chair at Rome, fortified with so much duty, love, and strength of her subjects, acknowledging no superior over her realms but the mighty hand of God; shall she forbear or fear to withstand and make frustrate his unlawful attempts, either by her sword or by her laws, or to put his soldiers, invaders of her realm, to the sword martially, or to execute her laws upon her own rebellious subjects civilly, that are proved to be his chief instruments for rebellion and for his open war? This is sure, that howsoever either he sitting in his chair with a triple crown at Rome or any other his proctors in any part of Christendom shall renew these unlawful attempts, Almighty God, [the King of Kings,] whom Her Majesty only honoreth and acknowledgeth to be her only sovereign lord and protector, and whose laws and gospel of His Son, Jesus Christ, she seeketh to defend, will no doubt but deliver sufficient power into His maiden's hand, His servant Queen Elizabeth, to withstand and confound them all.

And where the seditious trumpeters of infamies and lies have sounded forth and entitled certain that have suffered for treason to be martyrs for religion; so may they also at this time, if they list, add to their forged catalogue the headless body of the late miserable Earl of Desmond,[64] [the head of the Irish rebellion,] who of late, secretly wandering without succor as a miserable beggar, was taken by one of the Irishry in his cabin, and, in an Irish sort after his own accustomed savage manner, his head cut off from his body; an end due to such an arch-rebel. And herewith, to remember the end of his chief confederates, may be noted for example to others the strange manner of the death of Dr. Sanders, the Pope's Irish legate, who also, wandering in the mountains in Ireland without succor, died raving in a frenzy. And before him, one James Fitzmaurice,[65] the first traitor of Ireland next to Stukely the rakehell, a man not unknown in the Pope's palace for a wicked crafty traitor, was slain at one blow by an Irish noble young gentleman in defense of his father's country, which the traitor sought to burn. A fourth man of singular note was John of Desmond,[66] brother to the Earl, a very bloody faithless traitor and a notable murderer of his familiar friends, who, also wandering to seek some prey like a wolf in the woods, was taken and beheaded after his own usage, being, as he thought, sufficiently armed with the Pope's bulls and certain *Agnus Dei,* and one notable ring [with a precious stone] about his neck sent from the Pope's finger, as it was said; but these he saw saved not his life. And such were the fatal ends of all these, being the principal heads of the Irish war and rebellion, so as no one person remaineth at this day in Ireland a known traitor[: a work of God, and not of man]. To this number they may, if they seek number, also add a furious young man of Warwickshire, by name Somerville,[67] to increase their calendar of the Pope's martyrs, who of

[64] Gerald Fitzgerald, fifteenth Earl of Desmond, beheaded in 1583.

[65] James Fitzmaurice Fitzgerald, cousin of Gerald Fitzgerald, the leader of the 1579 invasion of Ireland, killed soon thereafter.

[66] Sir John Fitzgerald of Desmond, leader of the Irish revolt after the death of Fitzmaurice and until his brother joined the rebels, killed in 1581.

[67] John Somerville (1560–1583), a Roman Catholic layman, arrested for openly threatening to kill the Queen, died in prison, apparently a suicide.

late was discovered and taken in his way, coming with a full intent to have killed Her Majesty, whose life God always have in His custody. The attempt not denied by the traitor himself but confessed, and that he was moved thereto in his wicked spirit by enticements of certain seditious and traitorous persons, his kinsmen and allies,[68] and also by often reading of sundry seditious vile books lately published against Her Majesty[; and his end was in desperation to strangle himself to death: an example of God's severity against such as presume to offer violence to His anointed].

But as God, of His goodness, hath of long time hitherto preserved Her Majesty from these and the like treacheries, so hath she no cause to fear being under His protection, she saying with King David in the psalm, "My God is my helper, and I will trust in Him; He is my protection and the strength or the power of my salvation."[69] And for the more comfort of all good subjects against the shadows of the Pope's bulls, it is manifest to the world that from the beginning of Her Majesty's reign, by God's singular goodness, her kingdom hath enjoyed more universal peace, her people increased in more numbers, in more strength, and with greater riches, [and with less sickness,] the earth of her kingdoms hath yielded more fruits, and generally all kind of worldly felicity hath more abounded since and during the time of the Pope's thunders, bulls, curses, and maledictions than in any other long times before, when the Pope's pardons and blessings came yearly into the realm; so as his curses and maledictions have turned back to himself and his fautors, that it may be said to the blessed Queen [Elizabeth] of England and her people, as was said in Deuteronomy of Balaam, "The Lord thy God would not hear Balaam, but did turn his maledictions or curses into benedictions or blessings"; the reason is, "For because thy God loved thee."[70]

[68] Somerville implicated his wife, his father-in-law, Edward Arden, his mother-in-law, and a priest named Hugh Hall. All were arrested, tried, and found guilty. Arden alone was executed.

[69] Apparently Ps. 18:2.

[70] Deut. 23:5.

Although these former reasons are sufficient to persuade all kind of reasonable persons to allow of Her Majesty's actions to be good, reasonable, lawful, and necessary; yet because it may be that such as have by frequent reading of false artificial libels and by giving credit to them upon a prejudice or forejudgment afore grounded by their rooted opinions in favor of the Pope, will rest unsatisfied; therefore as much as may be, to satisfy all persons as far forth as common reason may warrant that Her Majesty's late action in executing of certain seditious traitors hath not proceeded for the holding of opinions either for the Pope's supremacy or against Her Majesty's regality but for the very crimes of sedition and treason, it shall suffice briefly, in a manner of a repetition of the former reasons, to remember these things following:

First, it cannot be denied but that Her Majesty did for many years suffer quietly the Pope's bulls and excommunications without punishment of the fautors thereof, accounting of them but as of words or wind, or of writings in parchment weighed down with lead, or as of water bubbles, commonly called in Latin *bullae,* and suchlike. But yet after some proof that courage was taken thereof by some bold and bad subjects, she could not but then esteem them to be very preambles or as forerunners of greater danger. And therefore, with what reason could any mislike that Her Majesty did for a bare defense against them, without other action or force, use the help of reviving of former laws to prohibit the publication or execution of such kind of bulls within her realm?

Secondly, when, notwithstanding the prohibition by her laws, the same bulls were plentifully (but in secret sort) brought into the realm, and at length arrogantly set upon the gates of the Bishop of London's palace, near to the cathedral church of Paul's, the principal city of the realm, by a lewd person [71] using the same like a herald sent from the Pope, who can, in any common reason,

[71] John Felton, Roman Catholic layman, who was hanged for this act, in 1570.

mislike that Her Majesty, finding this kind of denunciation of war as a defiance to be made in her principal city by one of her subjects avowing and obstinately maintaining the same, should, according to justice, cause the offender to have the reward due to such a fact? And this was the first action of any capital punishment inflicted for matter sent from Rome to move rebellion, which was after Her Majesty had reigned about the space of twelve years or more[, a time sufficient to prove Her Majesty's patience].

Thirdly, when the Pope had risen up out of his chair in his wrath from words and writings to actions, and had, contrary to the advice given by St. Bernard to [one of] his predecessors, that is, when by his messages he left *verbum* and took *ferrum,*[72] that is, left to feed by the word, [which was his office,] and began to strike with the sword, [which was forbidden him,] and stirred her noblemen and people directly to disobedience and to open rebellion, [which was the office of Dathan and Abiram,] [73] and that her lewd subjects by his commandment had executed the same with all the forces which they could make or bring into the field; who with common reason can disallow that Her Majesty used her royal lawful authority and by her forces lawful subdued rebels' forces unlawful, and punished the authors thereof no otherwise than the Pope himself useth to do with his own rebellious subjects in the patrimony of his Church[, as not many months past he had been forced to intend]? [74] And if any prince of people in the world would otherwise neglect his office and suffer his rebels to have their wills, none ought to pity him if, for want of resistance and courage, he lost both his crown, his head, his life, and his kingdom.

Fourthly, when Her Majesty beheld a further increase of the

[72] St. Bernard of Clairvaux, *De consideratione ad Eugenium,* lib. 4, cap. 3, advice to Pope Eugenius III, his disciple.

[73] Leaders, with Korah, of a revolt against Moses (Numbers 16).

[74] Gregory XIII had forcibly suppressed several bands of bandits active in the papal state in recent months.

Pope's malice, notwithstanding that the first rebellion was in her north parts vanquished, in that he entertained abroad, out of this realm, the traitors and rebels that fled for the rebellion and all the rabble of other the fugitives of the realm, and that he sent a number of the same in sorts disguised into both the realms of England and Ireland, who there secretly allured her people to new rebellions, and at the same time spared not his charges to send also out of Italy by sea certain ships with captains of his own, with their bands of soldiers, furnished with treasure, munition, victuals, ensigns, banners, and all other things requisite to the war, into her realm of Ireland, where the same forces, with other auxiliary companies out of Spain, landed and fortified themselves very strongly on the seaside and proclaimed open war, erecting the Pope's banner against Her Majesty; may it be now asked of these persons, favorers of the Romish authority, what in reason should have been done by Her Majesty otherwise than first to apprehend all such fugitives so stolen into the realm and dispersed in disguising habits to sow sedition—as some priests in their secret profession, but all in their apparel as roisters or ruffians, some scholars, like to the basest common people—and them to commit to prisons, and upon their examinations of their trades and haunts to convince them of their conspiracies abroad, by testimony of their own companions, and of sowing sedition secretly at home in the realm? What may be reasonably thought was meet to be done with such seditious persons but by the laws of the realm to try, condemn, and execute them? And specially having regard to the dangerous time, when the Pope's forces were in the realm of Ireland, and more in preparation to follow as well into England as into Ireland, to the resistance whereof Her Majesty and her realm was forced to be at greater charges than ever she had been since she was queen thereof. And so by God's power, which He gave to her on the one part, she did by her laws suppress the seditious stirrers of rebellion in her realm of England and by her sword vanquished all the Pope's forces in her realm of

Ireland, excepting certain captains of mark that were saved from the sword as persons that did renounce their quarrel and seemed to curse or to blame such as sent them to so unfortunate and desperate a voyage.

But though these reasons, grounded upon rules of natural reason, shall satisfy a great number of the adversaries (who will yield that by good order of civil and Christian policy and government Her Majesty could nor can do no less than she hath done, first to subdue with her forces her rebels and traitors, and next by order of her laws to correct the aiders and abettors, and lastly to put also to the sword such forces as the Pope sent into her dominions), yet there are certain other persons, more nicely addicted to the Pope, that will yet seem to be unsatisfied; for that, as they will term the matter, a number of silly poor wretches were put to death as traitors, being but in profession scholars or priests, by the names of seminaries, Jesuits, or simple schoolmasters, that came not into the realm with any armor or weapon by force to aid the rebels and traitors, either in England or in Ireland, in their rebellions or wars; of which sort of wretches the commiseration is made as though for their contrary opinions in religion, or for teaching of the people to disobey the laws of the realm, they might have been otherwise punished and corrected but yet not with capital pain. These kinds of defenses tend only to find fault rather with the severity of their punishments than to acquit them as innocents or quiet subjects. But for answer to the better satisfaction of these nice and scrupulous favorers of traitors, it must be with reason demanded of them (if at least they will open their ears to reason), whether they think that when a king, being stablished in his realm, hath a rebellion first secretly practiced and afterward openly raised in his realm, by his own seditious subjects; and when, by a foreign potentate or enemy, the same rebellion is maintained, and the rebels, by messages and promises, comforted to continue and their treasons against their natural prince avowed; and consequently when the same potentate and enemy, being author of the said rebellion, shall with his own proper forces invade the realm and subjects of the prince that is so lawfully and peaceably possessed; in these cases shall no subject favoring these rebels and yielding obedience to the enemy the invader be committed or punished as a traitor but only such of them as shall be found openly to carry armor and weapon? Shall no subject that is a spial [75] and an explorer for the rebel or enemy against his natural prince be taken and punished as a traitor, because he is not found with armor or weapon, but yet is taken in his disguised apparel with [scrolls and] writings or other manifest tokens to prove him a spy for traitors, after he hath wandered secretly in his sovereign's camp, region, court, or city? Shall no subject be counted a traitor that will secretly give earnest and prest money [76] to persons to be rebels or enemies, or that will attempt to poison the victual or the fountains, or secretly set on fire the ships or munition, or that will secretly search and sound the havens and creeks for landing, or measure the depth of ditches or height of bulwarks and walls, because these offenders are not found with armor or weapon? The answer, I think, must needs be yielded (if reason and experience shall have rule with these adversaries) that all these and suchlike are to be punished as traitors; and the principal reason is because [it cannot be denied but that] the actions of all these are necessary accessories and adherents proper to further and continue all rebellions and wars. But if they will deny that none are traitors that are not armed, they will make Judas no traitor that came to Christ without armor, coloring his treason with a kiss.

Now, therefore, it resteth to apply the facts of these late malefactors that are pretended to have offended but as scholars or bookmen, or at the most but as persons that only in words and doctrine and not with armor did favor and help the rebels and the enemies. For which purpose let these persons be termed as they list: scholars, schoolmasters, bookmen, seminaries, priests,

[75] Spy, scout.

[76] Money advanced to men enlisting in an armed force.

Jesuits, friars, beadmen,[77] romanists, pardoners, or what else you will, neither their titles nor their apparel hath made them traitors, but their traitorous secret motions and practices; their persons have not made the war, but their directions and counsels have set up the rebellions. [It is truly to be pondered that] the very causes final of these rebellions and wars have been to depose Her Majesty from her crown [; the Pope's bull hath roared it so to be]. The causes instrumental are these kind of seminaries and seedmen of sedition[; their secret teachings and reconciliations have confirmed it]. The fruits and effects thereof are by rebellion to shed the blood of all her faithful subjects. The rewards of the invaders (if they could prevail) should be the disinheriting of all the nobility, the clergy, and the whole commonalty that would (as they are bound by the laws of God, by their birth, and oaths) defend their natural gracious queen, their native country, their wives, their children, their family, and their houses. And now examine these which you call your unarmed scholars and priests wherefore they [first fled out of the realm, why they] lived and were conversant in company of the principal rebels and traitors at Rome and in other places where it is proved that they were partakers of their conspiracies. Let it be answered why they came thus by stealth into the realm. Why they have wandered up and down in corners in disguised sort, changing their titles, names, and manner of apparel. Why they have enticed and sought to persuade by their secret false reasons the people to allow and believe all the actions and attempts whatsoever the Pope hath done or shall do to be lawful. Why they have reconciled and withdrawn so many people in corners from the laws of the realm to the obedience of the Pope, a foreign potentate and open enemy, whom they know to have already declared the Queen to be no lawful queen, to have maintained the known rebels and traitors, to have invaded Her Majesty's dominions with open war. Examine further how these vagrant, disguised, unarmed spies

[77] Men who pray for others.

have answered when they were taken and demanded what they thought of the bull of Pope Pius the Fifth, which was published to deprive the Queen's Majesty and to warrant her subjects to disobey her, whether they thought that all subjects ought to obey the same bull and so to rebel. Secondly, whether they thought Her Majesty to be the lawful queen of the realm, notwithstanding the said bull or any other bull of the Pope. Thirdly, whether the Pope might give such license as he did to the Earls of Northumberland and Westmorland and other Her Majesty's subjects to rebel as they did, or give power to Dr. Sanders, a natural born subject but an unnatural worn priest, to take arms and move wars as he did in Ireland. Fourthly, whether the Pope may discharge the subjects of Her Majesty, or of any other princes christened, of their oaths of obedience. Fifthly, whether the said traitorous priest, Dr. Sanders, or one Bristow,[78] a rebellious fugitive, did in their books write truly or falsely in approving the said bull of Pius the Fifth and the contents thereof. Lastly, what were to be done if the Pope, or any other assigned by him, would invade the realm of England, and what part they would take, or what part any faithful subject of Her Majesty's ought to take.[79]

To these [few] questions, very apt to try the truth or falsehood of any such seditious persons, being justly before condemned for their disloyalty, these lewd unarmed traitors, I say, would nowise answer directly hereto, as all other faithful subjects to any prince Christian ought to do. And as they, upon refusal to answer di-

[78] Richard Bristow (1538–1581), prominent Catholic polemicist in exile. The book by him referred to, commonly called Bristow's *Motives,* was first published in Antwerp in 1574 under the title, *A Brief Treatise of Diverse Plain and Sure Ways to Find out the Truth in This . . . Time of Heresy, Containing Sundry Worthy Motives unto the Catholic Faith* (STC 3799), reprinted and revised several times.

[79] These six questions were put to a number of Jesuits and seminary priests on trial for treason in May of 1582. For a more extended copy of them and a number of answers see *Cobbett's Complete Collection of State Trials* (hereafter cited as *Cobbett's State Trials),* I (London, 1809), cols. 1078–1084.

rectly to these questions only, might have been justly convinced as guilty of treason, so yet were they not thereupon condemned but upon all their other former actions committed, both abroad and in the realm, which were no less traitorous than the actions of all other the spies and traitors, and of Judas himself afore remembered, which had no armor nor weapon and yet at all times ought to be adjudged traitors. For these disguised persons (called scholars or priests), having been first conversant of long time with the traitors beyond the sea in all their conspiracies, came hither by stealth, in time of war and rebellion, by commandment of the capital enemy, the Pope, or his legates, to be secret espials and explorers in the realm for the Pope, to deliver, by secret Romish tokens, as it were, an earnest or prest to them that should be in readiness to join with rebels or open enemies; and in like sort with their hallowed baggages from Rome to poison the senses of the subjects, pouring into their hearts malicious and pestilent opinions against Her Majesty and the laws of the realm; and also to kindle and set on fire the hearts of discontented subjects with the flames of rebellion; and to search and sound the depths and secrets of all men's inward intentions, either against Her Majesty or for her. And finally, to bring into a beadroll, or, as it were, into a muster roll, the names and powers, with the dwellings, of all them that should be ready to rebel and to aid the foreign invasion. These kinds of seditious actions for the service of the Pope and the traitors and rebels abroad have made them traitors, not their books, nor their beads, no, nor their cakes of wax which they call *Agnus Dei,* nor other their relics; no, nor yet their opinions for the ceremonies or rites of the Church of Rome; and therefore it is to be certainly concluded that these did justly deserve their capital punishments as traitors, though they were not apprehended with open armor or weapon.

Now if this latter repetition, as it were, of all the former causes and reasons afore recited, may not serve to stop the boisterous mouths and the pestiferous tongues and venomous breaths of these that are infected with so gross errors as to defend seditious subjects, stirrers of rebellion against their natural prince and country, then are they to be left without any further argument to the judgment of the Almighty God, as persons that have covered their eyes against the sun's light, stopped their ears against the sound of justice, and oppressed their hearts against the force of reason; and, as the psalmist saith, "They speak lies, they are as venomous as the poison of a serpent, even like the deaf adder that stoppeth his ears." [80]

Wherefore, with [Christian] charity to conclude, if these rebels and traitors and their fautors would yet take some remorse and compassion of their natural country, and would consider how vain their attempts have been so many years, and how many of their confederates are wasted by miseries and calamities, [and how none of all their attempts or plots have prospered,] and [therefore] would desist from their unnatural practices abroad; and if these seminaries, secret wanderers, and explorators [81] in the dark would employ their travails in the works of light and doctrine, according to the usage of their schools, and content themselves with their profession and devotion; and that the remnant of the wicked flock of the seedmen of sedition would cease from their rebellious, false, and infamous railings and libelings[, altogether contrary to Christian charity]; there is no doubt, by God's grace (Her Majesty being so much given to mercy and devoted to peace), but all color and occasion of shedding the blood of any more of her natural subjects of this land[, yea, all further bodily punishments,] should utterly cease. Against whose malices, if they shall not desist, Almighty God continue Her Majesty, with His spirit and power, long to reign and live in His fear and to be able to vanquish them all, being God's enemies, and [especially] her rebels and traitors both at home and abroad, and to maintain and preserve all her natural good loving subjects

[80] Ps. 58:3–4.

[81] Spies, scouts.

to the true service of the same Almighty God, according to His holy word and will.

Many other things might be remembered for defense of other Her Majesty's princely, honorable, and godly actions in sundry other things, wherein also these and the like seditious railers have of late time, without all shame, by feigned and false libels, sought to discredit Her Majesty and her government. But at this time, these former causes and reasons alleged by way of advertisements[, only for maintenance of truth,] are sufficient to justify Her Majesty's actions to the whole world in the cases remembered.

[2 Esdras 4.

Magna est veritas, et praevalet.

Great is truth, and she overcometh.] [82]

Finis.

[82] I Esd. 4:41.

A Declaration
of the favorable dealing of Her Majesty's Commissioners appointed for the examination of certain traitors and of tortures unjustly reported to be done upon them for matters of religion
1583

To the Reader

Good reader, although Her Majesty's most mild and gracious government be sufficient to defend itself against those most slanderous reports of heathenish and unnatural tyranny and cruel tortures pretended to have been executed upon certain traitors who lately suffered for their treason, and others, as well spread abroad by renegade Jesuits and seminary men in their seditious books, letters, and libels in foreign countries and princes' courts as also insinuated into the hearts of some of our own countrymen and Her Majesty's subjects; yet for thy better satisfaction I have conferred with a very honest gentleman whom I knew to have good and sufficient means to deliver the truth against such forgers of lies and shameless slanders in that behalf, which he and other that do know and have affirmed the same will at all times justify. And for thy further assurance and satisfaction herein, he hath set down to the view of all men these notes following.

Touching the rack and torments used to such traitors as pretended themselves to be Catholics upon whom the same have been exercised, it is affirmed for truth and is offered upon due examination so to be proved to be as followeth. First, that the forms of torture in their severity or rigor of execution have not been such and in such manner performed as the slanderers and seditious libelers have slanderously and maliciously published. And that even the principal offender, Campion himself,[1] who was sent and came from Rome and continued here in sundry corners

[1] Edmund Campion, S.J. See above, p. 17.

of the realm, having secretly wandered in the greatest part of the shires of England in a disguised sort to the intent to make special preparation of treasons, and to that end and for furtherance of those his labors sent over for more help and assistance, and cunningly and traitorously at Rome before he came from thence procured toleration for such prepared rebels to keep themselves covert under pretense of temporary and permissive obedience to Her Majesty, the state standing as it doth, but so soon as there were sufficient force whereby the bull of Her Majesty's deprivation might be publicly executed they should then join all together with that force upon pain of curse and damnation; that very Campion, I say, before the conference had with him by learned men in the Tower, wherein he was charitably used, was never so racked but that he was presently able to walk and to write, and did presently write and subscribe all his confessions, as by the originals thereof may appear. A horrible matter is also made of the starving of one Alexander Briant,[2] how he should eat clay out of the walls, gathered water to drink from the droppings of houses, with such other false ostentations of immanity.[3] Where the truth is this, that whatsoever Briant suffered in want of food, he suffered the same willfully and of extreme impudent obstinacy against the mind and liking of those that dealt with him. For, certain traitorous writings being found about him, it was thought convenient by conference of hands to understand whose writing they were, and thereupon, he being in Her Majesty's name commanded to write, which he could very well do, and being permitted to him to write what he would himself in these terms; that if he liked not to write one thing, he might write another or what he listed (which to do, being charged in Her Majesty's name, was his duty, and to refuse was disloyal and undutiful); yet the man would by no means be induced to write anything at all. Then was

[2] Alexander Briant, S.J., ordained a priest in Reims in 1578, executed with Campion in London in 1581.

[3] Monstrous cruelty, atrocious savagery.

it commanded to his keeper to give unto him such meat, drink, and other convenient necessaries as he would write for and to forbear to give him anything for which he would not write. But Briant, being thereof advertised and oft moved to write, persisting so in his curst heart by almost two days and two nights, made choice rather to lack food than to write for the sustenance which he might readily have had for writing and which he had indeed readily and plentifully so soon as he wrote. And as it is said of these two, so is it to be truly said of other, with this, that there was a perpetual care had, and the Queen's servants, the warders, whose office and act it is to handle the rack, were ever by those that attended the examinations specially charged to use it in as charitable manner as such a thing might be.

Secondly, it is said, and likewise offered to be justified, that never any of these seminaries or such other pretended Catholics which at any time in Her Majesty's reign have been put to the rack were upon the rack or in other torture demanded any question of their supposed conscience as what they believed in any point of doctrine or faith, as the mass, transubstantiation, or suchlike; but only with what persons at home or abroad and touching what plots, practices, and conferences they had dealt about attempts against Her Majesty's estate or person, or to alter the laws of the realm for matters of religion by treason or by force, and how they were persuaded themselves and did persuade other, touching the Pope's bull and pretense of authority to depose kings and princes; and namely for deprivation of Her Majesty and to discharge subjects from their allegiance, expressing herein always the kingly powers and estates and the subjects' allegiance civilly, without mentioning or meaning therein any right that the Queen, as in right of the crown, hath over persons ecclesiastical, being her subjects. In all which cases Campion and the rest never answered plainly, but sophistically, deceitfully, and traitorously, restraining their confession of allegiance only to the permissive form of the Pope's toleration. As for example, if they were asked whether they did acknowledge themselves the Queen's subjects and would obey her, they would say yea, for so they had leave for a time to do. But adding more to the question, and they being asked if they would so acknowledge and obey her any longer than the Pope would so permit them, or notwithstanding such commandment as the Pope would or might give to the contrary, then they either refused so to obey, or denied to answer, or said that they could not answer to those questions without danger. Which very answer without more saying was a plain answer to all reasonable understanding that they would no longer be subjects nor persuade other to be subjects than the Pope gave license. And at their very arraignment, when they labored to leave in the minds of the people and standers-by an opinion that they were to die not for treason but for matter of faith and conscience in doctrine touching the service of God, without any attempt or purpose against Her Majesty, they cried out that they were true subjects and did and would obey and serve Her Majesty. Immediately, to prove whether that hypocritical and sophistical speech extended to a perpetuity of their obedience or to so long time as the Pope so permitted or no, they were openly in place of judgment asked by the Queen's learned counsel whether they would so obey and be true subjects if the Pope commanded the contrary. They plainly disclosed themselves in answer, saying by the mouth of Campion, "This place" (meaning the court of Her Majesty's Bench) "hath no power to inquire or judge of the Holy Father's authority," and other answer they would not make.

Thirdly, that none of them have been put to the rack or torture, no not for the matters of treason or partnership of treason or suchlike, but where it was first known and evidently probable by former detections, confessions, and otherwise that the party so racked or tortured was guilty and did know and could deliver truth of the things wherewith he was charged. So as it was first assured that no innocent was at any time tormented. And the rack was never used to wring out confessions at adventure upon uncertainties, in which doing it might be possible that an innocent in that case might have been racked.

Fourthly, that none of them hath been racked or tortured unless he had first said expressly, or amounting to as much, that he will not tell the truth though the Queen command him. And if any of them being examined did say he could not tell or did not remember, if he would so affirm in such manner as Christians among Christians are believed, such his answer was accepted if there were not apparent evidence to prove that he willfully said untruly. But if he said that his answer in delivering truth should hurt a Catholic and so be an offense against charity, which they said to be sin, and that the Queen could not command them to sin, and therefore, howsoever the Queen commanded, they would not tell the truth which they were known to know, or to such effect; they were then put to the torture, or else not.

Fifthly, that the proceeding to torture was always so slowly, so unwillingly, and with so many preparations of persuasions to spare themselves, and so many means to let them know that the truth was by them to be uttered both in duty to Her Majesty and in wisdom for themselves, as whosoever was present at those actions must needs acknowledge in Her Majesty's ministers a full purpose to follow the example of her own most gracious disposition, whom God long preserve.

Thus it appeareth that, albeit by the more general laws of nations torture hath been and is lawfully judged to be used in lesser cases and in sharper manner for inquisition of truth in crimes not so near extending to public danger as these ungracious persons have committed, whose conspiracies and the particularities thereof it did so much import and behoove to have disclosed, yet even in that necessary use of such proceeding, enforced by the offender's notorious obstinacy, is nevertheless to be acknowledged the sweet temperature of Her Majesty's mild and gracious clemency and their slanderous lewdness to be the more condemned that have in favor of heinous malefactors and stubborn traitors spread untrue rumors and slanders to make her merciful government disliked under false pretense and rumors of sharpness and cruelty to those against whom nothing can be cruel and yet upon whom nothing hath been done but gentle and merciful.

Finis.

A True, Sincere, and Modest Defense of English Catholics That Suffer for their Faith both at Home and Abroad; against a False, Seditious, and Slanderous Libel Entitled: The Execution of Justice in England

Wherein is declared how unjustly the Protestants do charge Catholics with treason; how untruly they deny their persecution for religion; and how deceitfully they seek to abuse strangers about the cause, greatness, and manner of their sufferings, with divers other matters pertaining to this purpose.

Psal. 62.

Ut obstruatur os loquentium iniqua.

That the mouth may be stopped of such as speak unjustly.

Psal. 49.

Os tuum abundavit malitia, & lingua tua concinnabat dolos.

Thy mouth hath abounded in malice, and thy tongue hath cunningly framed lies.

THE PREFACE TO THE READER

ALBEIT the late pamphlet entitled *The Execution of Justice,* put forth in divers languages for defense or excuse of the violent proceeding against Catholics in England and for accusation as well of them at home as of us their fellows in faith abroad, passing forth without privilege and name either of writer or printer (even thence where such matter is specially current and might easily have been authorized), and moving indiscreet, odious, and dangerous disputes of estate, replenished with manifest untruths, open slanders of innocent persons, and namely with immodest malediction and seditious motions against the chief bishop, the prince of God's people; though (I say) it might rightly have been reputed an infamous libel, either to be contemned or with such freedom of speech refelled [1] as that manner of writing doth deserve; yet, considering the matter, meaning, and phrase thereof to be agreeable to the humor and liking of some in authority and the book not only not suppressed (as divers others of that argument, seeming over-simple to the wiser Protestants, of late have been) but often printed, much recommended, diligently divulged, and sought to be privileged in foreign places [2] where for shame they durst not publicly allow it at home; yea, and in a manner thrust into the hands of strangers and therefore like to proceed (though in close sort) from authority: we are forced and, in truth, very well contented and glad

[1] Refuted.

[2] [In France.]

it hath pleased God to give this occasion, or rather necessity, to yield (for the answer of the said book) our more particular account in the behalf of our Catholic brethren dead and alive, at home and in banishment.

Which we will do sincerely, as in the sight of Christ Jesus, the just judge of the world, and all His saints, in such humble, mild, and temperate manner as beseemeth our profession and the audience, which audience we crave with tears of the whole Church and Christian world, and of all that are placed in power and sublimity over us in our own country or elsewhere, that so our cause may be discerned both by God and man and our unspeakable calamities, either by the intercession of many relieved, or by the general compassion of all our faithful brethren made to us more tolerable. Loath we are, and odious it may be counted, to speak in such matter as must needs in some sort touch our superiors; but God's truth and man's innocency are privileged and may in humble seemly wise be defended against whomsoever. And our pen (God willing) shall be so tempered herein that it shall displease no reasonable reader, nor surely scare them (if it may be) against whom in our inculpable defense we are forced to write.

We have in this case examples enough of Christian modesty in the ancient apologies of holy Fathers in Christ His Church, as of St. Justin, Tertullian, Athanasius, Hilarius, and other, writing to their princes that persecuted either by error or infidelity the faithful people.[3] Whose style and steps so long as we follow we shall be blameless in the sight of all wise and good men and offend none to whom the plain truth itself is not odious. As on the other side we have in our adversaries' late books, for immodest

[3] Reference to St. Justin Martyr, *First Apology,* addressed to Emperor Antoninus Pius and his adopted sons (ca. 155), and *Second Apology,* addressed to the Roman Senate (ca. 161); Tertullian, *Apologeticum,* addressed to the prefects of the Roman provinces (ca. 197); St. Athanasius' tracts against the Arian party at the imperial court (339–359); St. Hilary of Poitiers' anti-Arian tracts (ca. 353–367).

railing, contemptuous phrase, slanderous speech, blasphemous words, false, reproachful, seditious matter, and all inhonest scurrility, what to abhor and detest and what to avoid in these our writings, which we would have most unlike theirs and not only allowable to our friends but (if it were possible and so pleased Our merciful Lord to give us grace in their sight) not ingrateful to our persecutors, whose salvation (as Christ knoweth) we seek in all these our endeavors, together with the maintenance of truth, more than our own defense and purgation.

Whereupon otherwise, for our own only honor and interest, we would not so formally stand against so honorable adversaries in this world, if we thought either their hearts (which are in God's hands) were not upon evident reason and remonstrance of our innocency inclinable to mercy and better consideration of their own state and ours; or that their accusation of us afflicted Catholics were not joined to the general reprehension of the whole Church and the principal pastors thereof, whom by the law of our Christian religion we ought to respect more than our own lives and in causes of our soul and conscience to obey above any earthly prince, by what other obligation soever we be bound unto him.

And as we would gladly pass in this our answer with such equability and indifferency that in defense of the spiritual power (which by our adversaries' importunity we are driven in manner against our wills to treat of) we might not justly offend the temporal, acknowledging in divers respects all humble duty to them both; so, writing nothing that any man shall be able to prove untrue, either in fact or faith, we trust in the reader's equity, be he Catholic or Protestant, that in so faultless and necessary a defense of ourselves and of our superiors, as also of the common cause of our Christian faith and conscience, he will not judge our writing seditious, slanderous, or infamous libeling (as the nameless author of this invective, against whom we treat, unchristianly and uncourteously calleth other our brethren's books), recording only the heavy persecution, torments, and deaths of Catholics in such simple, plain, and sincere sort as indeed all things were done, and so as no man living can truly either charge the reporters of fiction or falsehood or of any evil intention of defaming to strangers their superiors' dealings, in making relation of our dear country's most doleful calamities. For the things there done daily in public cannot otherwise be hidden from the world; and, seeing they are passed by law and order of pretended justice, there can be no cause why themselves should mislike the divulging thereof, except they acknowledge in their conscience some iniquity and dishonorable defect in their proceedings against the most innocent persons whom daily they torment and make away.

We are not so perversely affected (God be praised) as purposely to dishonor our prince and country, for whose love in Christ so many have so meekly lost their lives; or to reveal their turpitude, which we would rather cover (if it were possible) from the eyes of the world with our own blood. But we set forth the truth of all these actions for the honor of our nation, which otherwise, to her infinite shame and reproach, would be thought wholly and generally to have revolted from the Catholic faith and consented to all the absurdities and iniquities of this new regiment and religion, if none with zeal and extreme endeavor resisted such pernicious innovations. Where now, as well our own people as all strangers in the Christian world, perceiving the disorder to proceed but of the partiality of a few powerable persons abusing Her Majesty's clemency and credulity, do glorify Our Lord God that in so great a temptation all the clergy in manner and so many of the laity of all sorts constantly persist in their fathers' faith, to the loss of goods, lands, lives, honors, and whatsoever besides, and that the whole state (excepting the authority of the prince) may yet be rather counted Catholic than heretical. This is the honor of our nation in all places, which otherwise (for double revolt and recidivation into schism and for extreme persecution) would be counted remediless, hopeless, and of all other places most infamous.

Secondly, we set forth these things for the memory and honor of such notable martyrs as have testified the truth of the Catholic faith by their precious death, which was an ancient canon and custom of the primitive Church, which appointed certain special persons of skill and learning to note the days of everyone's glorious confession and combat, that their memories might afterward be solemnly celebrated forever among Christians.[4]

Thirdly, we do it to communicate our calamities with our brethren in faith and the Churches of other provinces standing free from this misery, both for their warning and our comfort and to excite in them Christian compassion toward us; that thereby and by their counsel and prayers we may find mercy and relief at God's hand, by the example of the Oriental Churches afflicted by the Arians, which, as we may read in St. Basil, in their like distresses made their general complaints by often letters and messengers to the west Churches, standing more entire and void of that heresy and persecution.[5]

Finally, we are forced to publish these things so particularly and diligently to defend the doings of the said holy confessors and their fellows in faith against the manifold slanders and calumniations of certain heretics or politiques,[6] unjustly charging them with treason and other great trespasses against the commonwealth, to avert the eyes of the simple from the true causes of their suffering and to disappoint the holy personages (if they could) of the honor done to martyrs in God's Church. For that is one special cause among many why they had rather make them away for forged treason or other feigned offenses than for profession of the truth, which in their heart they hate more than any

[4] [See St. Cyprian.]

[5] [See St. Basil, Epist. 69 & 70.] St. Basil the Great, Letters 92 and 243 in Migne.

[6] Opportunists or temporizers.

crime in the world. St. Gregory Nazianzen lively expresseth the condition of all heretics in the behavior of Julianus the Apostate, thus writing of him:

He, openly and boldly professing impiety, yet by color of clemency covered his cruelty; and lest we should attain to the honors done customably to martyrs (which he disdained to the Christians), he used namely this fraud and deceit, that such as he caused to be tormented for Christ's cause should be thought and reported to be punished, not for their faith, but as malefactors.[7]

For discovery, therefore, of this sinful and deceitful dealing of our adversaries (who, not contented with the death and torments of God's saints, would punish them by ignominy after their life), we are driven to this dutiful office of their and the Holy Church's defense, whose honor and innocency we may not bewray for a thousand deaths.

Wherein we are not much terrified by the vain and vulgar exordium of the author of this invective which we now must refute, who beginneth above all art (after their manner) with a common sentence, as meet for us and our matter as for him and his cause, telling us that it is a common usage of all offenders, and specially rebels and traitors, to make defense of their lewd and unlawful facts by covering their deeds with pretense of other causes, which speech, as it might be used where any such trespass could be proved, so is it fondly said where no crime can be avouched, as in the process of this treatise shall be (by God's grace) most clearly convinced. And it might not only be applied by the old heathen or heretical persecutors against the first apostles and martyrs of Christ, being falsely charged with the same crimes as we be now, and answered for themselves as we do, but may much more be verified and found in public persons and

[7] [Oratione in laudem Caesaris.] St. Gregory Nazianzen, Oration no. 7, *In laudem Caesarii fratris,* cap. 11, alluding to the Emperor Flavius Claudius Julianus, the Apostate (331–363).

commonwealths, when they err or commit iniquity, than in any poor, private, or afflicted persons, be they never so guilty. For princes and communities in disorder have a thousand pretenses, excuses, and colors of their unjust actions. They have the name of authority, the shadow of laws, the pens and tongues of infinite at their commandment. They may print or publish what they like, suppress what they list. Whereof private men, be they never so wicked or good, have not so great commodity.

For examples we need not to go far out of our own country and memory. For when Richard the Third, intending to usurp the crown of England, slew divers of the nobility first most cruelly, and afterward murdered unnaturally his own innocent nephews, what solemn libels, proclamations, orations were put forth to justify his abominable iniquity? When the last Duke of Northumberland for the like ambitious purpose would have disabled and defeated traitorously both the noble daughters of his own sovereign and master and by the title of his daughter-in-law possessed himself of the crown,[8] what a number of pamphlets and edicts were published on the sudden for coloring of that foul treachery and intolerable treason! When Orange and his confederates revolted not long since from their natural prince, the Scottish heretics from their lawful sovereign,[9] and other provinces for the same cause from the unity and common faith of the Church, who hath not seen the infinite libels for their excuse in wickedness? That, therefore, that may sometimes fall in private men's causes for covering their sin and shame happeneth far oftener and much more dangerously in powerable and public persons. And so it maketh no more against us than this writer himself whether he hath published his libel by authority (as he

[8] Reference to Northumberland's abortive attempt to make Lady Jane Grey queen on the death of Edward VI in 1553, in place of Henry VIII's daughters, Mary and Elizabeth.

[9] [Jamy, Murton, etc.] Reference to the revolt against Mary Stuart in 1567, led by James Stuart, the Earl of Morton, and others.

will not seem) or of his own peculiar head and affection, which rather we are content to suppose.

Howsoever it be, we will be bold to examine in the treatise following with such modesty and indifferency as is requisite in God's cause his whole reprehension; and in the meantime till he can prove us or our brethren guilty of any crime, other than the exercise and profession of the Catholic faith, we will say with our Savior: *De bono opere lapidamur,*[10] and with the Apostle: *De spe et resurrectione mortuorum judicamur,*[11] *et propter spem Israel his catenis circundati sumus.*[12]

❦

Chapter I

That many priests and other Catholics in England have been persecuted, condemned, and executed for mere matter of religion and for transgression only of new statutes which do make cases of conscience to be treason without all pretense or surmise of any old treasons or statutes for the same

Now to the principal points of the libel: we first affirm that the very front or title thereof (importing that no Catholics at all, or none of them whom they have executed, were persecuted for their religion), is a very notorious untruth and contradictory to the libeler's own words in his discourse following, where he confesseth underhand that some be corrected otherwise for religion.[1] Or (if they will stand in the contrary) we appeal to the con-

[10] [John 10:32]: "Many good works have I showed you from my Father; for which of those works do ye stone me?"

[11] [Acts 23:6]: "Of the hope and resurrection of the dead I am called in question."

[12] [Acts 28:20]: "Because that for the hope of Israel I am bound with this chain."

[1] Cecil, p. 13.

science and knowledge of all the Catholics and Protestants within the realm, who of their equity will never deny that most prisons in England be full at this day and have been for divers years of honorable and honest persons not to be touched with any treason or other offense in the world other than their profession and faith in Christian religion.

Secondly, we say and shall clearly convince that, contrary to the pursuit of the same libel, a number have been also tormented, arraigned, condemned, and executed for mere matter of religion and upon the transgression of new statutes only, without any relation to the old treasons so made and set down by Parliament in Edward the Third's time, by which they untruly avouch all our brethren were convicted.

And herein to deal particularly and plainly, we allege the worthy priest and Bachelor of Divinity, Mr. Cuthbert Mayne [2] (who suffered a glorious martyrdom at Launceston in the province of Cornwall, for that the case or cover only of an *Agnus Dei,* and a printed copy of that bull, now expired, which denounced to the Christian world the last Jubilee,[3] were found about him), condemned not by any old laws (as is deceitfully pretended to abuse the simple of our own nation and strangers that know not our lamentable condition) but by a late statute enacted the thirteenth year of the Queen's reign [4] which maketh it high treason to bring from Rome any beads, sacred pictures, *Agnus Deis,* bulls, or (as the express words of the said statute are) "any writing or instrument, written or printed, containing any thing, matter, or cause whatsoever," by which words they may condemn a man to

[2] Cuthbert Mayne, first of the English priests trained on the Continent at Douai (or elsewhere) to be executed by the Elizabethan government. He was executed on November 29, 1577.

[3] This year of jubilee had begun on Christmas of 1574. For a description of its proclamation and celebration, see Ludwig von Pastor, *Geschichte der Päpste,* 11th ed., IX (Freiburg and Rome, 1958), 142 ff.; in the Eng. trans., *The History of the Popes,* XIX (London, 1930), 199 ff.

[4] 13 Eliz. I, c. 2.

death as guilty of high treason though he bring from Rome but letters testimonial for a traveler's credit and commendation in journey: a thing unheard of in all ages, not credible to foreigners and a fable to the posterity, or rather a warning to the world to come, into what misery and barbarousness a kingdom that forsaketh the Church may be brought unto. And an honorable gentleman of an ancient family,[5] for only receiving the said blessed priest into his house, remaineth condemned at this day to perpetual prison and hath lost both lands and goods of great importance for that fact.

Likewise Thomas Sherwood,[6] a layman indicted, adjudged, and put to death for questions of the Queen's supremacy in causes spiritual and other articles made capital by the new laws only two years at the least before this fiction of conspiracy against the realm or person of the princess was made or heard of. The same year was a reverend priest named Mr. John Nelson[7] condemned and executed for affirming (being driven thereunto by the commissioners' captious interrogatories) the Queen's religion to be heretical and schismatical, which is made death not by the old laws of the realm, nor by any other of any Christian country, but only by a statute made in the said thirteenth year of the Queen's reign,[8] providing by a special clause that none shall affirm Her Majesty that now is (for it holdeth not in other princes' cases to come) to be an heretic or schismatic, under pain of incurring high treason and death.

After these, Mr. Everard Hanse[9] was indicted and so con-

[5] [Mr. Tregian.] Francis Tregian, b. 1548, spent twenty-eight years in prison, ended his life in exile in Spain.

[6] Thomas Sherwood, a student at Douai, executed in London, February 7, 1578.

[7] John Nelson, studied at Douai, ordained a missionary priest in 1576, executed in London, February 3, 1578.

[8] 13 Eliz. I, c. 1.

[9] Everard Hanse, sent as a missionary priest from Reims in 1581, executed in London, July 31, 1581.

demned to death (which he constantly suffered) only upon a statute made in the last Parliament of all [10] (by which it is made a crime capital to persuade any man to the Catholic religion), into the compass of which law they violently drew the blessed man by calumnious interpretation of his speeches, when he affirmed (being urged thereunto) that the Pope was his superior in causes spiritual "and had in such matters spiritual as good right as he ever had in England or hath at this day in Rome," for which words, though enforced from him, he was there presently indicted, arraigned, and condemned to death, and soon after most cruelly executed, whose case, together with that of Mr. Nelson, which goeth before, declareth what truth is in this libeler who writeth here in one place that none are for their contrary opinions in religion persecuted or charged with any crimes or pains of treason, nor yet willingly searched in their consciences for their contrary opinions. And again within a leaf after he repeateth the same untruth, saying: "Without charging them in their consciences or otherwise by any inquisition to bring them into danger of capital law, so as no one was called into any capital or bloody question upon matters of religion, but have all enjoyed their life as the course of nature would." [11]

Here may be named also Mr. William Lacy,[12] a worshipful gentleman, who was condemned to death not long since at York for that he confessed he had obtained a dispensation for bigamy of the Pope's Holiness to be made priest, and that according to the same dispensation he was made priest, either of which points by their late laws of religion are deadly. And the latter point they make treason, forsooth, by this strange sequel, that when men take Holy Orders in the Catholic Church they give their oath of obedience to the Pope, who is a foreign enemy to Her Majesty and to the realm, as these men affirm, and could the world ween

[10] 23 Eliz. I, c. 1.

[11] Cecil, pp. 9–10 and 11–12.

[12] William Lacy, received his dispensation and ordination in Rome, executed in York, August 22, 1582.

we were in such thralldom of this barbarous heresy? With this man was Mr. Kirkeman,[13] an happy priest, also martyred for that he acknowledged himself to have reconciled certain persons to the Catholic Church. For which likewise were put to death Mr. Thompson,[14] Mr. Hart,[15] and Mr. Thirkeld[16] afterward, in the same city of York, never charged nor suspected of any other treasons than of hearing confessions, absolving and reconciling sinners to the favor of God and to the unity of the Catholic Church again, which both in the priest that absolveth and in the party that is absolved they have made to be the crime of lese majesty under this false and most unjust pretense, that all parties so reconciled are assoiled[17] of their obedience to the Queen, and do adhere to her enemy and admit foreign jurisdiction, power, and authority, which is exercised in confession for remission of sins.

These be the treasons and none other for which the blood of God's priests is so abundantly shed in our poor country these years.

Add to these the two famous confessors, Mr. John Slade and Mr. John Body,[18] who both by certain interrogatories being driven to say their minds touching the Queen's challenge of supreme regiment ecclesiastical (contrary to the asseveration of this libeler set down before), for confessing their faith of the Pope's spiritual sovereignty, and for denying her to be head of the Church of England or to have any spiritual regiment, were con-

[13] Richard Kirkeman, ordained in Douai in 1578, executed with Lacy in York, August 22, 1582.

[14] James Thompson, ordained in Reims, executed in York, November 28, 1582.

[15] William Hart, ordained in Rome, executed in York, March 15, 1583.

[16] Richard Thirkill or Thirkeld, ordained in Reims in 1579, executed in York, May 29, 1583.

[17] Released, delivered.

[18] John Slade, a schoolmaster, and John Body, a former student at Oxford and Douai, were tried together for treason in Winchester. Slade was executed there, October 30, 1583, Body in Andover, November 2, 1583.

demned to death in public judgment at two divers sessions, and that at twice (a rare case in our country), the latter sentence being to reform the former (as we may guess in such strange proceedings), which they perceived to be erroneous and insufficient in their own laws. Whereupon one of them was executed at Winchester, the other at Andover in the same province, being never charged with disloyalty or old treasons, as not only by the records of their arraignment and condemnation we are able to prove, but also by their own speeches and by the whole action of their martyrdom, which is put in print by one of their own Protestants that was present [19] and is witnessed by thousands of others that both heard and saw their deaths and judgment. I will (for example's sake) allege something out of the said printed pamphlet of that which was said unto them by the enemy at their martyrdom. "Confess your fault" (saith one of the chief gentlemen [20] and ministers of execution there present), "for satisfaction of the world in the cause of your death." To which the holy confessor, J. Body, answered, after protestation of his loyalty in temporal things: "You shall understand" (quoth he), "good people, that I suffer death for denying Her Majesty to be supreme head of Christ's Church in England in causes ecclesiastical. Other treasons, except they make hearing the holy mass, or saying Ave Maria, treason, I have committed none." So his happy companion, Mr. Slade, condemned for the same only cause, was thus spoken unto in the hour of his agony by one Dr. Bennet,[21] a

[19] [The book is entitled: *The Several Executions of Slade and Body,* etc., imprinted in London, by Richard Jones, 1583.] STC 1062, a slightly different title, author listed only as "R. B."

[20] [Sir W. Kingsmel.] Probably Sir William Kingsmill, Kt., of Sydmonton, Hants.

[21] Probably Robert Bennet, Anglican clergyman, who was master of the Hospital of St. Cross, Winchester, in 1583, and a vigorous opponent of the Catholic seminarists in that area. Perhaps Bennet was also the "R. B." who wrote the Protestant pamphlet Allen quotes.

great minister of their new congregation: "Let not the Pope" (saith he), "that unworthy priest, be preferred before thine own natural princess, who is the lawful supreme head of the Church next under Christ." So said this minister, by whom we may not only perceive upon what statute and treason they were executed, but also (which in another part of this libel [22] is without shame most boldly denied) that indeed the Queen is commonly of Protestants called supreme head of the Church. So their preachers in pulpit do sound out daily, as all men know. And their writers in books dedicated to her (as Mr. Bridges against Dr. Sanders and Dr. Stapleton,[23] and others) do term her expressly. Whereof the wiser sort (as we may see by this libel) are so ashamed that they would have it given out (to strangers specially, who wonder at the monstrous title) that there is no such thing challenged of her or given her by the new laws of religion in England.

For which cause, and for that they had an intention straight to publish at home and in foreign parts that none were put to death for any such matter of faith or religion, they suppressed the said printed pamphlet of these two men's martyrdom and punished the author thereof, though he wrote in that point the plain truth as he heard and saw, but not discreetly enough nor agreeable to the politic practice they had then in hand, which was to persuade the world that none were put to death for their conscience, nor that the Queen challenged any such title of supremacy or headship over the Church, which latter point it seemeth convenient to the politiques of our realm to disavow with such vehemency in this libel as they give us the manifest lie for that we reprove them of it, for thus they write: "Which title (of headship of the Church) the adversaries do most falsely write and affirm

[22] [Page 10.] Cecil, p. 12.

[23] John Bridges, *The Supremacy of Christian Princes* (London, 1573), STC 3737, dedicated to Queen Elizabeth, "in earth next under God, of the Church of England and Ireland, in all ecclesiastical and temporal causes, the supreme head and governor."

that the Queen's Majesty doth now use, a manifest lie and untruth," etc.[24] Wherefore of this matter I am enforced in this place to speak a word or two by the way.

The truth is that in the first year and Parliament of the Queen's reign, when they abolished the Pope's authority and would have yielded the same authority with the title of supreme head to the Queen as it was given before to her father and brother,[25] divers specially moved by minister Calvin's writing (who had condemned in the same princes that calling),[26] liked not the term and therefore procured that some other equivalent but less offensive might be used. Upon which formality, it was enacted that she was "the chief governor as well in causes ecclesiastical or spiritual as civil and temporal." And an oath of the same was conceived accordingly, to be tendered at their pleasures to all the spiritual and temporal officers in the realm, by which every one must swear that in conscience he taketh and believeth her so to be,[27] and that no priest or other born out of the realm can have or ought to have any manner of power in spiritual matters over her subjects. Which oath is counted the very torment of all Eng-

[24] Cecil, p. 12.

[25] By the Act of Supremacy, 26 Henry VIII, c. 1, which uses the formula, "the only supreme head in earth of the Church of England, called *Anglicana Ecclesia*."

[26] John Calvin, Commentary on Amos (7:10–13), *Calvini Opera,* XLIII, 134: *Qui initio tantopere extulerunt Henricum regem Angliae, certe fuerunt inconsiderati homines, dederunt illi summam rerum omnium potestatem; et hoc me semper graviter vulneravit. Erant enim blasphemi quum vocarent ipsum summum caput ecclesiae sub Christo;* in the Owen translation published by the Calvin Translation Society, *Commentaries on the Twelve Minor Prophets,* II (Edinburgh, 1846), 349: "They who at first extolled Henry, King of England, were certainly inconsiderate men; they gave him the supreme power in all things; and this always vexed me grievously. For they were guilty of blasphemy when they called him the chief head of the Church under Christ."

[27] 1 Eliz. I, c. 1, section 9, the oath clause, cf. Cecil, p. 12, n. 25. For an authoritative account of the parliamentary debates on this act, which remain somewhat mysterious in many particulars, see J. E. Neale, *Elizabeth I and Her Parliaments, 1559–1581* (London, 1953), pp. 51 ff.

lish consciences, not the Protestants themselves believing it to be true. And of all true Catholics, as before it was deemed in her father, a layman, and in her brother, a child, very ridiculous, so now in herself, being a woman, is it accounted a thing most monstrous and unnatural and the very gap to bring any realm to the thralldom of all sects, heresy, paganism, Turkism, or atheism that the prince for the time by human frailty may be subject unto, all our religion, faith, worship, service, and prayers depending upon his sovereign determination, a thing that all nations have to take heed of by our example, for the redress of which pernicious absurdity so many of our said brethren so willingly have shed their blood.

In the first Parliament of Her Majesty's reign it was indeed in a manner thrust upon her against her will, because otherwise there could have been no color to make new laws for change of religion, and this title of chief governess was thought to be a qualification of the former term of headship. But in truth, it is all one with the other, or rather worse. For in some kind of improper speech the king may be called the head or chief of the church of his country, for that he is sovereign lord and ruler of both persons spiritual and temporal, all sorts bound to obey his lawful civil laws and commandments, and so in that sense is he head of the clergy and of all others.

But when in the new form of our statute it is expressly and distinctly added that she is the only supreme governor even in all causes, as well spiritual and ecclesiastical as temporal and civil; and furthermore enacted that all jurisdictions, privileges, superiorities, and pre-eminences ecclesiastical, as by any power spiritual have been or may be exercised, are taken from the Pope (to whom Christ gave them in most ample manner) and are united, or rather (as they say) restored, by an old decree to the crown of England—this can have no excuse, neither true or likely sense in the world, making indeed a king and a priest all one, no difference betwixt the state of the Church and a temporal commonwealth, giving no less right to heathen princes to be governors of the Church in causes spiritual than to a Christian king. It maketh one part of the Church in different territories to be independent and several[28] from another, according to the distinction of realms and kingdoms in the world. And finally it maketh every man that is not born in the kingdom to be a foreigner also in respect of the Church. These and a thousand absurdities and impossibilities more do ensue, which for brevity we omit. Only this which is in most men's memories we may not overpass: that the very same year that this new pre-eminence was given by law to the Queen and the oath accordingly ministered to many, some, having remorse of the matter, for to avoid danger pretended for their refusal that it seemed to them by the words of the oath and act that the Queen might minister also the sacraments, whereunto they would not swear by any means.

Whereupon in her next visitation of the clergy a special injunction was printed and published by her commandment[29] declaring that in truth she had no such intent, and that no such thing was implied in her title or claim of spiritual regiment, nor no other thing, nor more than was before granted to her father by the term of supreme head, requiring all her loving subjects to receive the oath at least in that sense and so it should suffice Her Highness. By which it is now clear by their own authentical declaration that we speak no untruth (as this libeler saith) nor abuse not the world when we say she is called and taken for the supreme head of the Church of England, albeit (the thing itself being far more absurd and of more pernicious sequel than the makers of the law, which were mere laymen and most of them unlearned, could then perceive), their followers now would disavow the same. For this article, therefore, as the famous Bishop

[28] Separate.

[29] In the "Injunctions of Elizabeth, 1559," reprinted in Henry Gee and William John Hardy, *Documents Illustrative of English Church History* (London, 1896), pp. 438–439.

of Rochester,[30] Sir Thomas More,[31] and a great number more in King Henry the Eighth his days, so did those two last named martyrs and divers others before them most gladly and constantly yield up their lives, and so consequently died for mere matter of religion only.

And to end this point, we lastly refer the adversary to the late martyrdom of Carter, a poor innocent artisan, who was made away only for printing a Catholic book, *De schismate,*[32] in which no word was found against the state, the quarrel only most unjustly being made upon a certain clause which by no likely honest construction could appertain to the Queen's person; viz., that the Catholic religion should once have the upper hand of heresy and Judith cut off the head of Holofernes,[33] which they in their extreme jealousy and fear of all things would needs wrest against Her Majesty.

And the place serveth here to say somewhat of the cause also of their racking of Catholics, which they would have strangers believe never to be done for any point of religion. As for example (say they, in the addition to the end of the libel), none is asked by torture what he believeth of the mass or transubstantiation or suchlike.[34] As though (forsooth) there were no question pertaining to faith and religion but touching our inward belief. Whereas, indeed, it concerneth religion no less to demand and press us by torture where, in whose houses, what days and times we say or hear mass; how many we have reconciled; what we have heard in confession; who resorteth to our preachings; who harboreth

[30] John Fisher, executed June 22, 1535, for failure to take the Oath of Succession, which included a clause acknowledging the King's headship of the Church of England.

[31] Executed on a similar charge, July 6, 1535.

[32] William Carter, printer and bookseller, executed January 11, 1584, for printing the translation, Gregory Martin, *A Treatise of Schism* (1578), STC 17508.

[33] Jth. 13:8.

[34] Cecil, p. 47.

Catholics and priests; who sustaineth, aideth, or comforteth them; who they be that have their children or pupils in the Society or seminaries beyond the seas; where such a Jesuit or such a priest is to be found; where Catholic books are printed and by whom, and to whom they be uttered in England. Which things, being demanded of evil intent and to the annoyance of the Catholic cause, God's priests, and innocent men, no man may by the law of God and nature disclose, though he be expressly commanded by any prince in the world, for that God must be obeyed more than man.

Yet these were the interrogatories for which the famous confessor, Mr. Briant,[35] was tormented with needles thrust under his nails, racked also otherwise in cruel sort, and specially punished by two whole days' and nights' famine, which they attribute to obstinacy, but indeed (sustained in Christ's quarrel) it was most honorable constancy. The like demands were put to the blessed martyrs Campion,[36] Sherwine,[37] and others upon the torture. And of this latter, namely, was asked where Father Parsons [38] and Campion were, and whether he had said mass in Mr. Roscarrock's [39] chamber, and what money he had given him. Mr. Thompson,[40] a venerable and learned priest, was put to torments only to get out of him to what end he kept certain superaltaries[41] and where he intended to bestow them. The said young man Carter, of whose martyrdom we last treated, was examined upon the rack upon what gentlemen or Catholic ladies he had bestowed or intended to bestow certain books of prayers and

[35] *Ibid.*, p. 46. [36] *Ibid.*, p. 17.

[37] Ralph Sherwine, ordained March 23, 1577, executed with Briant and Campion, December 1, 1581.

[38] Cecil, p. 17.

[39] Nicholas Roscarrock, a prominent English lay Catholic, jailed several times for recusancy.

[40] See above, p. 64, n. 14.

[41] Portable altars, which can be placed on top of unconsecrated altars or tables.

spiritual exercises and meditations which he had in his custody. Which may suffice to refute the adversaries' asseveration that none have been tormented for other matter than treason.

But the words of Mr. Thomas Cottam,[42] uttered in sense at the bar and thus verbatim left in writing, discovereth the case more plainly, to the shame of this cruel heresy for advancement whereof so shameful things be committed. Thus, therefore, he spake and avouched openly in the presence of the rack masters:

Indeed [quoth he] you are searchers of secrets, for you would needs know of me what penance I was enjoined by my ghostly father for my sins committed. And I acknowledge my frailty that to avoid the intolerable torment of the rack I confessed (God forgive me) what they demanded therein. But when they further urged me to utter also what my sins were for which that penance was enjoined me (a loathsome and unchristian question), I then answered that I would not disclose my offenses saving to God and to my ghostly father alone. Whereupon they sore tormented me and still pressed me with the same demand. And I persisted that it was a most barbarous, inhumane question and that I would not answer though they tormented me to death.

Thus spake Mr. Cottam at his arraignment, wherewith, the enemies being ashamed, the Lieutenant of the Tower there present began to deny the whole. Whereunto Mr. Cottam replied again thus:

And is not this true? Here is present Dr. Hammond[43] with the rest of the commissioners that were at my racking, to whose consciences I appeal. God is my witness that it is most true, and you know that Sir George Carey[44] did ask me these unnatural questions, deny it if

[42] Thomas Cottam, S.J., ordained in Reims in 1580, executed in London, May 30, 1582.

[43] John Hammond, LL.D., an active member of the ecclesiastical court of high commission and an examiner of Briant, Campion, and several other priests accused of treason.

[44] Sir George Carey, Knight Marshal of the Queen's Marshalsea, had also been an examiner of Catholics accused of treason. See references to his

you can. In truth all your torture and demands, every one, were of no other treasons but matter of mere conscience, faith, and religion, or else of such follies as I have rehearsed.

As for the moderation, great pity, and courtesy, which by your libel you would have the world believe Her Majesty's ministers have ever used in giving the torment to the persons aforesaid and other Catholics, the poor innocents have felt it, and Our Lord God knoweth the contrary. And we can put you in remembrance that you did it with extreme rigor and despite, commonly upon no due presumption nor reasonable suspicion of discovery of any important matter thereby. Look in your records what suspicion of treasons or great matters you could have in young Sherwood,[45] who was the first in our memory that was put to the rack for matters of conscience, then when no man dreamed of any these feigned new conspiracies.

See whether a portable altar be a sufficient cause to give the torture to a grave, worshipful person, not so much as suspected of treason or any disobedience, other than in cases of conscience. Whether books of prayers and meditations spiritual, or the printing and spreading of them, be a rack matter in any commonwealth Christian. Look whether your ordinary demands were of that weight and quality as were to be answered by constraint of the rack. Let the world see what one confession of treasonable matter you have wrested out by the so often tormenting of so many, and what great secrecies touching the state (which you pretend so earnestly to seek for) you have found amongst them all. No, no, nothing was there in those religious hearts but innocency and true religion. It is that which you punished, tormented, and deadly hated in them. If they would have in the least point in the world condescended to your desires in that, or

---

later activities of this sort, in *Unpublished Documents Relating to the English Martyrs, I, 1584–1603,* ed. by John Hungerford Pollen (London, 1908), *passim.*

[45] See above, p. 62, n. 6.

but once for your pleasures presented themselves at your schismatical prayers, all racking and treasons had been cleared and past.

Whereby all the world seeth you did all for religion, not as for any conscience that way (wherewith most of you are not much troubled), but because the particular state of a number dependeth on this new religion. Remember whether you laid not Mr. Thompson on the rack, against all good use and order, before you ever examined him. What presumptions had you so pregnant that you must rack the famous man, Father Campion, about the Irish commotion or collection of money for the maintenance of the same? Or of any knowledge he had of killing the GREATEST,[46] as you mystically speak in your book? Have you not ordinarily threatened men with the racks and dungeons? And sometimes brought them to the rack-house door, yea, and laid some on the rack without either cause or intent to touch them, but only by those terrors to drive them to deny their faith, or to confess where they had said mass, or other like things which you desired to know?

How often have you by famine and filthy dungeons tormented the happy young confessor, Mr. John Hart,[47] which could not now be after his condemnation for anything else but for his religion and because he would not yield to one Rainolds,[48] a minister with whom you appointed him to confer? For what other cause did you threaten the torture to Mr. Osborne [49] but to make him confess that he had said mass before the true noble con-

[46] [Fol. 2.] Cecil, p. 6.

[47] John Hart, S.J., ordained in Douai, March 29, 1578, imprisoned in London in 1580, banished in 1585.

[48] John Rainolds or Reynolds, Anglican controversialist, later president of Corpus Christi College, Oxford. For his account of this debate, see *The Sum of the Conference between J. Rainolds and J. Hart* (London, 1584), STC 20626.

[49] Edward Osborne, priest trained in Reims, jailed and examined in London, apparently in 1582. See J. H. Pollen, ed., *English Martyrs,* I, 27, for a record of his examination.

fessors of Christ, my Lord Vaux [50] and Sir Thomas Tresham? [51] And which is more intolerable, is not your rack used or threatened to force men by the fear thereof to speak things against truth by your appointment, and specially for false accusation of innocent gentlemen? John Nicholls, himself a Protestant and one of your own instruments, hath acknowledged so much in public writing,[52] affirming that Sir Owen Hopton,[53] Lieutenant of the Tower, enforced him to accuse divers gentlemen by name of high treason, whom he never knew; which he did, to avoid his threatened torments, as he writeth.

We speak nothing of the pitiful extremities you have brought divers unto by horrible fetters, stocks, dungeons, famine; [54] or of the death of well near twenty happy Catholics at once, infected and pestered in York prison, where they perished by the unmercifulness of the Protestants, of whom by no pitiful complaints they could obtain liberty or fresh air, for the saving their lives, without condescending to go to their abominable service. We tell you not here, again, that for the more affliction of Catholics (a thing to be marked and lamented of all Christian hearts), that you have profanely made choice of Sundays and great holidays to practice your torments upon them, after the old fashion of the pagans,

[50] William Vaux, third Baron Vaux, 1542?–1595, prominent Roman Catholic nobleman, protector of Campion and other priests.

[51] Sir Thomas Tresham, 1543?–1605, brother-in-law to Vaux, another prominent lay Roman Catholic and protector of Campion and other priests.

[52] [In his epistle to Dr. Allen set forth in print, fol. 10.] Reference, apparently, to *A True Report of the Apprehension of J. Nicholls, Minister, at Rouen* (Reims, 1583), STC 18537. John Nicholls had switched religious sides several times, had recently expressed a wish to return to Catholicism, and had sent Allen several letters of apology.

[53] Sir Owen Hopton is frequently referred to as charged with the torture and examination of missionary priests. See Richard Challoner, *Memoirs of Missionary Priests,* ed. by John Hungerford Pollen (New York, 1924), *passim.*

[54] [Thompson, Borschoe, Henslowe, Clifton.] On James Thompson, see above, p. 64, n. 14. Thomas Clifton was ordained as a missionary priest in Douai, 1579, and jailed soon after arrival in England, 1580.

rather than upon workdays; that you bring other Catholic prisoners near to the place of torment, to hear their brethren's sorrowful cries, and eftsoons [55] lead some, newly taken from the rack, under their fellow prisoners' windows and to their doors, that by hearing their pitiful complaints, sighs, and groans, proceeding of infinite pains, they may relent in religion.

Of all which inhumane dealing, we will not impeach the superior magistrate, much less the sovereign. But surely the inferior ministers of that pretended justice cannot be excused of most cruel and sacrilegious dealing toward God's priests and other innocent persons. And as for the particular handling of Father Campion and Mr. Briant (whom the libelers make examples of their mild and gentle entertainment upon the torture), we refer all indifferent readers to the said Briant's own Latin epistle [56] of that matter. And for the other, they say true indeed that after his first racking, and at the time of the Protestants' disputes with him in the Tower, he was not so bereaved of his hands but he might with pain write or subscribe his name. But afterward, upon his second or third racking, he was so benumbed that he could neither take the cup and lift it to his mouth nor draw off his cuff at the bar. Nor straight after his last torment nor many days following had he any feeling or use of his limbs. As he confessed to his keeper, asking him how he felt his hands: "Not evil" (quoth he), "for I feel them not at all."

The like we could prove of Mr. Paine,[57] the priest's, tormenting, and divers others. But this is enough to control these shameless untruths of the libeler and to make demonstration of the pitiful violences, slanders, and tribulations which our brethren

[55] Soon afterward.

[56] [In the end of the book of the persecution in England.] *De persecutione Anglicana libellus* (Rome, 1582), attributed to Robert Parsons, S.J.; pp. 111–117 contain Briant's letter and commentary.

[57] John Paine, ordained in Douai, 1576, executed in Chelmsford, April 2, 1582.

have constantly borne, and yet do bear, for profession of their faith, which to some rebuke of our nation we would never so particularly utter here and elsewhere if our blameless defense drove us not thereunto. And specially for that we would Christianly give warning to all princes and provinces that yet happily enjoy the Catholic religion and the only true liberty of conscience in the same to take heed by our miseries how they let this pernicious sect put foot into their states, which by promise of liberty and sweetness at the beginning entereth deceitfully, but when she is once in and getteth the mastery (as she often doth where she is not in season constantly resisted), she bringeth all to most cruel and barbarous thralldom, procuring her followers to hate and persecute the Church, their own only true and old mother, far more deadly than the heathens themselves do, and turneth all the laws made by godly Popes and princes for punishment of heretics and malefactors to the spoil and destruction of innocent men and Catholics for whose defense they were made.

Into which misery our country, to us most dear, being fallen, and having no other human helps to recover it and our prince and peers (excepting this case of heresy, of excellent good nature and clemency), with millions of souls that there do perish, we will not fear nor fail to pray and ask it of God with tears and blood, as we have begun, *donec misereatur nostri,*[58] till He be merciful both to us and to our persecutors.

Our days of affliction cannot be long. Their felicity will have an end. Both sides shall shortly have their doom, where the dealings of us all shall be truly discussed and the just shall stand with great constancy against them that vexed them. Interim,[59] in the testimony of a guiltless conscience in all things whereof we be accused by our adversaries, and in joyful expectation of that day, we will continue still this work of God to our own and our country's salvation, *per infamiam et bonam famam,*[60] as the apostle

[58] Ps. 123:2: "Until that He have mercy upon us." [59] Meanwhile.
[60] II Cor. 6:8: "By evil report and good report."

willeth us, and through other miseries whatsoever man's mortality is subject unto.

❦

Chapter II

That Father Campion and the rest of the priests and Catholics indicted, condemned, and executed upon pretense of treason and upon statutes made of old against treasons were never yet guilty of any such crimes but unjustly made away

HITHERTO we have made it clear that divers (contrary to the drift of this libel) have been condemned and put to death, either without all law, or else only upon new laws by which matter of religion is made treason. Now it followeth and is next to be considered whether such other as were accused and appeached of old treasons upon a statute made in the days of Edward the Third, in the twenty-fifth year of his reign,[1] were indeed guilty of any such crimes.

The intent of that law is to register divers cases that were to be deemed treason, in which the first and chief is to conspire or compass the death of the sovereign, or to levy men of arms against him, and thereof can be by open fact convinced. Upon which special clause Father Campion (good man) and his fellow priests and Catholic brethren were, to the wonder of the world, arraigned. Namely, indicted that at Rome and Reims the last day of March and May in the twenty-second year of Her Majesty's reign they compassed the Queen's death, the subversion of the state and invasion of the realm, feigning (for better coloring of the collusion) the foresaid places, days, and times when this conspiracy should be contrived.[2]

[1] 25 Edw. III, st. 5, c. 2.

[2] For a copy of this indictment, see *Cobbett's State Trials,* I, 1049. Pp. 1049–1088 contain documents pertinent to this trial.

Which forgery and false accusation is now so clearly discovered to all Englishmen of any consideration, Protestants and others, that for excuse of that foul sinful practice they have set out at length to strangers, as they did with like luck before at home, this late libel, by which God Almighty, the protector of His saints and our innocency, hath marvelously confounded themselves and justified the cause and conscience of His holy martyrs, as by the declaration following shall appear.

When the politiques of our country, pretending to be Protestants, saw the Catholic religion, contrary to their worldly-wise counsels and determinations and against their exquisite diligence and discipline and twenty years' endeavor (in which time they thought verily to have extinguished the memory of our fathers' faith), to be revived in the hearts of the greatest number, noblest, and honestest sort of the realm; and that neither their strange, violent, and capital laws for the Queen's spiritual superiority against the Pope's pre-eminence, the power of priesthood in absolving penitents, the saying and hearing of mass, having or wearing of *Agnus Deis* or other external signs of our society with the Catholic Church of all times and nations; nor the execution of many by death and other penalties and punishment, according to the said laws, would serve nor were of force to hold out of England the priests of the Society and seminaries, to whom Christ had given more apostolic spirit, courage, zeal, and success than of so small a beginning was looked for; by whom the Protestants began to fear lest great alteration in religion—whereon they think their new state (that is to say), the weal of a very few in comparison, dependeth—might ensue; they thought good by their long exercised wisdom to alter the whole accusation from question of faith and conscience to matter of treason. Which being resolved upon, they went about by divers proclamations, libels, and speeches, first, to make the people believe that all Catholics, and specially Jesuits and such priests and scholars as were brought up in the seminaries or colleges out of the realm, were traitors. And for their better persuasion gave out one while that by the said priests and others in banishment there was a marvelous confederation of the Pope, King of Spain, Duke of Florence, and others for the invasion of the realm. But that being shortly proved nothing, they feigned that the said Jesuits and priests were confederated with the Irish quarrel,[3] and to give more color of somewhat they sticked not to rack Father Campion extremely for search of that point.

But this fiction failing, they found out another as foul: that the death of the Queen and divers of the council was contrived (forsooth) in the seminaries of Rome and Reims, of which conspiracy in fine they resolved to indict them, as they did, and pursued them to death for the same with such evident partiality, default of justice and equity, as was in that court (once most honorable for justice) never heard or read of before.

Such as pleaded against them to make them odious in judgment discoursed (as this libel now doth) first of the nature and horror of rebellion in general, and then of a rebellion in the North for religion a dozen years before, when the parties there accused were young boys in the schools and universities of the realm; of the Pope's bull of excommunicating the Queen a good many of years before any of them came over sea or ever saw Pope, Rome, or Reims, yea, when some of them were yet Protestants in England. They discoursed also of the rebellion in Ireland by Stukely, Sanders, and others, none of which men divers there arraigned ever saw or knew in their lives; of their being made priests by the Pope's authority, and of their obligation and obedience to him, being the Queen's enemy; of their authority to absolve and reconcile in England, received from him; of their coming in at the same time when they were in arms in Ireland, as though they had not entered their native country and exercised those spiritual functions seven years before, or could not then exercise them but in favor of such as took arms against the Queen.

[3] [Hereof there was a special proclamation published in July, 1580.] Cf. Robert Steele, ed., *Tudor and Stuart Proclamations, 1485–1714,* I, 80, no. 751 (Against rebels and traitors in foreign parts), July 15, 1580.

And when these generalities were uttered only to make them odious and amaze the hearers with those that should have to judge of their guiltiness or innocency, the good fathers and priests made just exceptions against such vulgar invectives as could not touch them that there stood in judgment more than any other priest or Catholic in the realm, and many of the points such as they were sure none should have been arraigned of in King Edward the Third's time, upon whose statute nevertheless the indictment was pretended to be drawn, humbly praying the judge and bench that they would more directly, plainly, and sincerely pass on them for their faith and exercises of the Roman religion (for proof whereof they should not need to seek for so impertinent and farfetched matter), which they openly professed and desired to die for with all their hearts. Or if they would needs proceed against them as for treason, in the sense of the old laws of our country, that then it would please them to aggravate no farther to their disadvantage and death either other men's faults or matter of pure religion but to come to the indictment and to the particular charge of every person there arraigned, which was of conspiring the Queen's death. Whereof if they could by any proof or sufficient testimony of credible persons convict all or any of them, then their death to be deserved. If not, their innocent blood upon all that should be accessory to the shedding thereof, a crime that crieth for vengeance at God's hand when it is done but by private malice and mischief, but committed in public place of judgment by authority and pretense of law (as in the case of Naboth [4] and of Christ our Master) it is in the sight of God most horrible and never long escapeth public punishment, from the which Our Lord God of His mercy save our poor country, even by the prayers of these holy martyrs for whose blood it is otherwise highly deserved.

Therefore all other idle and vagrant speeches, odiously amplifying either the Pope's, Jesuits', seminaries', Doctor Sanders', or

[4] The Old Testament victim of Jezebel, stoned to death on false charges (I Kings 21).

any other man's peculiar actions for religion or otherwise, set apart (whereupon, as the counselors then at the bar, so now the writers of this libel, voluntary and vainly do only stand and make their rest), there is nothing in the world that can prove effectually these men's lawful condemnation nor avow the justice of that execution (which the libeler taketh upon him to do, but in truth no whit toucheth the matter), saving only such allegation and testimony as may convince Father Campion and his fellows with him arraigned to have compassed the Queen's destruction or invasion of the realm.

What other thing soever they were guilty of; or what affection soever they bear, in respect of their contrary religion, to their prince and state; or what treasonable opinions (as they fondly [5] call them) concerning the excommunication or depriving the Queen were afterward discovered in them; or what other reasonable cause in respect of the adversaries' fear and jealousy over the state or doubt of the times then troubled the officers then or the libelers now, to satisfy the people or the world abroad, do allege for their excuse: none of all these things can justify that execution, so long as the matter for which they were only indicted cannot be proved, nor the statute of King Edward the Third, upon which they pretend to have indicted them, is transgressed by them.

Therefore as the whole treatise of our adversaries' defense is too-too wide from the purpose, so specially are the four reasons, which, for the reader's ease (as they term it) and for the pith and sum of the whole discourse, they have put at the end of their libel in a rank together,[6] by which the discreet reader may take a taste of their deceitful dealing in the whole book.

Every reason should conclude that the priests were executed upon no charge of new religious treasons but upon old statutes only for matter of conspiracy, in which sense no one of them in truth doth conclude.

[5] Foolishly.

[6] Cecil, pp. 32–35.

And the first reason cometh only to this end: that Her Majesty, contemning the Pope's bulls for a good while, at length spying them to be dangerous, revived former laws for prohibition of them within her dominions. Which argument, being laid for the ground of all, hath neither the conclusion looked for against those priests in particular nor truth of narration in the premises. For neither were there any such bulls and excommunications which (they say) were tolerated or contemned for certain years; none at all (I say) of that kind published in her days before that one of Pius the Fifth mentioned in the next argument following. Neither were there extant any old statutes (that we know) to be revived against such excommunications in any such sense as they will seem to make them.

The second argument proveth only that Felton,[7] for publishing Pius the Fifth his bull, was by their laws condemned and put to death and was the first that was executed for matters coming from Rome. Whereupon how substantially it is inferred that Father Campion and his fellows were not condemned for religion but for transgression of old statutes of treasons, let the wise consider. And withal, let the learned in our laws determine whether the bringing-in of a bull of excommunication from Rome were treason in the days and by the statute of King Edward the Third.

Thirdly, they reason thus: the people raised rebellion in the North; ergo Her Majesty cannot be blamed for using force against them and punishing the authors of the same, which maketh little against the persons here named.

Fourthly, that the Pope stirred to rebellion and succored the Irish; therefore she hath great reason to search out all seditious persons, as priests and Jesuits be, and so to try, condemn, and execute them. Neither of which reasons have any further sequel in the sight of any reasonable and indifferent man than to punish them that are by lawful trial proved to be partakers of these ac-

[7] John Felton, Cf. Cecil, p. 32, n. 71.

tions; which was impossible to do in any of the priests' case arraigned, neither was any of the said commotions laid in particular to any one of them all at the bar, though impertinently such matters were for a deceitful flourish often (as in this libel) touched.

And whereas by prevention of some objections either made or that may be made that these poor religious priests, scholars, and unarmed men could not be any doers in the wars of England or Ireland, the libel maketh a solemn rhetorical tale for answer, that though they were not in the field to fight yet they might by their counsel, encouragement, and persuasion be partakers of the same crime and executed as accessory to the other treasons; which needed not so many superfluous words in so short a work, all the world confessing that the ministers, messengers, espials, and abettors of offenders are often no less punishable than the principal actors. But in sincere dealing it had been to be proved that Father Campion and those other holy men were secret workers and aiders of the Northern and Irish commotion, whereof neither now in this book nor then at the bar any one word is alleged.

All is full of wild and waste words artificially couched to abuse the ignorant that knew not the state of this disputation, all running to this odd issue: that Her Majesty hath reason to punish traitors; but no word to convince them of these or any other old treasons for which they were indicted, nor to reprove us that boldly, upon evident demonstration, yea, and certain knowledge, do testify before God and man that they were not guilty of those offenses of which they were indicted and for which they were by unlawful calumniation and violence cast away, as in the face of the world, but in the sight of Our Lord attained a precious death and the glory of the saints everlastingly.

When it came to the very point of the accusation, and all roving and railing talk against Pope, Rome, religion, seminaries, bulls, masses, preachings, reconciliations, *Agnus Deis,* and beads (with which they larded all their evidence, though of such things they professed not to condemn them), was to be set aside, and now by witnesses to be proved that they were guilty of the foresaid conspiracy against the Queen's person, etc., two or three such fellows [8] were sought out and procured to give testimony against them as first professed themselves to be heretics and therefore by St. Augustine's judgment [9] were not to be heard against a Catholic priest. Secondly (seeing heresy maketh no exception in England), they were known to be otherwise common cozeners, lost companions, salable for a sou and bought by the enemy to betray them and bear witness against them. Thirdly, some of them charged in the face of the court with shameful adultery, with double or triple murder, and other like horrible crimes pardoned for this purpose. Fourthly, they were discovered both then and afterward of notorious falsehood, incongruity, and discord of times, persons, places, and other circumstances and their iniquity eftsoons disclosed by their own fellow.[10]

And to see now the men of God, so many, so excellent for virtue, so famous for learning, religion, zeal, and devotion, to hold their lives upon the conscience of such notorious atheists and outcasts of the world; yea (as in Mr. Paine's [11] case), upon the bare word of one of them only, against divine and human laws (requiring two witnesses at the least): it was surely very pitiful to behold but not marvelous to us that considered the condition of our time and easily foresaw that these holy men's deaths were now designed and thought necessary by our politiques for conservation of their state, as the libeler here subtly insinuateth,[12] that it was to be done in regard of the dangerous time when the Pope's forces were in Ireland and more in preparation to follow as well into England (as he cunningly feigneth to make the necessity of this justice more excusable) as also into Ireland, as though he would say that by some one pretense or other, for

[8] These witnesses were J. Caddy or Cradocke, George Eliot, Anthony Munday, Sleidon or Sledd. See *Cobbett's State Trials,* I, 1056–1072, for record of their testimony.

[9] [Epist. 212.] St. Augustine to Pancarius, Letter no. 251 in Migne.

[10] [John Nicholls in his letters imprinted.] See above, Ch. I, p. 75, n. 52.

[11] See above, Ch. I, p. 76, n. 57.

[12] [Fol. 16.] Cecil, p. 34.

terror and example, they were to be found guilty and so dispatched.

Well, thus their good witnesses gave in evidence of things spoken and contrived in Rome and Reims which were known to be most false of all that were in either place the times and days by them named. And whatsoever was either truly or falsely testified to be done or said in either of the two places by any English there dwelling, it was unjustly applied to all and every one of these good men now standing in judgment. Yea, it served against some that were never in either place in their life, as against Mr. Forde [13] and Mr. Collington; [14] as also against Father Campion, that dwelt a thousand miles off in Prague,[15] occupied by his superiors in teaching and preaching, wholly estranged from all Englishmen and English affairs, otherwise than in his prayers, for above nine years together, not ever seen or known to divers that then were arraigned with him in judgment as conspirators in one and the same treason before they met there together at the bar, nor ever known to the witnesses themselves. The same served against Mr. Shert, that had not been in either place of many years before.[16] Against Mr. Briant also and Mr. Richardson,[17] that

[13] Thomas Forde, ordained in Douai in 1573, executed in London, May 28, 1582.

[14] John Colleton or Collington, ordained in Douai in 1576; tried with Campion and others in 1581 but acquitted when it was proved he was in England at the time of the alleged conspiracies in Reims and Rome; banished in 1584; later returned to England for further missionary work.

[15] Campion had, however, left Prague on March 25, 1580, arrived in Rome on April 5, to join other priests assembled for the mission to England, and proceeded with them to Reims, arriving on May 31. These dates correspond roughly with those specified in the conspiracy indictment against him. He had, furthermore, met Allen in Reims. See Richard Simpson, *Edmund Campion,* pp. 96 and 117 (in account of his travels), 280 (text of indictment).

[16] John Shert had visited both Rome, where he was ordained, and Reims, 1578–1579, but had been sent to England in 1579. He was executed May 28, 1582. See Richard Challoner, *Memoirs of Missionary Priests,* pp. 46–49.

[17] Laurence Richardson, alias Johnson, ordained in Douai in 1577, executed May 30, 1582.

never had been in Rome nor in Reims of eight months before the time wherein the false witnesses feigned the conspiracy to have been there contrived. Yea, and against Father Bosgrave it served also, that was neither seminary man, nor sent by the Pope or superior, nor acquainted with any other English priests that returned home nor of the cause of their coming, having been so long absent in the north parts of the world that he had in manner forgotten his own language, repairing home himself for his health only.[18] And yet all or the most part of these men, being so different amongst themselves in age, life, state, calling, place of abode, time of absence from their country, and in the cause, manner, and purpose of returning, were condemned together at one bar, for one and the selfsame particular treason, for conspiring (forsooth) Her Majesty's death at Rome and Reims, such and such days, which in itself hath most manifest contradiction.

But yet when these things were, for the impossibility of the fact, laid down and opened at the bar by the holy confessors themselves, it prevailed nothing, though otherwise also the evidence were given by such persons and of such matters as it was neither possible nor credible that they could be guilty. It was found sufficient for their condemnation that they had kissed the Pope's foot; that they were his scholars and had received *viaticum* [19] from him; that they had seen or spoken with cardinals in Rome and were made priests either there or at other places and finally sent home by authority of their superiors, accounted enemies in the present state of our country. Which things, together with the partial, unwonted, and unlawful dealing used in the proceeding of that day of their judgment, and the known inno-

[18] James Bosgrave, S.J., had taught in Moravia, Poland, and Lithuania before returning to England in 1580. He gave testimony at the trial which did not coincide with that of Campion and the others (*Cobbett's State Trials,* I, 1064, 1082) and which was consequently exploited by the government. He was nevertheless condemned, but reprieved, imprisoned, and banished from England in 1585.

[19] Traveling money or supplies for a journey.

cent quality and trade of the persons, cleareth them against this libel and all other false accusation whatsoever.

But most of all, everyone's sincere protestation, in the hour of their honorable conflict and martyrdom, that they were ignorant of all conspiracies and most innocent of that for which they were condemned in particular, cleareth them thoroughly in the judgment and conscience of every reasonable man, seeing it is not probable that such men would against their consciences and against the truth have avouched a falsehood at that instant, to the present and everlasting perdition of their souls, which would not relent in any point of their faith to save only their temporal lives.

And this is also an invincible proof of their innocency, and that all was for religion and nothing in truth for treason, that if they would have confessed the Queen to be their chief in causes spiritual or have relented in their religion they should have had life and pardon, which was proffered to every one of them, not only at the execution but often before. Yea, for once going to their heretical service, any of those whom they pretend to be so deep traitors might have been quit with favor, as also with great thanks and goodly preferments.

And plain it is that now at the hour of their death, being past further fear of man's laws, if they had meant anything against the Queen's person, or had received order by their superiors, or had thought it agreeable to their spiritual profession, to deal in other matters than religion and conversion of souls by preaching, persuasion, prayers, and other priestly means, they might have spoken their minds boldly now at their passage and departure from this world; as since that time we understand that a certain worshipful lay gentleman [20] did, who protested both at his arraignment and at his death that Her Majesty was not his lawful Queen for two respects: the one for her birth, the other for the excommunication, Her Highness having neither sought dispensa-

[20] [Mr. James Laborne, put to death at Lancaster], March 22, 1583. Also spelled Laburne, Layburne, Leyburne.

tion for the first nor absolution for the second. But none of all our priests made any such answer nor otherwise uttered any unlawful speech that might either offend Her Majesty or the state present, irritate enemy, or scandalize friend.

All their confessions both voluntary and forced by torments are extant in the persecutors' hands. Is there any word soundeth or smelleth of conspiracy?

They have all sorts and sexes of Catholics in prison for their faith and divers honorable personages only upon pretense of dealing and conversing with them. Hath any one of all the realm, in durance or at liberty, by fair means or foul, confessed that ever either priest or Jesuit persuaded them in confession or otherwise to forsake the Queen? That ever they were absolved on that condition? That ever they received *Agnus Deis* at their hands or other spiritual token for earnest or prest to rebel and join with the enemy, as this slanderous libel doth not so much avouch (for that were intolerable) as by guileful art insinuate, without all proof or probability?

Wherein, as at the place of their judgment, the magistrate professing that nothing should be prejudicial unto them that touched only their religion (yet indeed had no other matter for their conviction but the functions of their order and priesthood), so this libeler now, pretending their treasons to be old and of another sort and acquitting them for their Romish tokens, ceremonies, books, beads, and opinions (as he speaketh), yet cunningly windeth himself about in words and only condemneth them in the end for the same, not as capital (forsooth) in themselves but as serviceable to the Pope and applicable to the benefit of rebels at home or abroad. So cunningly they play in such men's lives and deaths as our country was unworthy of.

But now when these innocent persons were condemned, and so many of them as they thought was necessary for their practice executed,[21] because they perceived great scruples and suspicious conceits to rise in all men's hearts and heads about the fact and

[21] [Machiavellian policies.]

unwonted proceeding, no man either so evil or ignorant as to take them guilty of those crimes whereof they were appeached, and every man not so wise as to spy that it was done of necessary policy without much regard of conscience or divinity; knowing also that one John Nicholls, a minister and Protestant (who gave the first false overture of this sinful stratagem), touched by God, absented himself at their condemnation and death and afterward cried the innocent men mercy upon his knees, confessing both by word and letter authentically recorded [22] that partly upon his motion they had condemned innocent blood, and that himself was forced by certain persons in authority (whom for honor sake we will not name though he named them) to commence such a foul tragedy. Considering therefore all these things, and desiring to cover the foulness of the fact as much as might be, as well in respect of their own people, manifoldly discontented and specially impatient of such injurious proceedings, as also of strangers, to whom the rare virtues of Father Campion and of some of the others were known (besides other violent means by severe punishments and proclamations to stay the hard speeches and conceits of the people therein), they caused some of them that yet were not executed to be examined upon certain articles, six in all,[23] clean of another purport than their former accusation of killing the GREATEST (as our libel speaketh) all which articles do concern only the authority and fact of Pius the Fifth of famous memory in censuring the Queen by excommunication and deprivation for heresy, and what they thought or how far they allowed of the same.

Whereunto, because they did conjecture their answers would be odious in the sight of the simple, and specially of zealous Protestants (as it fell out indeed), they devised to publish and read them to the people at the martyrdom of the rest, that thereby they might at least conceive that they were worthy of death for other causes, though not for that whereof they were

[22] [In Rouen, 1583.] See above, Ch. I, p. 75, n. 52.

[23] For a text of these six articles, see *Cobbett's State Trials,* I, 1078–1079.

condemned, and so either less pity them or less mark the former unjust pretensed matter of their condemnation.

And this cunning course they have followed ever sith in defense of that pretended justice and is the whole conveyance of this libeler now, who, to defend the execution of their cruelty toward these saints of God, bestoweth his labor only to prove that they have been tried by the Six Articles concerning the excommunication, and that there was found a note after Father Campion's death touching the same bull, procured for the interpretation and force thereof, and brought from Rome by Father Parsons and the said Father Campion's suit; [24] that Mr. Hart confessed the bull in such and such sort to bind, and otherwise not to stand in force.[25] Whereby only he goeth about to persuade the world, and specially strangers unacquainted in our affairs, the said men to have been traitors and justly punished, as though new crimes either found out or done after the sentence of their death passed, yea, after the execution of the same, could justify their condemnation passed before.

But the world looked for some justification of that former judgment and verdict of court, which passed with such great solemnity against those innocent men before, upon transgression (as was pretended) of an old statute for compassing the Queen's death. For, as for all other, declamations and invectives, be they true or be they false, cannot excuse the fact from plain murder, nor condemn them after they be dead for other crimes than they were convicted of in their lives. Which the libeler himself confesseth in these express words, after all his idle work and words: "Upon refusal to answer to these questions directly" (saith he), "as they might have been justly convicted of treason, so yet were they not thereupon condemned" (which yet is false, for they have lately executed divers priests, as Mr. Haydock, Mr. Hemerford [26] and others, most cruelly, only about the matter of excommunication of the Queen) "but upon their other former actions

[24] Cecil, pp. 17–19.
[25] Cecil, p. 19.
[26] George Haydock, ordained in Reims in 1581; Thomas Hemerford or

committed both abroad and in the realm." [27] But what those actions were, and how they were proved to be committed particularly by those whom we avouch to be unjustly condemned upon old treasons and to be only killed for their religion: that should have been your whole endeavor (sir) to show, all other superfluous railing or recital of pretended offenses (for which yourself confess they were not condemned) being not of force to maintain the defense of your pretended justice, nor yet to stay the Christian world and Church of God from accounting them martyrs whom you have murdered.

Against whose holy ashes and memories you can struggle no more than the old heathen and heretical persecutors did, to defame those glorious men of the primitive Church whom they executed in pretense of like treasonable trespasses, who yet (notwithstanding their enemies' manifold endeavors to stay the honors due to them after their deaths) by Christ and His Church's judgment have gotten the victory over their adversaries and so remain as glorious in heaven and earth as their persecutors be infamous through all the world.

What worldly honor the two King Henrys of England had (I mean the Second and Eighth), which in the days of their reign no doubt was great; or what esteem soever the princess present and her greatest ministers have now, by the height of their room and fortune in this life, it is but a very dream, shadow, or fantasy to the glory of Thomas of Canterbury,[28] John of Rochester, Chancellor More,[29] Father Campion, and the rest, whom fame and felicity followeth upon their deaths and upon such contradiction of sinners seeking to disgrace them. As also, in the contrary part,

---

Emerford, ordained in Rome in 1583; both executed in London, February 12, 1584.

[27] [Fol. 18.] Cecil, pp. 38–39.

[28] Thomas à Becket, 1118?–1170, Archbishop of Canterbury, assassinated by knights in the course of a quarrel with King Henry II, canonized in 1173.

[29] John Fisher and Thomas More. Cf. above, Ch. I, p. 70, ns. 30, 31.

the persecutors' glory dieth with their authority, if not before; and they are commonly better known to posterity by executing of such men (though to their shame), than by other their facts in their life whatsoever. And so doth God protect His saints *a contradictione linguarum,*[30] from the gainsaying of tongues, and giveth them victory of the world by the fortitude of their faith in Him.

But of the Six Articles concerning the bull of excommunication, more shall be said in the next chapter and other places following, that their innocency therein also may appear and the slanderous libeler repressed every way.

Chapter III

That we now have great cause to complain of unjust persecution, intolerable severity, and cruelty toward Catholics in England; and their Protestants no reason to do the like for the justice done to them in Queen Mary's and other princes' days, and the cause of the difference

THE libeler, by sophistical reasons and popular persuasion going about to make men think the English persecution to be nothing so violent as is divulged nor anything comparable to the justice exercised toward the Protestants in the reign of the late Queen Mary, telleth of hundreds for our scores, as also of the qualities of them that then suffered, of their innocency in all matters of state and treason, and suchlike.

To which we say briefly, clearly, and to the purpose that we measure not the matter by the number, nor by the severity of the punishment only or specially, but by the cause, by the order of justice in proceeding by the laws of God and all Christian na-

[30] Ps. 31:20: "From the strife of tongues."

tions, and such other circumstances. Whereby we can prove Queen Mary's doings to be commendable and most lawful, the other, toward us and our brethren, to be unjust and impious.

The difference is in these points: You profess to put none to death for religion. You have no laws to put any man to death for his faith. You have purposely repealed by a special statute made in the first year and Parliament of this Queen's reign all former laws of the realm for burning heretics,[1] which smelleth of something that I need not here express. You have provided at the same time that nothing shall be deemed or adjudged heresy but by your Parliament and Convocation. You have not yet set down by any new law what is heresy or who is an heretic. Therefore you can neither adjudge of our doctrine as of heresy nor of us as of heretics. Nor have you any law left whereby to execute us. And so, to put any of us to death for religion is against justice, law, and your own profession and doctrine.

But nevertheless you do torment and punish us, both otherwise intolerably and also by death most cruel; and that (as we have proved) for *Agnus Deis,* for ministering the holy sacraments, for our obedience to the See Apostolic, for persuading our friends to the Catholic faith, for our priesthood, for studying in the Society or colleges beyond the seas, and suchlike, which you have ridiculously made treason but afterward (being ashamed of the foul absurdity) acknowledge them to be matters of religion and such as none shall die for. And therefore we most justly make our complaint to God and man that you do us plain violence and persecute us without all equity and order.

On the other side, Queen Mary against the Protestants executed only the old laws of our country and of all Christendom made for punishment of heretics, by the canons and determination of all Popes, councils, churches, and ecclesiastical tribunals of the world, allowed also and authorized by the civil and imperial laws and received by all kingdoms Christian besides. And who

[1] 1 Eliz. I, c. 1, section 6.

then hath any cause justly to be grieved? Why should any man complain or think strange for executing the laws which are as ancient, as general, and as godly against heretics as they are for the punishment of traitors, murderers, or thieves?

Secondly, we complain justly of persecution for that our cause for which we suffer is the faith of all our forefathers; the faith of our persecutors' own ancestors; the faith into which our country was converted and by which we are called Christian; the faith of the Catholic Churches and kingdoms round about us; the faith that we promised in our regeneration; and therefore cannot be forced from it nor punished for it by any law of God, nature, or nations.

Where contrariwise those that in our time or otherwise have fallen from that faith which not only their elders religiously received but themselves also for most part were many years brought up in, or if not, yet had they promised and vowed the same by their parents and spiritual sureties [2] (though Protestants) in their baptism, wherein solemn promise is both made and taken to follow the Catholic Church and faith, with abomination of all heresies and sects whatsoever; [3] these men (I say) though born of parents either Arians,[4] Macedonians,[5] Pelagians,[6]

[2] Godparents.

[3] Cf. the order for public baptism in the *Book of Common Prayer,* 1559 version, which includes in the charge to godparents the Apostles' Creed with its pledge of belief in the "holy Catholic Church" but does not include a clause requiring abomination of heresies and sects.

[4] Fourth-century heretics who held that Jesus Christ is a secondary divinity, not coeternal with the Father but created.

[5] The Pneumatomachi, followers of Macedonius, fourth-century patriarch of Constantinople, who denied the divinity of the Holy Spirit, claiming that the third person of the Trinity was no more than a ministering angel, citing as authority Heb. 1:14.

[6] Followers of the fifth-century British or Irish monk Pelagius, who felt that the moral strength of man's will is sufficient, without grace, when tempered by asceticism, to resist sin. He held that Christ's death is valuable only as an instrument of instruction and example to counter the bad example of Adam in committing the first sin.

Anabaptists,[7] Zwinglians,[8] Protestants, or other sect or opinion, are not permitted, and much less charged or bound (as the libeler full ignorantly surmiseth),[9] to hold that profession of peculiar heresy wherein they were first brought up, seeing they cannot be deemed to have professed that sect in their baptism (or, as idly this poor divine addeth, in their confirmation) which was first taught them by their masters of error, according to the time or place of their first education; but are to be instructed how that their profession in baptism was of the true, Catholic, received, and known Christian faith, dispersed over the world in Christ His Church, whereunto they afterward stand bound and consequently by all law both divine and human may be enforced, albeit their actual baptism or education were never so much amongst heretics.

So that, as no law of God or man can force us to be Protestants, no more can any reason be alleged nor just excuse made for either young or old why, being baptized or brought up amongst Arians or Calvinists, they may not be forced to return to the Catholic Church and faith again.

And we may marvel in what age or world those people were born which the libeler noteth to have been burned in Queen Mary's time, having never heard (as he saith) [10] of any other religion than that for which they suffered. For the sect which they pretended to die for was not extant in England above five or six years before in the short reign of King Edward the Sixth, or rather of his Protector.[11] For before that, in King Henry's days, the same profession was accounted heresy, and the professors thereof were burned for heretics, and that by public laws, no less

[7] Christian groups of the sixteenth century who denied the validity of infant baptism.

[8] Followers of Huldreich Zwingli, 1484–1531, initiator of the Protestant Reformation in Switzerland.

[9] [Fol. 9.] Cecil, p. 20.

[10] [Fol. 9.] Cecil, p. 20.

[11] Edward Seymour, first Earl of Hertford and Duke of Somerset, the Protector of England during the early years of the reign of Edward VI, beginning in 1547.

than in the reign of Queen Mary. But the truth is that because we Catholic Christian men do justly ground ourselves upon the former profession of our faith notoriously known to be and to be called Catholic, these men apishly would imitate our phrase and argument in a thing as far differing as heaven and hell.

Thirdly, we say that we have just cause to complain of this present persecution for that the manner of it is such, and the proceeding so conformable to the old pagan, heretical, and apostatical fashion and dealing against God's Church and children, that nothing can be more like.

They hated all Catholics and counted them traitors; so do you. They specially persecuted bishops, priests, and religious; so do you. They killed them indeed for their belief, but yet pretended other crimes more odious, and specially matters of conspiracy and rebellion against the civil magistrate; so do you. They drove the innocent, by captious interrogatories, into dangers of laws that never offended the laws; so do you. They pressed men by torments to deny their faith, under color of trying their secret intents against the prince; so do you. They punished and have put to death one Catholic for another man's fault of the same profession and, upon general supposals common to all of the same faith, made away whom they list; so do you. I refer the indifferent readers to the persecution of *Julianus Apostata,* of the Goths and Vandals in Italy and Africa.

It is not only the slaughter of many, and them specially the priests of God, which is most proper to heretical persecution, but the other infinite spoil of Catholic men's goods, honors, and liberty, by robbing them for receiving priests, hearing mass, retaining Catholic schoolmasters, keeping Catholic servants, mulcting them by twenty pounds a month (which by their cruel account they make thirteenscore a year) for not repairing to their damnable schismatical service; [12] by which a number of ancient gentlemen fall to extremity, either of conscience, if for fear they

[12] In enforcement of 23 Eliz. I, c. 1, "An act to retain the Queen's Majesty's subjects in their due obedience."

obey, or of their undoing in the world, if they refuse; the taking of their dear children from them by force and placing them for their seduction with heretics (which violence cannot be done by the law of God to Jews themselves); the burning of our priests in the ears; the whipping and cutting of the ears of others; carrying some in their sacred vestments through the streets; putting our chaste virgins into infamous places appointed for strumpets; and other unspeakable villainies, not inferior to any of the said heathenous persecutions. They have pined and smothered in their filthy prisons above thirty famous prelates; above forty excellent learned men; of nobles, gentlemen, and matrons a number; whose martyrdom is before God as glorious as if they had by a speedy violent death been dispatched; every dungeon and filthy prison in England full of our priests and brethren; all provinces and princes Christian witnesses of our banishment. In all this we yield them our bodies, goods, country, blood, and lives; and nothing will quench their hatred of our priesthood, faith, and profession. Thus in all causes we suffer, and yet they would not have us complain. They say all is sweet, clement, and merciful in this regiment. But as we said, we no otherwise complain of this persecution against us but as it is exercised for that faith and quarrel which the laws of God and man approve and justify in us; that it is done by the sheep and subjects of God's Church against their own prelates and pastors, to whom in causes of religion they are bound to obey by the express word of God.

When the lawful magistrate, bearing sword by God for punishment of offenders, putteth thieves, heretics, or murderers to death, who accounteth it cruelty? Who complaineth of persecution? But when, contrariwise, by any violent disorder, the malefactors get head and take heart in a commonwealth and kill a lawful officer, judge, or superior, that is a cruel and horrible fact, though it be done but in one or two persons, instead of a thousand wicked men executed by just laws. So when the prince and prelate proceed together against such as by the sentence and law of the Church of Christ are adjudged to be heretics and injuries to God, that is justice. But when the temporal prince or lay people rebel against their own bishops, to whom in spiritual matters they are bound by God's word to give ear under pain of damnation; yea, when mere laymen, and most of them wholly unlearned, disorderly take upon them to prescribe unto their own pastors what they should believe, how they should minister the sacraments, force upon them false and impious oaths and articles, and that in Parliament, where the bishops, by the laws of our country having the principal suffrages, and the rest of the whole Convocation, representing the Church of England, honorably and uniformly resisted; whom these men afterward deposed of their honors, took their pulpits, churches, titles, and prerogatives from them, imprisoned their sacred persons, and abused some of them, namely the noble confessor and Bishop of London,[13] by all sorts of villainy: this, lo, is a persecution indeed, where the sheep, subjects, and inferiors violently oppose themselves against them whom the Holy Ghost hath placed to be the guides, governors, and curates of their souls. Yea, when they depose, disauthorize, spoil, punish, imprison their own rulers, God's anointed priests, and give warrant by wicked laws to the temporal powers to visit, correct, judge, and discern of the doctrine of their masters in religion, that is a persecution, sedition, and rebellion in the highest degree.

And we may truly say hereof to our lost country with the prophet: *Populus tuus sicut hi qui contradicunt sacerdoti,*[14] the state of the persecution being wholly agreeable to the mutiny of Korah, Dathan, Abiram, and their confederates in the desert against their lawful priests and governors;[15] yea, properly

[13] Edmund Bonner, Bishop of London from 1540, twice refused the Elizabethan Oath of Supremacy, in 1559 and 1563, and was consequently kept in prison until his death in 1569.

[14] [Hos. 4]:4: "For this people are as they that strive with the priest."

[15] Numbers 16.

against the high priesthood of Aaron, as our country's revolt now is against the See Apostolic and all lawful spiritual regiment proceeding from the same.

And therefore the libeler, guilefully in respect of the simple, but fondly and falsely in our eyes, disproveth our lawful refusal to obey men before God and our resistance in matter of conscience by the example of Korah's conspiracy; which toucheth all their rebellions from the See Apostolic and Catholic Church and confirmeth all our endeavors for maintenance of the same against what adversaries soever.

And their rebellion is the more plain and persecution more hateful and intolerable for that they have not only unnaturally done this violence to their own spiritual rulers but thereupon also have chosen at their pleasures and intruded into their places a sort of greedy wolves; unordered apostates; amorous and godless companions; the very filth and chanel [16] of the realm, who for hatred of the Catholic faith from which they are renegades and through a kind of competency [17] or emulation of the true bishops (whose rooms by secular force they unjustly have invaded and do detain), bear such unquenchable malice to the true anointed clergy and to their obedient followers that they cease not to incite the powers of the realm against us and exercise themselves under the pretensed title of their usurped dignities and other temporal commissions, the greatest tyranny and cruelty in the world, standing in fear of their state so long as they see any true bishop or Catholic man alive. Whose actions are the rather intolerable for that they know and hath been proved in open court that they not only usurp those places against God's and the Church's laws, but that they were not made and invested according to the new laws of the realm [18] specially made for creation of them.

So as, our true pastors being vexed, spoiled, tormented, and

[16] Apparently a form of "canaille," meaning vile populace, rabble, mob.
[17] Rivalry, competition.
[18] Henry VIII, c. 20, reinstated by 1 Eliz. I, c. 1.

slain against law, nature, and all reason by temporal men having no authority in causes ecclesiastical, and by a new forged clergy that exerciseth no jurisdiction but by evident usurpation against both the canons of the Church and the laws of our country: who is of so dull a wit as not to see the difference of the discipline of the Church and realm done toward offenders in Catholic times and states by lawful authority both spiritual and temporal, and the unjust persecution of the Church and her children now, proceeding of neither lawful authority temporal nor spiritual?

Therefore let not the libeler here so much extol the equity and mercy used in Her Majesty's regiment to certain of the old principal clergy, because they put them not to death as they have done others sithence. Cicero will not stick to tell them what a benefit is done to an honest man when his purse is taken from him and yet his life saved, and what thanks are to be rendered in that case to the benefactor.[19] What courtesy soever was showed at that time more than afterward to such as followed (which in good sooth was no other than instead of a present quick dispatch on gibbet to allow them a long and miserable life, or rather a lingering and languishing death, in durance, desolation, and disgrace; a far worse kind of persecution, as St. Hilary noteth against Constans [sic] the Arian Emperor,[20] than any other). But whatsoever it was that moved them not to put such to present death as they have done some of the younger sort afterward, no difference of cause there was, the latter sort being indeed no more traitorous or disloyal than the former.

This may perhaps be the chief cause: that persecutors lightly[21] at the beginning use, of purpose and policy, gentle allurements, hoping that way to gain the grace of all sorts, which is the reason that Julian the Emperor in the beginning was much noted of

[19] Reference, perhaps, to Cicero, *Phil.* ii, 3.

[20] St. Hilary of Poitiers, *Contra Constantium Imperatorem,* cap. 5. Allen here confuses Constans with his Arian brother Constantius.

[21] Commonly, often.

clemency; but in fine, when he saw he could not extinguish the Christian faith by art, his former hypocritical lenity was at length turned into extreme fury.

In our country, at the first entrance of heresy, they had all the principal clergy and divers chief Catholics in prisons or places at commandment, where they could not exercise their functions; and being ancient men, most of them, they knew they could not live long. Whereof divers, having been in high offices hard before, had showed pleasures to some Protestants that should have else suffered for their heresies or treasons in Queen Mary's days; who now, by saving some of the said bishops' lives, thought to requite their courtesies in part. They little thought that, these old holy confessors being worn out by years and imprisonment, a new generation would rise to defend their old bishops' and fathers' faith.

Wherein perceiving now, after twenty-five years' struggling against God's Church, all their human counsels to be frustrate, and that they can have no rest in their heresy nor security of their state, depending (as they think) thereupon, they are now in greater fury and rage toward us, making challenge for our ancestors' faith, than they were with the said holy bishops. Though to say truth, in respect of the others' high calling and unction, to degrade only and imprison one of them was greater punishment than twenty deaths to us, being to them but punies [22] and their pupils and most obedient children of their pastoral dignity.

But where the libeler pretendeth us to be guilty of other treasons and trespasses than they were, and therefore punished by death rather than they, as also pressed by these new questions of the bull and other capital matters, as they never were, we avouch both assertions to be untrue; neither our treasons being other than matter of our conscience and religion more than theirs were, nor yet they (being indeed so quiet and obedient subjects as you confess them to have been) were always free from such or other

[22] Juniors, subordinates.

bloody and quarreling demands as now are put to us for entangling of our blood. Whereof as well the honorable confessor and Bishop of London[23] may be an example, before any excommunication of the Queen was heard of, as other prelates and prisoners of that time and rank convented afterward, about nine years ago, and had interrogatories concerning the bull of the very same sense and peril as these that quiet Catholic men are now tempted even to death withal.

As for the high praises and special testimony of wisdom, learning, and loyalty that it liked the maker of the libel to give in particular and in very nice fashion and migniard[24] terms to certain of the chief clergy; though it be but the sweet salve of Joab to Amasa,[25] kissing and killing both at once (for within six lines he crieth shame and reproach to them all), yet it is a condemnation to him and his fellows that presumed to dispossess so noble, wise, and learned prelates and to prefer the judgment and verdict of men ignorant and profane before such men's sentence even in matter of religion; and much more to put into their places a number of uncircumcised Philistines, taken of the rascality of the whole realm, and of such only as could and would fill My Lords of the Court's hands with the benediction given to Esau.[26] In respect of whom, or of any or all the rout that suffered for heresy in Queen Mary's days, the poorest and worst that be in trouble for religion at home or in banishment for the same abroad (of whom this libeler upon either his malicious heretical humor or artificial policy, to diminish their credit with the people or their grace with the princes and prelates abroad, under whose protection they live, speaketh so contemptibly and in part so reproachfully and slanderously) may be in all life and behavior accounted saints.

It is a shame to follow the libeler's folly in the pursuit of such

[23] Edmund Bonner. Cf. above, p. 99, n. 13.
[24] Dainty, delicate, mincing.
[25] II Sam. 20:9–10.
[26] Gen. 27:39–40.

childish things. But he compelleth us, and therefore we be forced to compare our cases and persons to theirs that were burned in our country for heresy and apostasy not long before.

The libel therefore maketh a glorious muster of archbishops (so he speaketh by *enalage numeri*); [27] for indeed there was but one, and he a notorious perjured and often relapsed apostate,[28] recanting, swearing, and forswearing at every turn, and at the very day and hour of his death sacrilegiously joined in pretended marriage to a woman, notwithstanding his vow and order (the very first and principal cause of the English calamity). Other bishops or clergymen were there none of all the pack that was burned (though two or three of them had unjustly usurped some prelates' rooms) but were of the basest (for most part), worst, and contemptiblest of both sexes. Insomuch that the very saint-woman whose child (as he saith upon lying Foxe's credit) burst out of her belly into the fire was naught [29] of her body and therefore to cover her incontinency would not utter to the officer her case nor claim (after the custom of our country) the benefit of her belly, but for the honor of her holy martyrdom (forsooth) went to the fire with the child in her womb, herself only knowing thereof: where Almighty God discovered her filth and shame, where she looked for the glory of a saint and of a virgin martyr;[30] of which sort there is none in all Foxe's martyrology nor commonly amongst Protestants' saints.

Now for these we yield unto the libeler: first, fourteen noble and most worthy bishops at one time, such as himself upon evil

[27] Change of number.

[28] [Cranmer.] Thomas Cranmer, 1489–1556, Archbishop of Canterbury, executed for heresy by the government of Mary.

[29] Immoral, unchaste.

[30] John Foxe, *Acts and Monuments,* book XI, "A tragical, lamentable, and pitiful history . . . ," reportedly occurring on the island of Guernsey in July of 1556, involving a woman named Perotine Massey. A Catholic polemicist, Thomas Harding, published an attack on the character of this woman, probably the source for Allen's, which was refuted at length in later editions of Foxe.

intent commended even now so highly (and indeed they were inferior in virtue and learning to none in Europe), who all were deprived of their honors and high callings and most of them imprisoned and spitefully used in all respects; besides the famous confessor Archbishop of Armagh,[31] Primate of Ireland, and a number of bishops of that country. Next we yield you in banishment two worthy English prelates of the same dignity, the one dead,[32] the other yet alive in Rome; [33] three elected bishops all now departed this life; we name the honorable Abbot of Westminster,[34] four priors or superiors of religious convents, with three whole convents put out of their possessions either into prison or out of the realm.

In the same case were a dozen of famous learned deans, which next to the bishops do hold the chief dignities in the English cathedral churches; fourteen archdeacons; above threescore canons of cathedral churches; not so few as an hundred priests of good preferment in Queen Mary's time, besides many [a] one made in our banishment and since martyred; fifteen heads or rectors of colleges in Oxford and Cambridge, men of great importance in those universities and in the commonwealth; and with them and the rather by their good example and provocation, not many years after, many of the chief professors of all sciences; and above twenty doctors of divers faculties for conscience sake fled the realm or were in the realm imprisoned. And both at the first and in divers years sithence hath many of the very flower of the universities come over both into the Society, seminaries, and other places famous for learning. Where through God's goodness

[31] Richard Creagh, Roman Catholic Archbishop of Armagh, was arrested and tried for treason in 1567, acquitted, rearrested after an escape, and imprisoned in the Tower of London, where he died in 1585.

[32] Richard Pate (d. 1565), Bishop of Lincoln, imprisoned early in the reign of Elizabeth I but soon released.

[33] Thomas Goldwell (d. 1585), Bishop of St. Asaph, left England for Rome in 1559.

[34] John de Feckenham. Cf. Cecil, p. 11.

and the great benignity of prelates, princes, and Catholic people they have passed their long banishment in honest poverty, and some in worshipful calling and rooms in universities with as much grace and favor as to foreigners could be yielded; in no place (thanks be to Our Lord God) impeached of crimes or disorder, whereof we can show the honorable testimony of the best where we have lived in all nations.

And for our Christian comportment both at home in affliction and abroad in banishment (though we be subject to infirmities as other sinful creatures be), we dare stand with all the Protestants in the world. Which we be forced against this infamous libeler to speak more liberally and confidently for that he so shamefully and against his own knowledge writeth that "very few are fled for religion other than such as were not able to live at home but in beggary, or discontented for lack of preferment, which they gaped for unworthily in universities and other places; or bankrupt merchants,"[35] etc. Where the poorest wretches and worst amongst us, that in this tedious time of twenty-five years' absence from our country will relent in religion and return to them, may be most welcome, received with joy and triumph, and made jolly fellows in their new synagogue. *Ita nusquam facilius proficitur, quam in castris rebellium,* as one saith.[36] So earnestly they woo every poor apostate, lewd scholar, and lost companion that for weariness of banishment, loose life, or impatience looketh homeward toward heresy or carnal liberty and license again. By which allurements yet the world knoweth how exceeding few you gain or get from us; whilst we in the mean space (through God's great grace) receive hundreds of your ministers, a number of your best wits, many delicate young gentlemen, and divers heirs of all ages, voluntarily fleeing from your damnable condition and seeking after God; and many of them also become priests or religious,

[35] Cecil, p. 5.

[36] [Tertullian], *De praescription ibus adversus haereticos,* cap. 41: "Nowhere is promotion easier than in the camp of rebels."

even now when you hate, contemn, and punish priests so deadly. This is the work of God, marvelous both in your eyes and ours; and cannot by human force, fear, or policy be dissolved.

Count your cards, therefore, better and look not only of so many famous clergymen and the daily increase of them against your violent laws (Sir Libeler), but count, if you dare for shame, among your beggars and bankrupts in Queen Mary's time (as you dishonestly term us now) so many noble and valiant earls, barons, knights, esquires, and gentlemen, that have either suffered prison, or, as their conscience led them, stood in arms for defense of their faith and Christian knighthood, not against their prince or country but against such as abused her weak sex and former years of her youth to the establishing of themselves and their heresy, or have forsaken their honorable callings, offices, and livelihoods in their countries for defense of their Christian faith; of which I could name you a noble number of all degrees, able and ready to defend by sword (excepting the respect they have to their prince and dear country) their religion and honorable actions against all the heretics in the world that defame them.

Whose most worthy order and knighthood the libeler seeketh to distain by naming the noble Earl of Westmorland,[37] whose peculiar life and actions, or any other particular person of what condition soever, though we go not about nor need to defend against malicious envy and detraction of heresy, yet surely, notwithstanding his youthful behavior whatsoever (which he learned there amongst you, and is not so strange in camp or court, you wot well, Mr. Libeler), he is able to prove that you slander him extremely. And we can witness that he liveth in good health and honorable charge in the service of the King Catholic; [38] as we also can tell you that the renowned Count of Northumberland [39] died a saint and holy martyr. For, what former quarrel or cause of his death soever there was, yet was he a true

[37] Charles Neville. Cf. Cecil, p. 4.
[38] Philip II of Spain.
[39] Thomas Percy. Cf. Cecil, p. 16.

martyr in that he was offered his life if he would alter his religion; as divers others were of the same action in the North and all other priests pretended to be condemned for other treasons.

Which life and living inasmuch as they refused for Christ and His faith when it was offered, they be in the number of saints and confessors no less than if they had died only for the same.

And therefore when the adversary chargeth Dr. Sanders and Dr. Bristow with treason for affirming such to be martyrs in this sense,[40] he showeth himself ignorant, as he is malicious in bidding us enroll Somerfield[41] in the number of our martyrs. As perhaps before God he is, if he were distract of his wits or furious (as all men say and the libeler confesseth), to whom cannot be imputed whatsoever he did in alienation of mind, and to his enemies shall be imputed murder whatsoever was done against him in that his state; or specially (which is the most common opinion proved by many probabilities) if the poor gentleman were dispatched of purpose and appointment (as the friar that accused the Duke of Lancaster was[42] and many other, and as the Protestants said John Hun[43] was in Lollards' tower) for prevention of the discovery of certain shameful practices about the condemnation and making away of the worshipful, valiant, and innocent gentleman Mr. Arden,[44] whose case like to Naboth's,[45] and his words of wishing the Queen in heaven (as it is reported), were so partially or rigorously scanned by the malice of his great

[40] Cecil, pp. 14–15, 29, 38. [41] John Somerville. Cf. Cecil, pp. 30–31.

[42] When Parliament met at Salisbury on April 29, 1384, a Carmelite friar accused John of Gaunt, Duke of Lancaster, of plotting to remove the King. At the Duke's request, the friar was arrested, and while in custody he was assassinated.

[43] Richard Hun, accused of heresy in 1514, imprisoned in the Lollards' tower in London, found hanged in his cell soon thereafter. The charge that he had been murdered was reported by John Foxe, *Acts and Monuments,* book VII, "The story of Richard Hun, martyr."

[44] Edward Arden, implicated by his son-in-law, John Somerville, in his plot to kill the Queen; executed in 1583.

[45] I Kings 21:13.

and potent professed enemy that many years hath sought his ruin, together with his zealousness in the Catholic faith, that they brought him to his most pitiful end, to the great regret of the whole country. But the importunity of the adversary hath brought us somewhat out of our intended course.

To return back, therefore, to our famous prelates, deposed in this Queen's days, the principal whereof was Archbishop of York and High Chancellor of the realm [46] (the Primate of Canterbury being deceased before). Which worthy man this libeler hypocritically commendeth for his loyalty,[47] though in religion differing from them, thereby to make the Queen's Majesty's mercy toward him a pattern (forsooth) of clemency not to be matched, as he wisely writeth, in Queen Mary's time. Which Queen notwithstanding pardoned a number of heretics and rank condemned traitors, both of life and lands, whom we could name and all the world knoweth yet alive. And further he addeth (which is a notorious untruth) that the said prelate voluntarily left his chancellorship and archbishopric. Where all wise men will witness with him and for him that he was most unjustly, with the rest of his suffragans and brethren bishops, for refusing to take that absurd oath of the Queen's supremacy and to use the new Calvinistical service in his province, deposed by violence from his spiritual function and dignity.

Whose courage and resistance for quarrel of God's religion (how loyal and obedient soever the libeler would make those men in comparison of us, thereby to insinuate that the more bloody rigor is used now toward us than in the beginning toward them) was such in them, and specially in the said Archbishop, that he worthily and as became his excellency refused to anoint or crown the Queen's Majesty that now is, though it appertained to his special office to do the same, the Metropolitan being dead, as hath been said before. And so did all the rest of the bishops refuse the same until with much ado they obtained the Bishop of

[46] [Dr. Heath, Archbishop of York.]

[47] Cecil, p. 10.

Carlisle [48] (the inferior almost of all the rest) to do that function. Which is here remembered by me for that the libeler of his good discretion recordeth it for special courtesy of that man toward his princess. Which refusal of him (specially that by office should have done the same), might in reason have been construed to as heinous and treasonable a purpose as most things that afterward have been done for the Catholic cause by any of the later years, if the malice of that time had been as ripe then as now it is against God's Church and priests.

The cause why they durst not then nor could be adduced by any human fear or authority to invest her was for that they had evident probabilities and arguments to doubt that she meant either not to take the oath or not to keep the same which all Christian kings (and specially ours in England) do make in their coronation for maintenance of Holy Church's laws, honors, peace, and privileges and other duties due to every state, as in the time and grant of King Edward the Confessor.[49]

They doubted also lest she would refuse, in the very time of her sacre,[50] the solemn divine ceremony of unction (accustomed in the consecration of all Christian princes), through the evil advices of certain young counselors, being then in the heat, prime, and pride of their heresy, whereby great scandal might arise and hurt to the realm. Which they the rather doubted because they saw (not long before) Her Highness, at her first entrance to that high estate, command a certain Bishop, even the same of Carlisle now named, standing ready to say mass before her (a strange case in a woman toward a bishop), not to elevate the holy consecrated Host but to omit that ceremony, because she liked it not.

[48] Owen Oglethorpe, Bishop of Carlisle. While he did crown Elizabeth, he refused to take the Oath of Supremacy, was deprived of his see, and died, all in 1559. Cf. Cecil, p. 10.

[49] For a text of this coronation oath, see Leopold G. Wickham Legg, ed., *English Coronation Records* (London and New York, 1901), p. xxxi. Edward the Confessor was King of the English, 1042–1066.

[50] Coronation.

Which the said Bishop, to his great honor, constantly refused to obey. A thing that in one of us poor men now perchance would be accounted high treason and disloyalty toward our sovereign.

And of this his courage in God's cause it never repented him; but for doing the other office at the coronation, when he saw the issue of the matter and both himself and all the rest of his sacred order deprived and the Church's holy laws and faith, against the conditions of her consecration and acceptation into that royal room, violated, he sore repented him all the days of his life; which were, for that special cause, both short and wearisome afterward unto him.

Otherwise, doubtless, all the bishops and the rest of the principal of the inferior clergy did stoutly and worthily as could be wished and as was possible in that sudden assault of heresy, fearing at the same time their personal peril so little that they were many of them of that mind that it should be good to use the censure of excommunication against Her Highness and some of her leaders into that revolt so dangerous and shameful to the state, so lately reconciled to the See Apostolic and by oath and promise of all estates confirmed.

But the wiser of the bishops, or at least the milder sort, persuaded the contrary for many inconveniences that might ensue; and so they rather resolved the matter to be remitted to the high pastor of Christ's universal Church than to be executed by them that were her subjects, not without peril perhaps of some further tumult, scandal, and trouble to the whole clergy; whom they would have interpreted to have done it of malicious and rebellious mind rather than of love and duty; of which all such censures indeed do proceed, howsoever the party affected and sick in soul (especially princes, except they be very well trained in the fear of God) accept the same; well remembering that many kings had killed their pastors in like cases.

All this we put down that no man be abused by the enemy to think that reverend prelates at the first were less zealous (which he calleth more loyal) or more obedient to the prince in lawful things than we, their scholars and offspring, be; or we less loyal than they and therefore more punishable than they were; though indeed their perpetual imprisonment and pining away in miserable desolation, their tossing and shifting from one superintendent's house to another, from one keeper to another, from one prison to another, subject to extreme wants and to a thousand daily villainies besides, whereof some of them now have tasted for twenty-five years together, is worse than any death in the world. This, then, is a true persecution indeed, when such men for such causes against all reason and laws be so vexed by such as owe them all reverence, duty, and obedience.

Such is also the miserable fortune of the Catholic nobility and gentry, whom this libeler saith they put not to death nor loss of their inheritance, though they hold opinion for the Pope's supremacy and defend that "the Queen's Majesty ought not to be the governor over all her subjects in her realm, being persons ecclesiastical; which opinions" (saith he) "are nevertheless in some part by the laws of the realm punishable in some degrees." [51] Yet such is their misery (we say) that, notwithstanding these fair and false speeches of the enemy, they be far more injured than the clergy; even themselves more vexed, spoiled, dishonored with fines, mulcts, bonds, penalties, imprisonments, arraignments amongst thieves, pretense of praemunires, misprisions, discontentments, evil affections, and contrary religion to the state; pursued by the vilest and most abject men, by ministers, spies, and promoters; assailed and robbed in their own houses and chased from the same into woods, yea, sometimes into waters (we speak of knowledge) and at length into banishment. Which who seeth not how miserable a thing it is, when their whole families must either perish of famine at home or beg in strange lands abroad; in which case both their goods are seized on (as the world knoweth) and their possessions fall to the prince's hands or into

[51] Cecil, pp. 12–13.

the fist of some lost companion which shall upon favor obtain the gift to make spoil of the same.

And yet this good writer so nicely, to color their cruelty toward Catholic gentlemen, setteth down the matter as though cases of conscience, religion, or of the See Apostolic were but in some degrees, in some little part, punished and not with loss of lands nor death at any time persecuted; when he and all the world knoweth that they may and do by those wicked laws of theirs disinherit, put to perpetual prison and to death, divers of the laity. We refer them to the worshipful Mr. Tregian's [52] case, who liveth in prison so many years of alms after the spoil and rapine of so goodly possessions. We refer them to the laymen put to death of late at Winchester and Andover; [53] to so many fled for religion of the best nobility and gentry, wholly sacked and spoiled of all they possessed; and so many hundreds more, vexed, pillaged, and spoiled at home as they have not wherewithal to expel famine from themselves and their families. And which is yet more, we tell you that there can never a Catholic nobleman in the realm, if by any show of religion or moderation in life he give the enemy the least suspicion in the world of his good affection that way, be sure of his life, lands, and state one day. For by one false pretense and calumniation or other they will entrap him, imprison him, and in fine (except God marvelously protect him) they will overthrow him and his whole family and transfer all his honors sometimes to his chiefest enemies. Yea, all this often against the princess' will, being led against her own natural inclination to such things by the violent domination of certain that overrule her and the whole realm, so as no Catholic can be sure of his lands or life longer than the adversary list.

God knoweth we do not amplify in the sight of strangers the calamities of Catholics in our country; whose chains, dungeons, spoils, flights, disgraces, deaths if all the world could see with

[52] Francis Tregian. See above, Ch. I, p. 62 and n. 5.

[53] John Slade and John Body. See above, Ch. I, p. 64 and n. 18.

their eyes, as we do feel, all the princes Christian would take compassion and account our complaints most just and necessary.

Wherein our miseries are multiplied that such libelers as these do by false reports and misconstruction of our sentence in religion guilefully go about to defame us with foreigners. As, for example, when here this fellow saith that there be divers gentlemen Catholics in England that hold, "The Queen ought not to be governor over any her subjects in her realm, being persons ecclesiastical, and yet are not prosecuted to death for the same,"[54] etc. For their prosecution and persecution I have made it plain before. But for their holding of any such assertion, I must and do say that it is slanderous and most untrue. For there is a great difference to say she is not to rule the bishops in causes ecclesiastical or in matter of ministering the sacraments, preaching, and doctrine, and to say she is not queen or governor over the clergy, or that priests or ecclesiastical persons be not her subjects. For they are also bound, yea, even monks and religious, as St. Chrysostom saith[55] (which this libeler in another place allegeth ignorantly to prove that in all matters such ought to obey their temporal princes),[56] they are bound (I say) to order and obedience of their kings and to observe their temporal and civil laws made for peace, tranquillity, and temporal government of their people and to do them all honor and service in that behalf; as the libeler right well knoweth that all Catholic bishops and prelates of the Church ever have done and do at this day, both in our realm and in all other realms abroad to their lawful kings, yea, to heathen kings also; though in matters of religion and of their spiritual charge neither heathen nor Christian kings be their superiors or ought to direct them but rather to take direction from them.

Thus then, over and above all former recounted calamities, by opprobrious tongues, lying lips and pens, we be persecuted for defense of our fathers' faith and the Church's truth. The cause

[54] Cecil, p. 13. [55] St. John Chrysostom, Homily 23 on Romans (13), ver. 1.
[56] Cecil, p. 22.

whereof putteth the difference between our martyrdom and the due and worthy punishment of heretics; who, shedding their blood obstinately in testimony of falsehood against the truth of Christ and His holy Spouse and out of the unity of the same, are known malefactors and can be no martyrs but damnable murderers of themselves.

One only thing belonging to this passage is yet behind, which we must answer, too, briefly. The adversary telleth us that the martyrs of their sect in Queen Mary's time "denied not their lawful queen nor maintained her enemies, as ours do."[57] A strange boldness to avouch a lie without necessity which all the world can disprove at the first sight! For how say you (sir), was not your Archbishop[58] (named here for the principal of all your martyrs) convicted and condemned openly of high treason? Even for waging soldiers for Duke Dudley[59] (a hateful name to England since Henry the Seventh's time, ever aspiring, but still unfortunate to itself and followers) against the Princess that was then and Her Highness that is now?

Was not your next martyr, superintendent Ridley,[60] an high traitor, publicly preaching and proclaiming at Paul's Cross in London both Queen Mary and this Queen to be bastards and to have no right title to the crown? Did not your famous superintendent now of York[61] (yet no martyr, howsoever he hath

[57] Cecil, p. 21.

[58] Thomas [Cranmer].

[59] John Dudley, Duke of Northumberland, leader in the plot to make Lady Jane Grey, his daughter-in-law, queen in place of Mary on the death of Edward VI in 1553. His father, Edmund Dudley, had been an unpopular financial official in the government of Henry VII and was put to death for treason by the government of Henry VIII in 1510. His son, Robert Dudley, Earl of Leicester, survived the collapse of the Grey plot to become a favorite of Elizabeth I and a power in her government.

[60] Nicholas [Ridley], Bishop of London, jailed in 1553, following the sermon to which Allen alludes, executed for heresy in 1555.

[61] Edwin [Sandys], later Archbishop of York, was Vice-Chancellor of Cambridge in 1553, the time of this incident. He was imprisoned for his part in the Grey plot but soon released, made his way to the Continent

suffered of late some heavy crosses for other causes of homely quality), boldly publish the same in Cambridge; as also your confessor Jewel of Salisbury [62] had done the like in Oxford if he had not been in time prevented? Were not all the pack of your Protestants confederated or acquainted with Wyatt's conspiracy and open rebellion against their prince and country,[63] with other wicked attempts against the state of that time, as they have been sith, well near against all the states and provinces christened? But of this you must needs hear more anon.

But it is a world to see the cunning winding of this libeler. For being ashamed, as it seemeth, or else in doubt of that which he had boldly affirmed before, now cometh to foist in a word to salve all (as he thinketh) and that is that "at their death they denied not their Queen," [64] etc. And in such deceitful cobbling-in[65] of words he passeth no line lightly without fraud. But for answer hereof we say that what they did at their death or the day after God knoweth; but it is plain that in their life they were notorious rebels, as most of that sect be. And how many of our men (I pray you, sir), of whose lives and deaths so great numbers can bear witness, denied their obedience or meekly prayed not for the Queen at the very place and time of their execution? Every one of them, as they lived exemplarily for duty and loyal behavior to all their superiors both temporal and spiritual, so yielded they their happy life and blood in all apostolical patience,

---

in 1554, and returned to England on the accession of Elizabeth. In 1581 he had been blackmailed in an apparently trumped-up marital scandal, perhaps the later "crosses" Allen mentions.

[62] John Jewel, Bishop of Salisbury, had been deprived of a fellowship at Oxford in 1553, made his way to the Continent in 1555, and returned to England in 1559, to become an Elizabethan bishop and a prominent writer in defense of Anglicanism.

[63] An armed rebellion led by Sir Thomas Wyatt against the government of Mary in January of 1554, in protest against the Queen's marriage to Philip II of Spain. It was easily crushed in a few weeks.

[64] Cecil, p. 21.

[65] Putting together roughly or clumsily.

peace, and meekness for the faith wherein they, our country, and all converted nations in the world were baptized and for the very same belief wherein the old glorious martyrs of God's Church gave up their lives.

This faith, this Church, this cause, severeth our true martyrs from the notorious malefactors of the contrary side. And so giveth us just cause to complain of persecution and the enemy no reason at all, of what number, name, obstinacy, age, or quality soever they be that have suffered for their heresy.

Chapter IV

That our priests and Catholic brethren have behaved themselves discreetly and nothing seditiously in their answers to the questions of the bull of Pius the Fifth; and that they cannot lawfully be pressed nor put to death as traitors by the true meaning of the old laws of the realm for the same, with examination of the Six Articles proposed about the said bull

In times of heretical regiment, where politiques have all the government, though religion be sometimes pretended as a thing whereof they make their advantage for the affairs specially intended, yet indeed the first and principal care is of their temporal state and so consequently of the prince's and their own well-being in this life; the lot whereof they often prefer, with Esau, before the weal of the world to come, the blessing of Jacob,[1] or the kingdom of Christ, which is His reign and regiment spiritual in the Church, the house of His glory and our salvation in earth.

Contrariwise, in Christian Catholic commonwealths the chief respect is and ever was (as it ought to be) of the honor of God,

[1] Gen. 25:29–34, account of Esau's sale to Jacob of his birthright for some food.

the good of Holy Church, the salvation of the souls of their people, and so to pass through these secular things as eternal joys be not lost and put in hazard.

In which difference of things you shall easily perceive that in the days of disorder and error the faults done against the prince, or so said to be done, are far more odious and punishable than whatsoever is directly done against God; against the commonwealth than against the Church; against the body than against the soul; more ado about Caesar's tribute than about God's due.[2] As in the time and regiment of Jeroboam, when all the care was how to manage matters so that the kingdom of Israel might be severed from Judah and so established in itself that no spiritual union by worship in Jerusalem might reduce the divided tribes to their former state again, and all things tending to that reunion were grievously punished, but matters of faith and religion wholly contemned.[3]

In our country, when God and His kingdom had the first place, the terrene state the second (as in truth it ought to be; and where it is otherwise, whatsoever is pretended, Christ hath no place at all), then were the crimes committed against God first and principally punished; as heresy, blasphemy, schism, and suchlike; and secondly, treasons and trespasses done against the prince and country; whereof Queen Mary's days and regiment may be an example, when without the forgery of new or false treasons the lately named Archbishop[4] and other principal heretics, being convicted of conspiracy and open traitorous actions, might have justly suffered for the same but yet were rather burned for heresy, as for their more heinous crime and which a Christian prince ought to regard far more than anything committed against his regality.

But now, and ever when the superiority temporal hath the preeminence and the spiritual is but accessory, dependent, and wholly upholden of the other, error in faith is little accounted of,

[2] Mark 12:17.

[3] I Kings 12:26–33 and *passim.*

[4] Thomas Cranmer.

whatsoever their pulpit men (to make themselves and their patrons sport) brawl of such matters; and all our doings, endeavors, and exercises of religion are drawn to treasons and trespasses against the Queen; themselves protesting, in all their doings, that they meddle not with us for our doctrine whatsoever; thereby either insinuating that our religion is true, and indeed by the judgment of their own conscience not punishable, or else that they care not for it nor what we believe, no further than toucheth their prince and temporal weal; wherein yet they wipe so hard as they draw blood.

For, finding no errors, heresies, or false opinions concerning God and His worship worthy to condemn us of, and being ashamed of their statutes of new treasons (as it seemeth), they have found out a new fault and a term for the same, not usual either in writers of our schools and divinity or in their own laws, which they call traitorous assertions, treasonable and malicious opinions against the Queen, as in a former like pamphlet, evil affection or evil disposition toward Her Majesty; which is now the only and proper point they pursue against us both in judgment and writing. For which, as of late they have put divers to death, so by the same they try (as they say) whether papists be traitors or no and accordingly to use them. And for better trial thereof they propose unto all men whom they list make away or otherwise endanger certain demands which in effect are these that ensue: [5]

1. Whether the bull of Pius the Fifth against the Queen's Majesty be a lawful sentence and ought to be obeyed by the subjects of England?
2. Whether the Queen's Majesty be a lawful queen and ought to be obeyed by the subjects of England, notwithstanding the bull of Pius the Fifth or any other bull or sentence that the Pope hath pronounced or may pronounce against Her Majesty?
3. Whether the Pope have or had power to authorize her subjects

[5] Cf. *Cobbett's State Trials,* I, 1078–1079, for a slightly different text of these questions, and Cecil, p. 38.

to rebel or take arms against her or to invade her dominions; and whether such subjects, so doing, do lawfully therein?

4. Whether the Pope have power to discharge any of Her Majesty's subjects or the subjects of any Christian prince from their allegiance or oath of obedience to Her Majesty or to their prince for any cause?

5. Whether Dr. Sanders in his book of *The Visible Monarchy of the Church* [6] and Dr. Bristow in his book of *Motives* [7] (writing in allowance, commendation, and confirmation of the said bull of Pius the Fifth) have therein taught, testified, or maintained a truth or a falsehood?

6. If the Pope do by his bull or sentence pronounce Her Majesty to be deprived and no lawful Queen, and her subjects to be discharged of their allegiance and obedience unto her, and after, the Pope or any other by his appointment and authority do invade this realm, which part would you take, or which part ought a good subject of England to take?

Wherein if you say nothing or refuse to answer somewhat in contempt or derogation of the See Apostolic, then are you judged no good subject but a traitor. Whereby let all princes and people Christian bear witness of our miseries and unjust afflictions, who are enforced to suffer death for our only cogitations and inward opinions, unduly sought out by force and fear, and yet not condemned by any Christian school in the world nor uttered by us but upon forcing interrogatories; we having committed nothing by word or deed against our prince or laws, but doing all acts of honor and homage unto her and suffering meekly what punishment soever she would lay upon us for our religion. For so most part of all sorts of Catholics have done both in England and Ireland for this twenty-five years' space; only a very few nobles of both countries taking once arms for their defense in all this long time of intolerable affliction (the like patience you shall hardly find in Protestants, as their furious rebellions against their sov-

[6] Cf. Cecil, p. 13, n. 27. [7] Cf. Cecil, p. 38, n. 78.

ereigns in France, Flanders, and Scotland do testify); our nobles and gentlemen, having borne all those anguishes of body and mind, with loss of honors, country, lands, and liberty for so long time, have both at home and abroad obeyed her with such loyalty as subjects ought to do their sovereign, never took arms in all England upon the bull of Pius the Fifth nor any time since the publication thereof (contrary to the deceitful division of those times, things, and actions set down by the libeler, placing that after which was done before the bull was published), but have showed themselves in all cases as serviceable as before.

The clergymen, also, whether religious, priests, or students of the two colleges in Rome and Reims, whether they were in the service of their country at home or in the schools absent, did all in manner (notwithstanding the said censure of His Holiness) use all due reverence and respect, uttering in no preaching speech or book, no, nor at the hour of their death and martyrdom, nor ever before in any their confessions to the magistrate, any disloyal word against Her Majesty. No (which we further avouch), not any one priest of the Society or seminaries can be proved by the adversary to have absolved in secret confession any one man living from his allegiance or to have ever either in public or private dissuaded any one person in the realm from his obedience in civil causes to the Queen.

Furthermore, it is certain that never priest had any such commission given hitherto by either the Pope's Holiness or such other superiors in religion or college to deal in any such matters touching the Queen; neither is there any such thing implied in either the authority or act of reconcilement, howsoever the jealous enemy hath found knots in those rushes that of themselves are smooth. As the contrary is doubtless most true, the governors of the students always of purpose prohibiting and, as much as in such numbers of all sorts (not all ever having discretion to season their zeal) could be, providing that in the course of our school questions and controversies concerning the Pope's pre-eminence no matter of depriving or excommunicating princes should be disputed; no, not so much as in generalities, and much less the particularizing of any point in our Queen's case. Which matter, notwithstanding it be determinable by divinity and do come in course to be handled in schools as other questions do, yet because it is incident to matter of state (as now our country most unfortunately standeth), and consequently might be interpreted by the suspicious to be meant of her whose case men liked least to deal in, it was thought best to pass over all with silence.

Which moderation was kept in all places and persons of our nation, two only learned men of great zeal and excellency indeed —Dr. Sanders and Dr. Bristow—excepted, who had their special reasons to do as they did, which we will neither defend nor reprove. But many Catholics were sorry therefor and wished the matter so offensive had never been touched but committed only to higher powers, and especially to God's judgment, that He might, either in this world or the next (where both Popes and princes must come to their accounts), discern of the controversy betwixt our two superiors, the one being our spiritual head and sovereign, who is the higher and in matter of religion rather to be obeyed, the other our temporal prince, to whom likewise in such sort and matter as the Holy Scriptures appoint us we owe all duty and obeisance.

Whereupon afterward not only Dr. Bristow omitted in his second edition or abridgment of his book [8] that odious point, not fit at that time to be handled, but Dr. Sanders also (though his former treatise was not, of any stranger Catholic and learned, in any nation misliked, being more free therein because they be not entangled by authority and sway of laws as we are), yet called he in and suppressed to his life's end a very learned book made in defense of Pius the Fifth his sentence and printed above fourteen

[8] Richard Bristow, *Demands to be Proponed of Catholics to the Heretics, . . . Taken Partly Out of His Late English Book of Motives to the Catholic Faith* (Antwerp, 1576). Allison and Rogers *Catalogue,* no. 148.

years since; no copy thereof that is known being now extant.[9] Which course of moderation all Catholics of all sorts, both spiritual and temporal, have followed ever since, restraining (as much as in them lay) the rigor of that sentence.

And the blessed martyr Father Campion himself, as is recited in the story of his arraignment, falling in talk with a certain principal cardinal in Rome at his first arrival there (a dozen years sithence and not many after the bull was published), he being asked of English affairs, and how the Catholics so much distressed held yet out, and what effect the excommunication had, answered that the bull was troublesome to them and cause of the Queen's more heavy hand upon them, insinuating that it were good it were mitigated, so that it should not bind the subjects but that they might obey her as their lawful princess, notwithstanding any contrary sentence of the See Apostolic before given.[10] Which good office of speech and meaning the adversaries were not ashamed to charge him withal in his judgment.

As their folly and partiality are also so great herein that in this libel they specially put down to prove both the said good Father and his Superior, the Reverend Father Robert Parsons, guilty of treason, for that they made special suit unto His Holiness that now is to qualify the censure of his predecessor, at least so far that it might not bind or make culpable any her Catholic subjects in conscience for obeying and serving her as their sovereign; howsoever it stood against the Protestants, who neither looked nor cared to be discharged of it, as the Catholics, for conscience sake, most desired to be free.[11] They knew His Holiness would not wholly alter that censure, the case standing with the principal

[9] Joseph Gillow, *Bibliographical Dictionary,* V, 478, gives the title as Nicholas Sanders, *Pro defensione excommunicationis a Pio V. latae in Angliae Reginam* (Louvain, 1570), 8vo, and also says that "no copy is known to exist." Cf. Thomas McNevin Veech, *Dr. Nicholas Sanders and the English Reformation, 1530–1581* (Louvain, 1935), p. 103, for comment.

[10] For text of this account of Campion's, see *Cobbett's State Trials,* I, 1057.

[11] See Cecil, p. 18, for text of relevant clause of this petition.

party as it did before his predecessor's sentence. They knew the Queen and Protestants themselves made no account thereof nor desired to be loose. They knew it singularly pertained to the safety of her person and the quiet of the state that the Catholics were persuaded they might lawfully obey her as their Queen and governess, notwithstanding the said sentence. They knew the subjects would gladly do that with safety of conscience, as a way far more secure for both themselves and the Queen, which they did before only for fear. They knew they could not profitably proceed in their spiritual work of confessing, converting, and reconciling the subjects to the Holy Church, except they might by apostolic warrant resolve them for their lawful obedience to the Queen. They thought good, where neither the Pope could be induced, without the repentance of the party, to call in the censure, nor the Queen to yield to any condition that way, rather thus to seek for mitigation than to leave it in full force still; and finally, rather thus by moderation and sweetness to temporize betwixt both their superiors, to see whether God might not move the heart of Her Majesty, wholly lying in His hand, to enter into some good conditions for her reuniting to the communion of the Christian world, the only way of saving her realm in this world and her soul in the next.

Alas, what evil office have these good fathers done herein? What treason is committed more now than if they had desired His Holiness to have discharged the Queen and Protestants also of all bond of that bull? How could either they or the rest of the priests do more dutifully and discreetly in this case than to provide that all such with whom they only had to deal might stand free and warranted in their obedience and commit the rest that cared not for excommunication to the judgment of God?

By all which we may see the notable, discreet, and sincere dealing of Catholics all this while, about fifteen years, that this sentence hath been extant and published, and their manifold endeavors to mitigate and ease the burden thereof in all such as might thereby have remorse to obey and acknowledge the Queen's regality. Never writing of the matter, nor dealing in it, but to the end of pacification, public rest, and security of the state, brought into brandle[12] and doubt by this unhappy alteration in religion. And so they might have had all the learned of our nation either silent in the question of the excommunication or mitigators of it still, had not the unwise and very impolitic importunity of certain in government (seeking by all direct or indirect drifts the blood of poor Catholics) forced men to their needful defense and interpretation of their meaning herein; yea, verily, to seek with diligence the truth of the matter, which of purpose they did let pass before as a thing impertinent to their edification or salvation.

Which they did the rather for that Pius the Fifth, the author thereof, being departed, his successor, Gregory the Thirteenth, that now happily sitteth in the apostolic throne, never revived the same (that we know of), but by connivance and expectation of our Queen's and country's return to Holy Church's peace and to the society of other Christian kings suffered the sentence after a sort to die, specially so far as it concerned the Catholics (as is said);[13] even as the like censure of excommunication and deprivation published by Paul the Third against King Henry the Eighth[14] did pass over in peace to his dying day by the patience of other Popes following; and the many hopes and proffers which the said King made of his return to the Church's obedience again,

[12] Unsteadiness, wavering.

[13] A legal brief had been drafted, perhaps by Antonio Possevino, S.J., shortly before Campion and Parsons had presented their petition in 1580. This brief developed a thesis, similar to Allen's, that the excommunication of Elizabeth was no longer in force. But it also argued that she remained a public enemy of the Church. See J. H. Pollen, *English Catholics,* p. 294.

[14] The bull *Ejus, qui, immobilis,* August 30, 1535, text published in *Bullarum, diplomatum, et privilegiorum sanctorum romanorum Pontificum,* Turin ed., VI (1860), 195–203; hereafter cited as *Bullarum,* Turin ed.

though, prevented by death, it pleased not God to make him worthy of the same.

And this was the Catholics' honest desire and behavior touching the excommunication ever since the publishing thereof, until now of late, when by their interrogatories and new order of most bloody, unlawful, and unwise search of men's consciences, not deeds, words, or writings, but very inward opinions, thoughts, and cogitations of heart, are wrung out of men by the questions before rehearsed. Whereby not only divers holy priests that have suffered but also some other, being strangely and cunningly brought into this odious and dangerous matter of state and pressed against their wills to say their cogitations, they did notwithstanding as much as was possible avoid anyways so to determine or answer as might be prejudicial to their allegiance; which they observed not only whilst they had hope of life but even after their condemnation also and at the very last hour of death.

Some meekly and discreetly declined from the question one way, some another, but all with great show of honesty, fidelity, and innocency. One (as Father Campion) answered they were controversies and questions not determinable in that court but in school.

Another, that he thought the Pope, that gave the sentence, might err in some cases, that is, though not in doctrine, yet in fact, for want of informations, proofs, and other circumstances needfully in such cases to be observed; but whether he did err or no and abuse his authority in this censure, that he referred to God, himself not being sufficient to judge of his superior's doings.

Some said they never saw the bull in their life and therefore could not answer of the sense or force thereof nor be guilty of any crime toward Her Majesty contained in the same; no, nor should ever have much thought or heard of it had not the other now revived the matter.

One or two answered that they were not so learned as to

discuss *ex tempore* all those matters contained in their demands, but that they esteemed of all in general as the Holy Catholic Church teacheth, which is (said they) the Roman Church.

Some said there were or might be causes, as if a prince should fall to apostasy, Arianism, or suchlike that deserved excommunication and deprivation; in which case the Pope might discharge the subjects from their obedience; but of the Queen's particular case they would not talk at all.

To be short, some, being demanded what they would do or advise others to do if the matter should come to battle for religion, as it fell out in Ireland, answered they would do when that happened (which they trusted would not so chance) as good priests ought to do, that is, pray for peace and that truth and justice in war might prevail.[15]

In all which you see, on the one side, how carefully all men eschewed to utter their opinions in any other words but such as could, in truth, no way give offense to the Queen or state; on the other, into what marvelous perplexity the ministers and maintainers of heresy are brought that cannot but by such violent means be secure in their sect nor uphold their foul practices against God, the Church, and their own country.

Let our Christian brethren of all nations judge of the causes, means, and measure of our calamities. We never procured our Queen's excommunication; we have sought the mitigation thereof; we have done our allegiance notwithstanding; we have answered, when we were forced unto it, with such humility and respect to Her Majesty and council, as you see; no man can charge us of any attempt against the realm or the prince's person. Yet, not content with this, they will know what we will do hereafter if such or such a thing should chance; they will sound all the Catholics' hearts in the realm, and (which is more than anti-Christian violence) they will punish them as traitors by death

[15] *Cobbett's State Trials,* I, 1078–1084, includes official transcripts of a number of these replies summarized by Allen.

most cruel for their only thoughts—yea (which God Himself doth not), for future faults never committed nor perhaps ever like to come to pass.

Which search of men's future facts or intentions, whereof themselves have neither knowledge nor rule beforehand, is unnatural, intolerable, and to commonwealths most pernicious, and were able to make all the Catholics of the realm to be wholly desperate, not finding their loyal behavior (showed in all kind of office and service to their prince) sufficient to save their lives, but may be examined of these captious and deadly chapters, of their inward opinions and purposes to come, when the magistrate, or any man's one powerable enemy, list require it. Especially now, when their vulgar ministers give it out generally that all those whom they call papists be in their hearts traitors, and this libeler saith those foresaid questions are most proper to try them.[16]

Into such thralldom of body and soul hath that barbarous heresy brought us, and them also into those hazards of their state, which they pretend to be the causes of these their so extraordinary proceedings, as may be thought were never before used nor lawful by nature or custom of any civil country in earth.

Some such demands the Scribes and Pharisees and other of the Jews' sectaries proposed in times past to our Savior, to entrap Him in speech and to drive Him to utter some treasonable words or conceit against the Emperor's regality over the people of God, which they presumed to be evil thought of of divers, and specially of the better and more exact zelators [17] of the law, notwithstanding that either for fear or other causes every one seemed in all exterior offices to obey. Of which tempting questions, though Christ by His divine wisdom easily discharged Himself, nevertheless they ceased not still to exclaim: *Hunc invenimus prohibentem tributa dare Caesari;* [18] as others did afterward the

[16] Cecil, p. 38.

[17] Zealous defenders or supporters.

[18] Luke 23:2: "We found this fellow . . . forbidding to give tribute to Caesar."

like of St. Stephen and St. Paul; and even so now our English Sadducees are not satisfied but by blood, never resting till they have pressed or sucked out something, at least for men's intentions or other casual events to come, that may sound against their duties to the Queen. Such is our present menage [19] of state in England, and into such terms are we brought of extremity.

When all other pretenses, practices, forged crimes, and false witnesses against priests or Catholics do fail, then are these made just quarrels of their death and the highest treasons in the world: viz., to affirm upon their unreasonable and importune demands that if (which God forbid) the Queen, by supposal, should fall to Arianism, apostasy, or atheism (whereunto man's frailty is subject), she might be deprived and her subjects discharged of obedience to her. This is the only treason which they have tried out of Catholics, which for all that in truth cannot be treason, how plainly or voluntarily soever it were spoken, much less being wrested out by commandment and subtle drift of interrogatories.

The libeler saith nothing is punished in us for question of conscience or religion; but yet this is such in the sight of all reasonable men in the world. For it is a mere matter of divinity, if not defined for us, yet at least disputable in school, as themselves will confess. It concerneth the Pope's supremacy and power apostolical, for which this libeler affirmeth and repeateth often that none be endangered of life or limb in England. This proposition (I say) or any other equivalent to it: viz., that the Pope hath power to excommunicate or deprive a prince in case of heresy or apostasy, and consequently to absolve his subjects from their oath and obedience to him; or to stand in defense of themselves and the Catholic faith against him, cannot be proved treason by the statute of Edward the Third,[20] upon which only he saith we be condemned for traitors. Whosoever should avouch the same, in any Christian country in the world, or in our own country in the time of the said King Edward had held the same opinion, should

[19] Management, administration. [20] Cf. above, Ch. II, p. 78 and n. 1.

not, nor could not have been convicted of treason, treasonable assertion, or evil affection to the prince or country; because it standeth with the honor and safety of the whole commonwealth and the rulers thereof so far to be subject and obedient to Christ and His Church that they count themselves no longer to stand or reign rightfully than they stand and reign for the advancement of God's truth and kingdom in earth, which is His Church.

What treason had it been to Queen Mary (whose regiment, for an example of their grief and our contentment, this libeler so often allegeth) if in school, book, or pulpit it had been affirmed that for heresy or atheism a prince or herself might be deposed?

If in the famous University of Paris or honorable College of Sorbonne that conclusion of divinity were defended, that the Pope in case of heresy might censure their king, would that trouble His Most Christian Majesty,[21] who desireth no longer to reign than he doth advance the glory of Christ? The like might be said of the other great monarch of Spain, who would not have his own issue (which God Almighty bless) succeed him, if it were not Catholic. No more would the Emperor's Sacred Majesty; no, nor the Pope's Holiness (in spiritual affairs and regiment of our souls superior to all the rest) count any of his own subjects traitors for holding that in case of heresy or apostasy he might be deposed or lose the right of his place and dignity.

We ask here the libeler by what law or custom, canon civil or national, of our country or other, is this made treason? Or why it should be more treason in England than in any other place? Seeing no law hitherto hath passed by authority against the same, nor any opinion to be counted prejudicial to any prince or state; no assertion treasonable that is true in divinity, for that no truth agreeable to God's law and man's can be contrary to the lawful sovereignty of any power or potentate in earth.

But you will say (and that is all you can say) that though the general proposition that princes for heresy may be deposed were

[21] The King of France.

true; yet the application thereof to Her Majesty in particular may be treason, for that it is made high treason by act of Parliament in the thirteenth year of the Queen's reign for any to call her an heretic or a schismatic, under pain of death.[22]

To which we answer, first, that our affirming that she may be deposed for heresy doth not at all avouch her to be one; no more than the like assertion of the King of Spain would imply him to be such an one or us to think him such an one. And, therefore, if your own conscience accuse yourselves or give you suspicion that whatsoever is said toucheth you, it is you that apply the general speech to your own particular, and not we. Secondly, we say that your said law may bind us that be subjects not to speak so unreverently of her to whom God hath given power over us in this life as to call her heretic, infidel, or schismatic (for those be the terms of your statute) though we should know her damnably to err in religion; but the Pope is not subject to that law, but he may according to the authority given unto him determine by the laws of God and Holy Church who is an heretic; and so will the learned of foreign schools, whether you will or no, apply the definition of heresy or of an heretic to what person they please.

As for us and our brethren executed, you know none ever called the Queen heretic voluntarily, contemptuously, or maliciously, as your statute runneth, but when they were driven by you of set purpose to offend the law, so to have some quarrel to make them away.

For example of your charitable and no less politic dealing in such matters, we will set down the holy martyr John Nelson's case.[23] This man, being brought before the magistrate, was demanded what religion he was of. To which when he boldly answered that he was a Catholic, they further asked what he

[22] 13 Eliz. I, c. 1.

[23] John Nelson, ordained on the Continent in Binche, June, 1576, executed in London, February 3, 1578. Cf. the very similar account of his examination in Richard Challoner, *Memoirs of Missionary Priests*, pp. 7–11.

thought of that religion and service which was used in England; and to that, when he answered that he took it to be heretical and schismatical, then (quoth they) "What is schism?" "A voluntary revolt" (said he) "from the Roman and Catholic Church." "Well, then," said the magistrate, "go to; what thinkest thou of the Queen, is she a schismatic or no?" (For of anything said before, they had no just pretense of law to condemn him of treason.) The man of God answered that he never so called her, for reverence of her high dignity; nor could tell (for that he knew not Her Majesty's meaning) whether this religion were established by her special commandment and authority or no; and, therefore, humbly prayed them not to urge him wittingly to commit any crime, wherein hitherto he had never offended. But they would not so cease but said they could well resolve him in that, that indeed this English religion was established by her and by her maintained. The confessor refused still to answer, saying that he knew not so much, for all that, of her mind and conscience, but it might proceed rather of some of her ministers more than of herself; in which sort (as St. Augustine noteth) a man may be deceived by heretics but yet properly no heretic; *haereticis credens, et non proprie haereticus.*[24] But because they would needs have the poor man's death, they left him not so. "But what," say they, "if she were the author of this religion, then whether were she a schismatic or heretic, or no?" The confessor being loath to exasperate the prince on the one side, and more loath to offend God or give scandal on the other, after he had paused a while and asked strength from above, finally he said: "If she be the setter-forth and defender of this religion, then she is a schismatic and heretic indeed." And so they got the holy person into the compass of their law, for which afterward he was martyred.

Now we do appeal to the equity of all Christian people how loath our brethren be to offend by word or deed the honor of the Queen, and after what a shameful captious sort they be forced to

[24] Cf. similar statement in St. Augustine, *De utilitate credendi,* cap. 1.

do or say that which the enemy chargeth them withal, even to death. Alas, it is not Catholics that apply those universal truths of schools to the particular case of our state, but it is their own uneven drifts, questions, fears, and suspicions that make them imagine and convert all to themselves. As also it is their error in regiment (well near, as may be doubted, incorrigible) that hath brought themselves to these perplexities and us to these coacted [25] miseries and complaints.

Lastly, we say that howsoever any one Catholic or other hath been driven or shall be forced hereafter to offend against the said statute of supremacy or heresy, or against any new law made in that behalf; yet in equity they cannot be pursued to death for that cause, seeing our adversary protesteth here publicly in his libel that no other trespasses shall be objected to us as matter capital, saving treasons so made by the old laws of the realm. As we for our parts eftsoons [26] do protest and avow before God (seeing we are now enforced to treat of these affairs) that whatsoever we have said or shall say in this our defense or remonstrance touching the former articles and demands about the bull neither hath been nor shall be by us anywise spoken, meant, or applied against our natural princess or country; howsoever any suspicious, malicious, or guilty mind shall peradventure [27] construe or apply the same. Neither shall the matter be otherwise treated of by me in this place but in such general terms as the schools use, without touching any particular person now living; referring the application of all to God's Church and to the chief pastors thereof, and to the conscience of every good Christian reader to whose hands this book may chance to come. As, on the other side, we will not busy ourselves to defend every private man's writing or action concerning the matter of the excommunication, but will without partiality and personal quarrel, for a common apology of us all, declare and prove these assertions of the Pope's power and superiority over kings in cases of heresy,

[25] Forced, compelled. [26] Again or often. [27] Perhaps, possibly.

apostasy, and other like to be agreeable to God's word, and not treasonable nor undutiful to any prince or state in the world, but beneficial to all and every commonwealth under heaven whose government is contained within the prescript of Jesus Christ our Redeemer's law.

But first, before we come to the declaration of Catholic doctrine concerning [the] Church's authority in censuring and deposing princes for matter of religion, it shall not be amiss, perhaps, to set down the judgment and practice of Protestants in the same case. Which, though it weigh little or nothing with us, as being altogether both done and spoken of seditious and partial affection to their heresy and against the lawful magistrate of God; yet the adversary, seeing his own masters against him, shall well perceive that the resisting of princes and magistrates in cause of religion, as also the subjects' taking arms for their defense in such a case, is no way to be accounted treason but most lawful, according to their new gospel.

And first, their grand master, John Calvin, putteth down his oracle, as a conclusion approved of their whole sect and confraternity, in these words: *Abdicant se potestate, terreni principes, dum insurgunt contra Deum: imo indigni sunt qui censeantur in hominum numero. Potius ergo conspuere oportet in illorum capita, quam illis parere, ubi sic proterviunt ut velint spoliare Deum suo jure,* etc.[28] Which in English is thus: "Earthly princes do bereave themselves of all authority when they do erect themselves against God, yea, they are unworthy to be accounted in the number of men; and therefore we must rather spit upon their heads than obey them when they become so proud or perverse that they will spoil God of His right"; and to the same place I further refer the reader for his instruction.

For declaration of which text, and for cutting off all cavilation

[28] [In Dan. cap. 6. ver. 22.25.] John Calvin, *Praelectiones in librum prophetiarum Danielis,* 6:22, in *Calvini Opera,* XLI, 25–26, a wording slightly, but not significantly, different from Allen's.

about the interpretation of his words, their brother Beza shall speak next, who alloweth and highly commendeth in writing the fighting in France for religion against the laws and lawful King of that country, saying in his epistle dedicatory of his New Testament to the Queen of England herself that "the nobility of France (under the noble Prince of Condé) laid the first foundation of restoring true Christian religion in France, by consecrating most happily their blood to God in the battle of Dreux." [29] Whereof also the ministers of the reformed French churches (as their phrase is) do give their common verdict, in the confession of their faith, thus: "We affirm that subjects must obey the laws, pay tribute, bear all burdens imposed, and sustain the yoke even of infidel magistrates, so, for all that, that the supreme dominion and due of God be not violated." [30]

Zwinglius, likewise a cater-cousin to the Calvinists in religion, writeth thus: [31] "If the Empire of Rome, or what other sovereign

[29] [In editione. An. 1564.] The quotation is a partial translation of the concluding paragraph of Beza's letter dedicatory to Queen Elizabeth, printed in the 1565 Estienne folio edition of his Greek and Latin New Testament (Folger Library Acc. No. 179585). The complete paragraph: *Genevae, Anno a nato Jesu Christo, MDLXIIII, Decembr. XIX, quo die ante biennium Gallica nobilitas illustrissimo principe Condensi duce, tuis & illustrissimorum quorundam Germaniae principum subsidiis freta, non procul Druidum urbe, fortissime praeliata, prima restituendae in Galliis Christianae religionis fundamenta sanguine suo feliciter Deo consecravit.*

[30] [The opinion of the Congregation. Art. 39.] The quotation is taken from the Confession of Faith of the Reformed Churches of France, adopted by their 1559 National Synod, subsequently reaffirmed and slightly modified several times. Cf. the text in John Quick, *Synodicon in Gallia Reformata,* I (London, 1692), p. xv, Article 40 (sic): "Therefore we affirm that obedience must be yielded unto their laws and statutes, that tribute must be paid them, taxes and all other duties, and that we must bear the yoke of subjection with a free and willing mind, although the magistrates be infidels; so that the sovereign government of God be preserved entire. Wherefore we detest all those who do reject the higher powers, and would bring in a community and confusion of goods, and subvert the course of justice."

[31] [The sentence of Zwinglius. Lib 4. Epist. Zwinglii & Oecol. fol. 186.] From Zwingli's letter to Konrad Sam and Simpert Schenk, August 18,

soever, should oppress the sincere religion and we negligently suffer the same, we shall be charged with contempt no less than the oppressors thereof themselves. Whereof we have an example in the fifteenth of Jeremiah, where the destruction of the people is prophesied, for that they suffered their King Manasseh, being impious and ungodly, to be unpunished." [32]

And more plain in another place: "When kings," saith he, "rule unfaithfully and otherwise than the rule of the Gospel prescribeth, they may, with God, be deposed, as when they punish not wicked persons, but specially, when they advance the ungodly, as idle priests, etc., such may be deprived of their dignity, as Saul was." [33]

And what our English Protestants write or think of this matter, you shall well perceive by their opinion and high approbation of Wyatt's rebellion in Queen Mary's days. Whereof one of their chief ministers called Goodman thus speaketh in his treatise entitled, *How Superior Magistrates Ought to Be Obeyed:* "Wyatt did but his duty, and it was the duty of all others that profess the Gospel to have risen with him for maintenance of the same. His cause was just, and they all were traitors that took not part with

---

1530, in *Huldreich Zwinglis Sämtliche Werke* in *Corpus Reformatorum* (Berlin, *et al.,* 1905—), XI, 68–70. His precise words: *Romanum imperium, imo quodque imperium, ubi religionem sinceram opprimere coeperit, et nos illud negligentes patimur, iam negatae aut contemptae religionis non minus rei erimus, quam illi ipsi oppressores. Exemplum est apud Ieremias 15., ubi exterminium comminatur Deus Israëli, quod Mannassem permisissent impune esse pessimum.*

[32] Jer. 15:4–9.

[33] [Art. 42. explanat. fol. 84.] From Zwingli's *Auslegen und Gründe der Schlussreden,* 1523, explaining his famous 67 articles. For complete Swiss German text of article 42 and gloss, see *Zwinglis Werke,* edition cited, II, 342–346. For text of the article alone, see Philip Schaff, *The Creeds of Christendom* (New York, 1877, and reprints), III, 204. The Latin text: *Quando vero perfide et extra regulam Christi egerint, possunt cum Deo deponi.* It is one of a group of articles on the magistrate.

him. O noble Wyatt! Thou art now with God, and those worthy men that died for that happy enterprise," [34] etc.

What the Scottish ministry defineth in this question is plain, by the verdict of John Knox, their mightiest prophet, the argument of a treatise of this matter being set down by himself thus: "If the people have either rashly promoted any manifest wicked person or else ignorantly chosen such an one as after declareth himself unworthy of regiment above the people of God (and such be all idolaters and cruel persecutors), most justly may the same men depose and punish him." [35]

So Luther also, the Protestants' Elijah, being asked his opinion of the Almains' [36] confederacy made at Smalkalde against Charles the Fifth, their lawful and noble Emperor, answered that "indeed he was in doubt for a time whether they might take arms against their supreme magistrate or no; but afterward, seeing the extremity of things, and that religion could not otherwise be defended nor themselves, he made no conscience of the matter but either Caesar, or any waging wars in his name, might be resisted." [37]

[34] [Goodman's opinion. Cap. 14. a. pag. 204 ad pa. 212.] Christopher Goodman, *How Superior Powers Ought to Be Obeyed of Their Subjects* (Geneva, 1558), STC 12020, facsimile reprint by Columbia University Press, ed. by Charles H. McIlwain (New York, 1931). Allen's quotation is actually a paraphrase of sentences on p. 204, plus a direct quotation of one on p. 206.

[35] [Jo. Knox. Ibidem. pag. 77.] John Knox, *The Appellation of John Knox from the Cruel and Most Unjust Sentence* (Geneva, 1558), STC 15063, fol. 78, proposition 4, a wording slightly, not significantly, different; cf. copy in *The Works of John Knox,* ed. by David Laing, IV (Edinburgh, 1895), 540.

[36] Germans.

[37] [Sled. Hist. lib. 8.] Johannes Sleidanus, *Commentariorum de statu religionis et reipublicae, Carolo Quinto Caesare, libri XXVI.* Several editions, including English translations. For one version of this opinion by Luther in a wording slightly different from Allen's, see *A Famous Chronicle of Our Times, Called Sleidan's Commentaries* (1560), STC 19848, lib. 8, fol. 100v.

Sleidan also recordeth that the Duke of Saxony and the Landgrave gave this reason of their taking arms against their supreme magistrate: "Forasmuch," say they, "as Caesar intendeth to destroy the true religion and our ancient liberty, he giveth us cause enough why we may with good conscience resist him, as both by profane and sacred histories may be proved." [38]

The same writer reporteth the like of the ministers of Magdeburg; declaring how the inferior may defend himself against the superior, compelling him to do against the truth and rule of Christ's laws.[39]

By all which you see that to resist the magistrate, defend themselves in cases of conscience, and to fight against the superior for religion, is a clear and ruled case and no treasonable opinion at all against the prince, if we will be judged by Protestants, wherein their known facts be far more notorious than their writings. For that Beza and other the chief ministers of the French Calvinical Congregations were themselves in field against two or three of their natural liege lords and kings.[40]

Zwinglius, also, the unfortunate father of our English faith, was killed in the battle,[41] as all the world knoweth; and thereby it is evident that the instance of Dr. Sanders, who followed of zeal the late commotion in Ireland, cannot be so much objected to the Catholics' reproach as the adversary would have it seem; whose report, notwithstanding, of the manner of his death is also a very slanderous untruth.

The Protestants of Flanders held it for a most certain truth (by

[38] [Lib. 21.] From their September 2, 1546, reply to an imperial proscription and ban, in Sleidan, lib. 18 (sic).

[39] [Lib. 22.] Reference to the confession published by the Magdeburg ministers in April, 1550, summarized by Sleidan, lib. 22, fol. 345v. of edition cited, in words close to Allen's: "It is lawful for the inferior magistrate to defend himself against the superior, compelling him to forsake the truth."

[40] In the first war of religion in France, 1562–1563, Beza and other ministers accompanied the Huguenot armies led by Condé.

[41] Of Kappel, 1531.

the approbation also and solicitation of England) that they might rebel against their supreme magistrate for religion, when by force of arms they altered all and deposed their sovereign. Which ought the more to weigh with the English Calvinists for that (as I have signified) their pudding lay also in that fire. As likewise it is well known that themselves have been the chiefest procurers and doers in the depriving of the lawful and anointed Queen of Scotland and for her further affliction have kept her also in captivity these fourteen years together.

And here in these cases of their own, no treasonable propositions, no resisting of "God's anointed," no disobeying the king "as being the most precellent,"[42] no overruling the person "that acknowledgeth no superior in earth, but holdeth only of God" (for all these terms the libeler seemeth to make great advantage of against the resisters of our Queen and deposing of Her Majesty by the See Apostolic), can have place or bear sway. But when it cometh to a point of their own fresh and flourishing religion, then neither unction, nor lawful succession, nor any other princely prerogative, can serve lawful magistrates or save them from their subjects' fury; the English brethren ever specially assisting the rebellion, as well by their divinity as otherwise by force of arms, to their power.

The question, therefore, is not (neither is it material to the purpose which the libeler so much flourisheth very idly) of the prince's lawful creation or consecration, but whether a prince lawfully invested and anointed may be for any cause, namely for matter of religion, resisted by his subjects. We say that the Protestants of all sects do both hold and practice it, England itself specially allowing of the same. And, therefore, there is no treason in this case, if we follow the present divinity of England; nor new example, if we respect the furious attempts and rebellions of Scotland, Flanders, France, and Germany against their superiors for maintenance of their heresies, and all well allowed by the

[42] Excellent.

ministry of every province. And upon these examples you should look (my masters of England) when you make so much ado for one poor commotion made in defense of the Catholics, in twenty-six years' space of the greatest persecution and tribulation that ever was since the Goths' and Vandals' times. Where if the Queen had holden her ancestors' faith and had ruled over so many Protestants but a quarter of the time, afflicting them as she hath done Catholics (though perhaps not herself so much as her unmerciful ministers), Her Majesty should have seen other manner of attempts against her state and quietness than have fallen by Catholics either in England or Ireland in this her reign. Which her long prosperity in government proceedeth specially of the said Catholics' timorous conscience, quietness of nature, love of order and obedience, and great detestation of garboils, stirs, and troubles.

Which the very heretics themselves have often reproachfully and scornfully imputed unto them openly, saying to some of great account whom they had afflicted extremely: "What will you, or what dare you do? Your hearts we know and your wishes; but you are very cowards and beasts that be papists. We stand in no fear of your forces or whatsoever you can do against us." Yea, the very ministers will out of pulpits protest that the papists shall never have the world for them, come what change of prince or laws soever, for they will fight for it to death.

Which challenge and vaunt they make on every hand so boldly, and yet very indiscreetly, because they see the Catholics more sad, grave, honest, and quiet-natured men, consisting of devout and aged persons and of godly women; whereas the Protestants now in possession of state, goods, and government are risen (most of the principal) by alteration, spoil, and faction; their chief followers youthful persons, venturous and desperate; and the rest, both of laity and specially clergy, entangled by the present commodities and pleasures (which this new religion yieldeth in all fleshly lusts and turpitude), are impatient, vindictive, restless, and furious; and in a very few (in comparison of Catholics and quiet men) make a great show and a terrible muster in the sight of quiet, honest, and peaceable persons.

Now these violent and factious men, when the prince and laws go for them, they make their advantage thereof; but if they be against them, they break all bonds of obedience, despise domination, make spoil and havoc of all things, and run headlong into all most detestable disorders.

If you mark them you shall perceive they make their market most in the minority of princes or of their infirmity; as in England in King Edward's time; in France under the deceased two young brethren of His Majesty that now is; [43] in our country, again, by the infirmity of the princess' sex that now reigneth, otherwise truly of most excellent gifts, but always a woman, easily seduced and not hardly led and drawn by those whom she either trusteth or feareth, in which case commonly the more gentle or innocent the sovereign is, the more violent is the government, through the abuse of their simplicity by the tyranny of such as occupy under them principal authority.

How this sort of men abused the years, sex, and benignity also of the noble lady now Queen of Scotland, whose fortune thereby hath been so hard as the world now seeth; and withal, how they have abused her most high and excellent son's minority, to the advancement of their sect and selves, no man can be ignorant. And now when that rare prince is come to years of knowledge and thereby like to espy and punish the wicked treachery and treasons of those that have so abominably abused his infancy and mother's sex, they barbarously, by the counsel of wicked ministers (the rascality of the realm), seized upon his royal person,[44] and, sithence being delivered by God from his enemies' hands, they

[43] Francis II (1559–1560) and Charles IX (1560–1574), brothers to Henry III (1574–1589).

[44] Reference to the Ruthven raid of 1582, in which King James VI was seized by Protestant nobles.

stick not to tell him to his face that he was erected by them to defend this new and barbarous Gospel of theirs; and only upon fear of his further years they seek to put his noble person in daily danger.

This, lo, is the devotion of Protestants toward their princes, agreeable to their former opinions recited before. But of their divinity we make no further account than is requisite for this dispute now in hand with their fellow Protestants, and with those specially of England, who are the principal protectors of all these practices colored by religion, whereof yet they have no further care than concerneth only their own interest. But it is sufficient for us that with these men (if we may believe either their words or deeds) it is no treason to resist the sovereign for defense of religion, nor no treasonable assertion to hold that a lawful prince may be deposed in case of revolt from God. And so say also on the other side all Catholic men and schools in the Christian world concerning this point. But yet here is the difference between Catholic Christians and rebellious heretics: that these good fellows, following their own deceitful wills and uncertain opinions without rule or reason, do adjudge, by their private folly and fantasy, that thing to be error or idolatry which indeed is true religion, and do condemn for God's enemies such their lawful sovereigns as Holy Church (which herein must be our chief informer and judge) doth allow for most just, godly, sacred, and Catholic princes.

The Catholics, contrariwise, as men of order and obedience, not trusting their own particular imaginations or partial affections, which might lead opinionative and restless brains to raise rebellion at their pleasure under pretense of religion (whereof the Protestants have given us pitiful examples these years past, whensoever the wicked desired change of governors and estate), do commit the direction of matters so important to the Church and to the chief governors of their souls, who can judge by the Scriptures, canons, and councils what is heresy; who is an heretic; what prince is worthy to be excommunicated; who to be deprived; who is incorrigible; who may be expected in hope of amendment; who not; in what season and sort, to the least disturbance and most benefit and safety of the kingdom or place annoyed by such unworthy princes, the thing must be executed.

The Church is not partial in these things, as we that be subjects may be; it is not decent that inferiors should determine at their pleasures of their superiors. What way, therefore, can we take in Christian religion more seemly and sure in conscience for these affairs than to hearken to the high priest of God's Church, by whose direction our consciences, in this case, cannot lightly err, or surely not so perniciously, when we follow them to whom Christ hath given the charge of our souls, and must render account thereof to Him as to the supreme bishop of all, by Whom and for Whom only all kings do reign. Catholics, therefore (as you see), agree with the other in the point of deposing and resisting kings for religion, but yet do differ in the manner, as far as reason and conscience differ from fury and frenzy.

About which matter I will now set down some Catholic writers, albeit but few, for brevity's sake; yet of such excellent credit as shall be able to instruct and satisfy any reasonable conscience in this case; as also to be our brethren's defense against all those that charge them so deadly with these treasonable propositions.

Thomas Aquinas, that glorious saint and clerk, whose only sentence weigheth more than all the Protestants' wits and words in the world, saith thus: *Postquam princeps est denuntiatus apostata, omnes inferiores et subditi absoluuntur a praestito juramento et obedientia illi debita;* [45] that is to say: "After a prince is one [sic] denounced to be an apostate, all his inferiors and subjects are assoiled of their oath made unto him and of their

[45] For succinct analysis of this doctrine of St. Thomas Aquinas, supported by another, very similar, proof text (*Summa Theologica*, 2, quaest. 12, art. 2) see R. W. and A. J. Carlyle, *A History of Mediaeval Political Theory in the West*, V, *The Political Theory of the Thirteenth Century* (New York, 3rd printing, n.d.), pp. 350–351 and n. 2.

obedience due unto him." This case, therefore, is plainly resolved upon by the greatest of all the school doctors and therefore can be no treasonable assertion or opinion. Upon which words of St. Thomas, the famous professor of our own time Francis Toledo writeth further thus:

Nota [saith he] *quod eadem est ratio de excommunicato, quia cum primum quis est denuntiatus excommunicatus, omnes subditi absoluuntur ab ejus obedientia. Licet enim sit notorium crimen principis, non absoluuntur vasalli a juramento, ut bene dicit Cajetanus, ante denuntiationem ab Ecclesia; qua facta, non solum sunt absoluti ab obedientia, sed tenentur non obedire; nisi forte propter periculum vitae, vel damnum bonorum temporalium. Et sic de Henrico octavo in Anglia factum est: cui etsi subditi postquam denuntiatus esset excommunicatus, tenebantur non obedire; tamen quia is crudelis erat, et illos vel vita vel bonis privasset, excusati fuerunt subditi illi adhuc obediendo.*[46]

Which is in English:

Note [saith he] that albeit St. Thomas named only an apostate, yet the reason is all one in the prince's case that is excommunicated. For as soon as one is denounced or declared an excommunicate, all his subjects be discharged of their obedience. For though the crime of a prince be notorious, yet before declaration thereof be made by the Church, the vassals are not assoiled from obedience, as Cajetanus well holdeth; which declaration being made by the Church, they are not only discharged of their loyalty but are bound not to obey him any more; except it be for fear of their lives or loss of their temporal goods. As it was in England in the time of Henry the Eighth, whom though the subjects were bound not to obey after he was denounced excommunicate, yet for that he was a cruel man and

[46] [Toledo's opinion of a prince excommunicat. in 2.2.] Quotation from a work by Francisco Toledo (1532–1596), Spanish theologian and exegete. The Cajetan Toledo refers to was Tommaso de Vio Gaetani, called Cajetan, best known for his dealings with Luther, also an authoritative commentator on St. Thomas.

would either have killed or spoiled them, they were excused in obeying him.

Thus doth this notable schoolman write; neither do we know any Catholic divine of any age to say the contrary.

We will not allege the canon laws,[47] which, for that they be the decrees specially of Popes, whom our adversaries account partial, shall weigh little with them, though they be authentical in all the lawful tribunals of the Christian world and make all heretics (not only after they be namely and particularly denounced, but by the law itself, *ipso facto,* as soon as they be heretics, or *de jure* excommunicated for the same) to be deprived of their dominions, though the subjects, until denunciation, need not take knowledge thereof.

Only it is not good to omit the definition and words of the famous general council of Lateran, celebrated above 300 years since; [48] wherein there were patriarchs and archbishops 70, bishops 412, and other prelates 800. In all, of the most chosen learned men of all nations, 1,282; with the ambassadors of the Roman Emperor, of the King of Jerusalem, of England, of France, of Spain, and of Cyprus, as also of other Christian states; than which there can be no surer judgment upon earth; which assembly, representing the whole Christian world, would never agree upon any assertion traitorous. These, then, are the words of their most renowned decree, put only in English for brevity's sake.

If any lord temporal, required and admonished by the Church, neglect to purge his state from heretical filth, let him be excommunicated by the metropolitan and conprovincial bishops. But if he contemn to come to order within one year's space, let relation be made to the supreme bishop, that from thenceforth he may declare all his subjects to be discharged of their fealty toward him and give up his land to

[47] [Cap. alius cum sequen. xv. q. 5. Cap. fin. de haeret.] Reference, apparently, to Gratian, *Decretum,* c. 15. 6. 4, 5.

[48] The Fourth Lateran Council of 1215.

be possessed by Catholics; which Catholics without all contradiction (when they have driven out the heretics) shall have and hold the same and so preserve it in purity of faith (the interest and right of the chief lord ever remaining safe and whole, so that himself give no impediment to the execution of this decree). And the same law to take place in such also as be sovereign lords and have no superiors.[49]

Thus both schools and laws speak and resolve for the matter in hand, both Catholics and Protestants agreeing that princes may for some causes, and especially for their defection in faith and religion, be resisted and forsaken; though in the manner of executing the sentence and other needful circumstances Protestants follow faction and popular mutiny, we reduce all to law, order, and judgment.

But for the further clearing of this cause we mean now, in the next chapter (by the help of God), to declare and plainly deduce all that hitherto hath been said in the premises from Holy Scriptures and warrant of antiquity, that all indifferent men may see how far we be from treason or undutifulness to our princess in these our opinions, especially when by a certain violence we be coacted to utter the same.

Chapter V

Of excommunication and deprivation of princes for heresy and falling from the faith; specially of wars for religion; and of the office and zeal of priests of the old and new law in such cases

PRINCES, being not subject to superiors temporal, nor patient of correction or controlment by their inferiors, may easily fall to grievous disorders, which must tend to the danger and ruin of whole countries.

[49] [Cap. 3 de haeret.]

In respect whereof great spirit, power, courage, and freedom of speech have been from the beginning granted by God, as well ordinary to priests as extraordinary to some prophets and religious persons in all ages and times, both of the New and Old Testament.

So by God's great providence (who by His prophet warned kings to take discipline, and to serve Him in fear, lest in His ire He should suffer them fall to iniquity),[1] the first kings of His peculiar people had lightly some prophets or priests, in manner as overseers, that might from time to time charge them boldly, and as it were by office, with their enormities, and namely with their fall from faith and the God of their fathers, to denounce[2] His threatenings, yea, and execute the same upon them at some times if need so required. Which ministers of their Lord God all godly princes did hear, honor, and obey; as contrariwise the kings that were wicked and disloyal to God have ever sought cruelly their death and destruction, that so their wickedness might pass without controlment.

Saul, the first temporal king that ever the Jews (being then God's peculiar) had, though chosen and inspired by God, was for all that led and directed by Samuel so long as he was in order.[3] But afterward for aspiring to spiritual function and other disobedience was by God's appointment and sentence (pronounced by the said Samuel) deposed of his kingdom and another named David anointed by him. Which Saul now after his deprivation, or after, as it were, his excommunication by Samuel, was invaded by an evil spirit that provoked him to kill not only David, that was now made the rightful owner of his crown, but also to seek for Samuel's death; yea, and to command all the holy priests of Nob (fourscore-and-five in number, as Holy Scripture recounteth) to be slain and murdered in most pitiful wise as traitors to him and favorers of David, the competitor of his kingdom. And so it was

[1] [Ps. 2]:10–11.

[2] Announce publicly, in a warning manner.

[3] [I Sam. 10, 15, 16.]

done at last; though at the beginning his guard refused to execute so vile and horrible an act; and in this sort he remained enemy many years against God and Samuel and kept the kingdom by tyrannical force notwithstanding his deposition.[4]

David, nevertheless, in whom was the right of the crown, was lawfully up in arms, with one of the principal priests, whose name was Abiathar, that escaped the foresaid murder; not of such power as the pretensed king was; till at length the usurper (whom, as St. Augustine deduceth, he might lawfully have killed, but would not) [5] being slain in battle,[6] David obtained his right, first of a part of the kingdom, and afterward of all the rest; which Ishbosheth did for two years, by the pretended right of Saul his father, usurp.[7]

By which it is plain that the priests and prophets of God, being the executors of His sentences and rule of the people in such doubtful and partial times of variety for claim and competency, are most subject to the hatred of usurpers, as also to death and danger for the same.

You see in what sort also Jeroboam, King of Israel, had a special prophet sent to him to denounce the intended judgments of God against him and his posterity, for his schism and separation of his people from the old ancient true worship of God in Jerusalem, and for erecting of a new altar in Bethel (in which all schism and division from the Apostolic See is properly prefigured), and for creating of a wicked clergy out of Aaron's order; I mean new, hungry, base, and inordered priests (the pattern of heretical ministers) thrust up out of the array and orderly succession and creation of apostolic priesthood; a crime so highly afterward both in him and his stock (according to God's former denunciation) revenged that none of his house was left to piss

[4] [I Sam. 22.]

[5] [August. contra Adamantium.] St. Augustine, *Contra Adimantum Manichaei discipulum,* cap. 16, 6.

[6] I Sam. 31.

[7] II Sam. 1–5.

against a wall.[8] Yet he fondly sought to apprehend the man of God and to kill him for bringing this news, which he accounted high treason against his regality. Ozias also, or Uzziah, King of Judah, puffed up with intolerable pride (as the Scripture saith), and not contented with his kingly sovereignty but presuming to execute spiritual and priestly function, was valiantly by Azariah and fourscore priests with him assailed and thrust out of the Temple by force. At what time, for that he threatened the priests of God and resisted them with violence, he was stricken with a filthy leprosy, and so not only thrust out of the Temple but by their authority severed also from all company of men (a special figure of the priests' power to excommunicate for heresy as well princes as others in the new law); and finally the regiment of his kingdom was committed to his son.[9] A clear example that priests may use arms and repress impiety by forcible ways, where it may serve to the preservation of religion and the honor of God.

But the office and zeal of good priests is notably recommended unto us in the deposition of the wicked Queen Athaliah. She, to obtain the crown after Ahaziah, killed all his children; only one, which by a certain good woman's piety was secretly withdrawn from the massacre, saved and brought up within the Temple for seven years' space. All which time the said Queen usurped the kingdom; till at length Jehoiada, the high priest, by opportunity called to him forces both of the priests and people, proclaimed the right heir that was in his custody, anointed and crowned him king, and caused immediately the pretensed Queen (notwithstanding she cried treason, treason, as not only just possessors but wicked usurpers use to do) to be slain with her fautors at her own court gate.[10] Thus do priests deal and judge for the innocent and lawful princes (when time requireth), much to their honor and agreeable to their holy calling.

No man can be ignorant how stoutly Elijah (being sought to death by Ahab and his queen Jezebel, that overthrew holy altars

[8] [I Kings 13, 14.] [9] II Chron. 26:16–21. [10] [II Kings 11]:1–16.

and murdered all the true religious that could be found in their land) told them to their face that not he or other men of God whom they persecuted but they and their house were the disturbers of Israel and slew in his zeal all the said Jezebel's false prophets, fostered at her table, even four hundred at one time, and so set up holy altars again.[11] How he handled the idolatrous King Ahaziah his captains and messengers, wasting them and a hundred of their train by fire from heaven till the third captain was forced to humble himself upon his knees unto him.[12]

How he had commission to anoint Hazael, King of Syria, Elisha, a prophet for himself, and Jehu, King of Israel, [13] and so to put down the son and whole house of Ahab;[14] which thereby lost all the title and right to the kingdom forever.

This prophet and his successor Elisha were so famous in this service of God for the chastisement of irreligious princes that in the Holy Writ it is thus said of the former: "He cast down kings, destroyed them, and plucked the honorable from their seats." [15] And of the second, in the same place that: "He never feared prince, nor could be overcome by any." [16] And in another place: "Whosoever escapeth the sword of Jehu, the sword of Elisha shall slay him." [17]

By which examples of Holy Scriptures we see, first, that anointed and lawfully created kings may be deposed; secondly, for what causes they were deprived; thirdly, that as in the creation and consecration of kings, so also in their deprivation, God used the ministry of priests and prophets, as either ordinary or extraordinary judges or executors of His will toward them.

For though neither these priests nor prophets were superiors to their own kings or sovereigns in their temporal states and regiments, nor lords or masters of their crowns and kingdoms; yet for that they held their dignities and sovereign authorities of God,

[11] [I Kings 18.]
[12] [II Kings 1.]
[13] [I Kings 19]:15–16.
[14] [II Kings 9.]
[15] [Ecclus. 48]:6.
[16] [Ecclus. 48]:12, 13.
[17] [I Kings 19]:17.

and were bound to occupy and use the same, with what forces soever they had, to the advancement of His religion and to the true worship and honor of their supreme Lord and Master; as also to the benefit and preservation of His people in faith and fear of Him, the priests and prophets (that then had the principal and direct charge of men's souls and religion and were in spiritual matters superiors to their own princes) rightly opposed themselves in all such actions as tended to the dishonor of God, destruction of religion, and to the notorious damage of the souls of them over whom they did reign, and in the behalf of God executed justice upon such as, contrary to their obligation and first institution, abused their sovereign power, to the destruction of true religion and advancement of idolatry, heresy, or suchlike abomination. In which cases, and all other doubts and differences betwixt one man and another, or betwixt prince and people, that priests, and namely the high priest, should be the arbiter and judge and the interpreter of God's will toward His people, is most consonant both to nature, reason, the use of all nations, and to the express Scriptures.

For in God's sacred law thus we read: *Si difficile et ambiguum apud te judicium esse prospexeris inter sanguinem et sanguinem, causam et causam, lepram et non lepram,* etc.

If thou foresee the judgment to be hard and ambiguous betwixt blood and blood, cause and cause, leprosy or no leprosy, and find variety of sentences among the judges at home, rise and go up to the place which the Lord thy God shall choose, and thou shalt come to the priests of Levi's stock and to the judge that shall be for the time; thou shalt ask of them, and they will judge according to the truth of judgment; and thou shalt do whatsoever they say that have the rule of the place which God shall choose, and shall teach thee according to His law; thou shalt not decline neither to the right hand nor left. And if any shall be so proud as not to obey the commandment of the priest that shall for that time minister unto the Lord thy God, by the sentence of the judge let that man die, and so thou shalt remove evil from Israel, and all the people hearing shall fear and take heed that hereafter they wax not proud.[18]

Thus far in the holy text, generally, without all exception, subjecting in cases of such doubts as are recited all degrees of faithful men, no less kings than others, to the priests' resolution. Yea, immediately order is given how their kings (which yet were not when that was written, but afterward by their motion to be created) should be elected; that none could be chosen to rule over them, being the people of God, that were not true believers and worshippers of Him, according to the ceremonies of their law and religion. Which laws they might not take, make, or moderate themselves, but receive of the priests of the Levitical tribe; and thereby learn to fear God and keep His words and ceremonies; expressly also appointing and warning them, or as it were covenanting with them and him whom they should create or have for their king, that he should not against God's express commandment bring back at any time His people into Egypt, that is to say, from the liberty of His faith and true service to the bondage of idolatry and false religion.[19]

Which condition was afterward to be implied in the receiving of any king over the people of God and true believers forever, *videlicet:*[20] that they should not reduce their people by force or otherwise from the faith of their forefathers and the religion and holy ceremonies thereof, received at the hands of God's priests and none other: insinuating that, observing these precepts and conditions, he and his son after him might long reign; otherwise, as by the practice of their deposition in the books and time of the kings it afterward appeareth (whereof we have set down some examples before), the prophets and priests that anointed them, of no other condition but to keep and maintain the honor of God and His true worship, deprived them again when they brake with their Lord and fell to strange gods and forced their people to do the like.

[18] [Deut. 17]:8–13. [19] Deut. 17:14–20. [20] Namely.

And this it was in the old law. But now in the New Testament, and in the time of Christ's spiritual kingdom in the Church, priests have much more sovereign authority and princes far more strict charge to obey, love, and cherish the Church; of which Church it was said by prophecy: "Kings shall be thy foster fathers and queens thy nurses"; [21] and again: "Kings' breasts shall nourish thee, and every kingdom that serveth not thee shall perish." [22] In which Church without fail is the supereminent power of Christ's priesthood, Who with His iron rod bruiseth the pride of princes that rebel against His Spouse and kingdom in earth, like a potter's potsherd; [23] and hath right in His Church over all kingdoms, to plant and pluck up, to build and destroy, [24] afore whom all kings shall fall down and all nations do Him service.

Now Christ's priestly prerogative, passing His own regal dignity (much more excelling all other human power of the world), in most ample and exact terms is communicated to the chief priest and pastor of our souls, [25] and secondarily to the rest of the governors of the Church, [26] in other manner of clauses than any earthly princes can show for their pretensed spiritual regiment. Fie on that secular pride and willful blind heresy, so repugning against God's express ordinance and yet is of wicked sect-masters and flatterers upholden, to the external calamity of themselves and of millions of others!

Now all Christ's sheep, without exception, be they princes, be they poor (if they be Christian men), are put to Peter's feeding and government. [27] Now the keys of heaven be delivered to Christ's Vicar in earth, to let in, to lock out; to bind, to loose; [28] to punish, to pardon. Now we be commanded every one (be we kings, be we Caesars) to obey our prelates and pastors and to be subject to them as to those that must make account to God for our souls; [29] wherein what Christian prince may except himself?

[21] [Isa. 49]:23.
[22] [Isa. 60]:16; 12.
[23] [Ps. 2]:9.
[24] [Jer. 1]:10.
[25] [Matt. 16]:18–19.
[26] [Matt. 18]:18–20.
[27] [John 21]:15–17.
[28] [Matt. 16]:19.
[29] [Heb. 13]:17.

Now they have full authority to forbid us the company of heretics, blasphemers, idolaters, and suchlike; [30] and not so much as to salute them, much more not to obey them. And lest any man should think this power to be so merely spiritual that it might not in any wise be extended to temporal or corporal damage or chastisement of the faithful in their goods, lives, possessions, or bodies, being mere secular things, and therefore not subject to their pastors' spiritual or priestly function, it is to be marked in the holy apostles' first execution of their commissions and authority that, though their spiritual power immediately and directly concerneth not our temporal affairs, yet indirectly (and as by accident) it doth not only concern our souls but our bodies and goods, so far as is requisite to our souls' health and expedient for the good regiment thereof and the Church's utility, being subject to their spiritual governors.[31]

Therefore St. Peter, being but a mere spiritual officer and pastor of men's souls, yet for sacrilege and simulation struck dead both man and wife.[32] St. Paul struck blind Elymas the Magician.[33] So did he threaten to come to his contemners in rod of discipline.[34] So did he excommunicate a principal person in Corinth for incest; not only by spiritual punishment, but also by bodily vexation, giving him up to Satan's chastisement.[35] As he corporally also corrected and molested with an evil spirit Hymenaeus and Alexander for blasphemy and heresy.[36] Finally he boldly avoucheth that his power in God is to revenge all disobedience and to bring under all lofty hearts to the loyalty of Christ and of the Apostles and Saints in this life.[37] *Nescitis* (quoth he) *quoniam angelos judicabimus, quanto magis saecularia?* "Know you not that we shall judge angels, how much more secular matters?" [38]

In all which there is no difference betwixt kings that be faithful

[30] [I Cor. 5]:9–11.
[31] [II John];[Titus 3.]
[32] [Acts 5]:1–10.
[33] [Acts 13]:6–11.
[34] [I Cor. 4]:21.
[35] [I Cor. 5]:1–5.
[36] [I Tim. 1]:20.
[37] [II Cor. 10]:5–6.
[38] [I Cor. 6]:3.

and other Christian men; who all, in that they have submitted themselves and their scepters to the sweet yoke of Christ, are subject to discipline and to their pastors' authority, no less than other sheep of His fold.

And although the state, regiment, policy, and power temporal be in itself always of distinct nature, quality, and condition from the government ecclesiastical and spiritual commonwealth called the Church or Body Mystical of Christ; and the magistrate spiritual and civil divers and distinct; and sometimes so far that the one hath no dependence of the other, nor subalternation to the other in respect of themselves (as it is in the Churches of God residing in heathen kingdoms, and was in the apostles' times under the pagan emperors); yet now where the laws of Christ are received and the bodies politic and mystical, the Church and civil state, the magistrate ecclesiastical and temporal, concur in their kinds together (though ever of distinct regiments, natures, and ends), there is such a concurrence and subalternation betwixt both that the inferior of the two (which is the civil state) must needs (in matters pertaining any way either directly or indirectly to the honor of God and benefit of the soul) be subject to the spiritual and take direction from the same

The condition of these two powers (as St. Gregory Nazianzen most excellently resembleth it) [39] is like unto the distinct state of the same spirit and body or flesh in a man, where either of them having their proper and peculiar operations, ends, and objects, which in other natures may be severed (as in brutes, where flesh is and not spirit; in angels, where spirit is but not flesh), are yet in man conjoined in person; and nevertheless so distinct in faculties and operations that the flesh hath her actions peculiar and the soul hers; but not without subalternation or dependence. Where we see evidently that in case the operations of the body be con-

[39] [In Orati. ad popul. trepidantem et Impera. commutum.] Perhaps St. Gregory Nazianzen, Oration no. 17, *Ad cives Nazianzenos gravi timore perculsos, et praefectum irascentem.*

trary to the end, weal, and just desires of the soul, the spirit may and must command, overrule, and chastise the body and, as superior, appointeth fasting and other afflictions, though with some detriment to the flesh: commanding the eyes not to see, the tongue not to speak, and so forth. So likewise the power political hath her princes, laws, tribunals, and the spiritual her prelates, canons, councils, judgments, and these, when the princes are pagans, wholly separate, but in Christian commonwealths joined, though not confounded; nor yet the spiritual turned into the temporal, or subject by perverse order (as it is now in England) to the same; but the civil (which indeed is the inferior) subordinate, and in some cases subject to the ecclesiastical. Though so long as the temporal state is no hindrance to eternal felicity and the glory of Christ's kingdom, the other intermeddleth not with her actions but alloweth, defendeth, honoreth, and, in particular commonwealths, obeyeth the same.

Yet where it is otherwise and the temporal power resisteth God or hindereth the proceeding of the people to salvation, there the spiritual hath right to correct the temporal and to procure by all means possible that the terrene kingdom give no annoyance to the state of the Church, which, now adorned in the New Testament with the power of Christ's priesthood and with several and distinct officers appointed by the Holy Ghost, must needs so far excel the terrene state and domination as the sun passeth the moon, the soul the body, and heaven the earth. By reason of which excellency and pre-eminence above all states and men, without exception of prince or other, Our Lord proclaimeth in His Gospel that whosoever obeyeth not or heareth not the Church must be taken and used no otherwise than as a heathen.[40]

This being so plain, and in truth so beneficial to the very kings and commonwealths themselves that the preservation of both specially standeth upon this concurrence with the Church and

[40] [Matt. 13.]

priesthood, and with the due subalternation of the temporal to the spiritual regiment; and which all kings (that be not for punishment of their own and their people's sins obdurate and prepared by God's judgment to be an example of His power and justice) most gladly acknowledge. Yet there be so many either flatterers of princes that so say, or heretics that so think, that the ministers of Christ's most dear Spouse, of His very Body Mystical, His kingdom and house in earth (whom at His departure hence He did endow with most ample commission and sent forth with that authority that His Father before gave unto Him), have no power over princes to denounce or declare them to be violators of God's and the Church's laws, nor to punish them either spiritually or temporally; not to excommunicate them, nor to discharge the people of their oath and obedience toward such as neither by God's laws nor man's a true Christian may obey.

Wherein it may please the gentle readers to inform their consciences partly by that is said before, and specially by that which followeth. Where they shall find that straight upon the first conversion of kings to the faith, as the good and godly have ever obeyed the Church and submitted themselves to ecclesiastical censures and discipline, so the evil and obstinate could never orderly discharge themselves from the same without evident note of injustice, tyranny, and irreligiosity, and were either in fine brought to order and penance, or else to confusion both temporal and eternal.

About thirteen hundred years ago Babylas, Bishop of Antioch, excommunicated the only Christian King or Emperor that then was (as some count Numerius, as others Philip) for executing a prince that was put to him for an hostage. Whereupon, as evil kings sometimes do, he martyred his Bishop; whom St. Chrysostom and others reckon for the most famous martyr of that time, because he gave both by his constancy and courage in God a notable example to all bishops of their behavior toward their princes and how they ought to use the ecclesiastical rod of correction toward them, whatsoever befall to their persons for the same.[41]

After the said prince had murdered his own pastor, then holy Pope Fabian, for that he was the general shepherd of Christendom (or as some think Fabius, the successor of Babylas), pursued the said Emperor by like excommunication and other means till at length he brought him to order and repentance.[42]

Afterward St. Ambrose, Bishop of Milan, excommunicated the elder Theodosius the Emperor; put him to public penance among the rest of the people; commanded him to put off his kingly robes; to leave his imperial throne in the chancel and to keep his place among the laity; and prescribed him after eight months' penance to make a temporal law for proviso against the occasions of such crimes as the said Emperor had committed and for which he was excommunicated.[43]

This was another world than we now are in; marvelous courage and zeal in bishops for God's cause; much humility and obedience in princes. Then was there no flatterer so shameful, nor heretic on earth so impudent, as to make the temporal kings above all correction of God's Church and their own pastors; nothing being more common in the histories of all ages than that princes have received discipline.

As when Anastasius the Emperor was excommunicated by

[41] [Chrisost. in vita Baby.] St. John Chrysostom, *In sanctam Babylam, contra Julianum, et contra gentiles. Acts of the Martyrs* gives the name of the emperor as Numerianus; Eusebius suggests it was Philip the Arabian (244–249).

[42] [Nicep. li. 5. cap. 25.] Nicephorus Callistus, *Ecclesiastical History,* lib. 5, cap. 26 (sic). Fabian was Pope (236–250); Fabius was Bishop of Antioch (ca. 251).

[43] [Soz. lib. 7. cap. 24; Theo. lib. 5. cap. 17; Amb. li. 5. epist. 28; Au. de civit. Dei li. 5. cap. 26.] Sozomen, *Ecclesiastical History,* lib. 7, cap. 25 (sic); Theodoret, *Ecclesiastical History,* lib. 5, cap. 17; St. Ambrose, Letter to Emperor Theodosius, no. 51 in Migne; St. Augustine, *De civitate Dei,* lib. 5, cap. 26.

Symmachus,[44] Lotharius and Michael, Emperors, by Nicholas the First,[45] and particular princes by their provincial bishops; as we see in the records of all nations. Therefore we will stand only upon more famous and ancient examples.

Innocentius the First excommunicated Arcadius the Emperor and his wife, Queen Eudoxia, for that they disobeyed and persecuted their Bishop, St. Chrysostom. We will report the judicial sentence briefly, because it is much to the purpose and full of majesty:

O Emperor [said Pope Innocentius well near 1200 years ago], the blood of my brother John Chrysostom crieth to God against thee. Thou hast cast out of his chair the great Doctor of the world; and in him by thy wife's (that delicate Dalila) her persuasion hast persecuted Christ. Therefore I (though a poor sinful soul), to whom the throne of the great Apostle St. Peter is committed, do excommunicate thee and her, and do separate you both from the holy sacraments, commanding that no priest nor bishop, under pain of deprivation, after this my sentence come to their knowledge, give or minister the said sacraments unto you.[46]

Thus did this blessed Father (whom St. Augustine exceedingly commended in his time)[47] deal with this Emperor and wicked Queen, the cause of her husband's fall and offenses, and at length brought them to penance. But when in process of time some

[44] Anastasius I, Emperor of the East, 491–518, a monophysite, was sharply criticized by Pope Symmachus, 498–514.

[45] Pope Nicholas I, 858–867, disciplined King Lothair II of Lorraine for marital irregularities and the Eastern Emperor Michael for ousting the Patriarch Ignatius and replacing him with Photius.

[46] [Nicepho. li. 13. cap. 34; Georg. Patriarcha. in vita Chris.] Nicephorus Callistus, *Ecclesiastical History*, lib. 13, cap. 34; presumably Georgius Alexandrinus, *Vita S. Joannis Chrysostomi* (discussed in Migne, PG, XLVII, xxiii–xl). Pope Innocent I, 401–417, worked for years to secure restoration of St. John Chrysostom as Bishop of Constantinople.

[47] But more for his opposition to the Pelagians, *passim*, in Augustine's works.

princes, through God's just judgment and the people's sin, were fallen to such contempt of religion (as it lightly happeneth by heresy and apostasy) that excommunication, being only but a spiritual penalty, or other ordinary ecclesiastical discipline, would not serve; then as well bishops as other godly persons, their own subjects, did crave aid and arms of other princes for their chastisement; as most holy and ancient Popes (even in these old days when the Protestants confess them to have been godly bishops) did incite Catholic kings to the same; that those whom the spiritual rod could not fruitfully chastise they might by extern or temporal force bring them to order and repentance, or at least defend their innocent Catholic subjects from unjust vexation.

There is no war in the world so just or honorable, be it civil or foreign, as that which is waged for religion; we say for the true, ancient, Catholic, Roman religion; which by the laws of Holy Church and all Christian nations is adjudged to be the only true worship of God and unto the obedience of which all princes and people have yielded themselves, either by oath, vow, or sacraments, or every of these ways. For this it is godly and honorable to fight, in such order and time as we be warranted in conscience and law by our supreme pastors and priests, and not for wild condemned heresies against most lawful Christian Catholics, kings and priests, as the rebellious Protestants and Calvinists of this time do, without all order, law, or warrant of God or man. As the arms taken for defense of godly honor and inheritance in such sort and difference from heretical tumults, as is said, are so much more commendable and glorious, for that no crime in the world deserveth more sharp and zealous pursuit of extreme revenge (whether it be in superiors or subjects) than revolting from the faith to strange religions.

"Whosoever seeketh not after the Lord God of Israel, let him be slain," said King Asa, admonished by Azariah the prophet, "from the highest to the lowest without exception." [48] And all the

[48] [II Chron. 15]:13.

people and many that followed him and fled to him out of Israel from the schism there did swear and vow themselves in the quarrel of the God of their forefathers. And they prospered and deposed Queen Maachah, mother to Asa, for apostasy and for worshipping the venerous god called Priapus.[49]

For that case also in Deuteronomy express charge was given to slay all false prophets and whosoever should avert the people from the true worship of God and induce them to receive strange gods and new religions, and to destroy all their followers were they never so near us by nature.[50] And in the same place, that if any city should revolt from the received and prescribed worship of God and begin to admit new religions it should be utterly wasted by fire and sword.[51] Neither pertaineth this to poor men only, but to the governors and leaders of the people most of all; as we see in the book of Numbers, where Moses, by the commandment of God, caused all the princes of the people to be hanged upon gibbets against the sun for communication in sacrifice with the Moabites, and the rest of the people every one by the hand of his neighbor to be put to the sword for the same fault; wherein Phinehas, the priest of God, by slaying a chief captain with his own hands, deserved eternal praise and the perpetuity of his priesthood.[52] By Moses, also, his appointment, the faithful Levites slew 33,000 of their neighbors, brethren, and friends for committing idolatry and forsaking the true God. Marry, in all this (as you see by the examples alleged) the prophet and priests must direct them for the cause and action, that they err not of fantasy, partiality, pride, and pretense of religion, as heretics and rebels do, but the quarrel must be for the old faith, service, and priesthood, against innovation, and directed and allowed by those which by order and function have charge of our souls.

[49] II Chron. 15:14–16. The King James version accuses her only of making "an idol in a grove."

[50] Deut. [13]:1–11. [51] Deut. 13:12–18. [52] Num. [25]:1–13.

As we read also in the book of Numbers that the captain and all the people were commanded to go in and out, that is, to proceed in wars according to the order of Eleazar the priest.[53] Such were the wars of Abijah and other kings of Judah, that fought most justly and prosperously against the schismatical Israelites and justly possessed the cities which they conquered in those wars.[54] As also Edom and Libnah revolted from King Joram for religion, even because he forsook the God of their forefathers and could never be recovered to the same again.[55] Wherein also the example and zeal of the children of Israel was very notable; that they would have denounced war against the tribe of Reuben and Gad, only for erecting (as they took it) a schismatical altar out of the only place where Our Lord appointed that sacrifice should be done unto His honor.[56]

So much more since Christ's law and religion was established, divers great and honorable fights have been made for the faith against princes and provinces that unjustly withstood and annoyed the same.

So in the old times of the primitive Church, the Christian Armenians lawfully defended themselves by arms against their Emperor Maximinus.[57] And the Catholic people of divers provinces have often by force defended and kept their bishops in their seats against the infidels; but specially against the commandment of heretical emperors; yea, and resisted them in defense of their churches and the sacred goods of the same. As the citizens of Antioch defended their church against the Emperor Galerius his officers. St. Basil and St. Ambrose's people defended them against the invasions of heretics.[58] And not the people only,

[53] Num. [27]:21.

[54] [II Chron. 13.]

[55] [II Chron. 21]:8–11; [II Kings 8]:20–22.

[56] Josh. 22:10–34.

[57] [Euseb. li. 9 cap. 6.] Eusebius, *Ecclesiastical History,* lib. 9, cap. 8 (sic).

[58] [Nazian. de laud. Basi.; Amb. li. 5. Epist.] St. Gregory Nazianzen, Oration 43, *In laudem Basilii Magni;* St. Ambrose, perhaps Letter no. 20, to Marcellina.

which may do things of headiness, without counsel or consultation (of whom St. Ambrose saith, being willed to assuage their fury, that it lay in him not to incite them himself, but had no means oftentimes to repress them), but the bishops of countries so persecuted by heretical princes have justly required help of other Christian kings and nations.

For so holy Athanasius (who knew his duty to his sovereign well enough and in what case he might resist him) asked aid against Constantius, the Arian and first heretical Emperor (whom Pope Felix declared to be an heretic), of his own brother Constans, Catholic Emperor of the West; for fear of whose arms the said Arian restored Athanasius and other Catholic bishops to their churches and honors again; though after this Catholic Emperor's death the other more furiously persecuted Athanasius than before.[59]

Likewise against Valens, the Arian Emperor, Petrus, successor to Athanasius and brother to St. Basil, did seek to the Pope of Rome for succor, as all other afflicted bishops and Catholics ever did.[60] So did Atticus, Bishop of Constantinople, crave aid of Theodosius the Younger against the King of the Persians that persecuted his Catholic subjects and was thereby forcibly deprived and his innocent subjects delivered.[61]

So did holy Pope Leo the First persuade the Emperor, called Leo also, to take arms against the tyrant of Alexandria for the delivery of the oppressed Catholics from him and the heretics

[59] [Theod. li. 2. cap. 5. 13; Socrat. li. 1. cap. 13; Soz. lib. 4. cap. 7; Damas in Pontif.] Theodoret, *Ecclesiastical History,* lib. 2, cap. 3, 10 (sic) and *passim;* Socrates, *Ecclesiastical History,* lib. 2, cap. 22, 26 (sic) and *passim;* Sozomen, *Ecclesiastical History,* lib. 3, cap. 20 (sic) and *passim; Liber Pontificalis,* once attributed to Pope Damasus, section on Pope Felix II (2nd L. Duchesne ed. [Paris, 1955], I, 211).

[60] [Socr. lib. 4. cap. 17. 30; Sozo. li. 6. cap. 19.] Socrates, *Ecclesiastical History,* lib. 4, cap. 22 (sic); Sozomen, *Ecclesiastical History,* lib. 6, cap. 19.

[61] [Socr. lib. 2. cap. 18; Nicepho. lib. 14. cap. 21.] Socrates, *Ecclesiastical History,* lib. 7 (sic), cap. 18; Nicephorus Callistus, *Ecclesiastical History,* lib. 14, cap. 21.

Eutychians; who then threw down churches and monasteries and did other great sacrileges. Whose words for example's sake I will set down: "O Emperor" (saith St. Leo), "if it be laudable for thee to invade the heathens, how much more glorious shall it be to deliver the Church of Alexandria from the heavy yoke of outrageous heretics, by the calamity of which Church all the Christians in the world are injured." [62]

In brief, so did St. Gregory the Great move Gennadius the Exarch to make wars specially against heretics as a very glorious thing.[63] And so ever have holy bishops most intermeddled in cases of heresy and injuries done unto God's Church (as a thing properly subject to their correction), by excommunication, or what other way soever God hath given them commodity of; which all is to be used and executed according to the differences of times and persons.

The holy bishops might most lawfully (and so sometimes they did) excommunicate the Arian emperors and have warranted their Catholic subjects to defend themselves by arms against them. But they always did not so, because they had no means, by reason of the greater forces of the persecutors. As there is no question but the Emperors Constantius, Valens, Julian, and others might have been by the bishops excommunicated and deposed and all their people released from their obedience if the Church or Catholics had had competent forces to have resisted.

Yea, the quarrel of religion and the defense of innocency is so just that heathen princes, not at all subject to the Church's laws and discipline, may in that case by the Christians' arms be resisted and might lawfully have been repressed in times of the pagans and first great persecutions, when they vexed and oppressed the

[62] [Leo. Epi. 75; Evag. lib. 2. cap. 8.] Pope Leo I, the Great (440–461), letter to Eastern Emperor Leo I (457–474), no. 156 in Migne, cap. 5; Evagrius Scholasticus, *Ecclesiastical History,* lib. 2, cap. 8 ff.

[63] [Lib. 1. ep. 71.] Letter of Pope Gregory I, the Great (590–604), to Gennadius, Patriarch and Exarch of Africa, lib. 1, no. 74, in Migne.

faithful; but not otherwise (as most men think), if they would not annoy the Christians nor violently hinder or seek to extirpate the true faith and course of the Gospel. Though St. Thomas seemeth also to say that any heathen king may be lawfully deprived of his superiority over Christians.[64]

Howsoever that be, plain it is that kings that have professed the faith of Christ and the defense of His Church and Gospel may be and have been justly both excommunicated and deposed for injuries done to God's Church and revolt from the same; as sometimes also for other great crimes tending to the pernicion [65] of the whole people subject unto them.

But to speak specially of matter of religion and the crimes thereunto belonging, Leo the Third was excommunicated and deprived of all his temporalities in Italy by Gregory the Second. For defect also in religion and of the Church's defense were the Greek emperors discharged and the empire translated to the Germans by Pope Leo the Third. As afterward divers German emperors for notable injuries done to God's Church, for sacrilege, and for heresy, by godly discipline of the Church and by the diligence of sundry Popes have been brought to order, or in fine deposed; or else, where they would not obey Christ's Vicar, either in themselves or in their posterity, have been notoriously by God confounded. As Frederick the First, Frederick the Second, Otto the Fifth, Lewis the Third, Lewis the Fourth, and whom we name last (because we must say somewhat more of him), Henry the Third (or, as some call him, the Fourth), by Gregory the Seventh, which example the libeler and other heretics most mention, [66] for that the said Henry so obstinately resisted (though otherwise by the invincible courage and constancy of the Pope often brought to penance and extremity), that in fine by arms he drove the said Pope out of his see and placed an Antipope, that is

[64] [See S. Thomas. 2. 2. quaest. 10. art. 10.] St. Thomas Aquinas, *Summa theologica,* c. 2, quaest. 10, art. 10.

[65] Total destruction, ruin.

[66] Cecil, pp. 23–25.

to say, one so opposite to Christ's Vicar as Antichrist shall be against Christ. Which by arms and patronage of this wicked Emperor usurped and occupied the apostolical throne against the true Pope Gregory the Seventh, whom the libeler (after the vulgar vein of rebellious heretics) vouchsafeth not the name of Gregory the Seventh, but calleth him commonly Hildebrand; as the heretics, when they were in arms in Germany against their Emperor, would not name him Charles the Fifth, nor Emperor, but Charles of Ghent.

And now because this good and notable Pope was not able in fine to resist the Emperor's forces (the which Emperor, as all the histories of that time record, was a most wicked, sacrilegious, simoniacal, and heretical person), the adversaries of God's Church do triumph (as the libeler here doth) over the blessed man; as Herod might have done over John Baptist, whose admonition was taken in so evil gree [67] that it cost him his life; as also the executing of the Church's sentence, which is God's, hath done to many a prophet and bishop in the world.

By which event of things whosoever measureth the right of causes will make a good religion and a good defense of the execution of justice. For so most tyrants might be justified, for a time, against all the saints of God. This Gregory, say they, was in fine banished by the Emperor; and so was St. Chrysostom by Arcadius and Eudoxia, and died in banishment, as Gregory the Seventh did; yet they were but homely Christians that would justify the Emperors and condemn St. Chrysostom.

And indeed this Pope, whom they specially hate because (as it may be thought) he was the first man that authentically condemned the Berengarians' heresy and in open disputation refuted it, though certain of the said Emperor's flatterers and enemies of the See Apostolic (as the fashion of our heretics is at this day) wrote slanderous libels against him, yet was he a very notable good man and learned and did suffer whatsoever he did suffer for

[67] With such ill will.

mere justice, in that he did godly, honorably, and by the duty of his pastorship whatsoever he did against the said Emperor. Whereof we could allege all the best writers of those days, or near that time, but that we should be tedious. Of whom yet this one grave testimony of Baptista Fulgosius, a noble and learned man that was Duke of Genoa above an hundred years past, we shall not let to set down as we find it in Latin:

Constantissimus habitus est Gregorius septimus Pontifex, qui quod Henricum tertium Imperatorem propter aperta nimis simoniae crimina, pro pastorali officio reprehendebat, gravibus ab eo injuriis affectus est: itaque injuriarum magnitudine compulsus, Henricum Gregorius ut haereticum Imperii honore privavit. Cum autem Henricus solvi ecclesiastica censura non emendatione vitae sed armis quaereret; alium creare Pontificem enixus, capta Urbe obsidere Gregorium coepit. Quae mala cum Gregorius pateretur, nunquam tamen a justo proposito dimoveri potuit.[68]

That is:

Gregory the Seventh was notable for his constancy; who, for that according to his pastoral charge he had admonished Henry the Third, Emperor, to leave his known impiety of simony, was by manifold intolerable injuries vexed by the said Emperor and by the greatness of his wickedness was compelled to deprive him, as an heretic, of his imperial dignity. But Henry, seeking not by amendment of his life but by arms to be absolved from the censure, he went about to set up a new Pope and besieged the city of Rome and brought the Pope into great distress. In all which miseries Gregory could never be removed from his just purpose.

So he writeth of the parties both and of the horrible crimes for which the Emperor was most justly in the sight of all good men

[68] Battista Fregoso, *Bap. Fulgosii factorum dictorum que memorabilium libri IX* (Paris, 1578), but many other editions with varying titles, [lib. 3. cap. ult.], i.e. cap. 8, fol. 118v. in this edition. The reference to the emperor should obviously be to Henry IV, not Henry III.

deposed.[69] Thus Trithemius reporteth in brief of the wickedness of this Emperor: *Episcopatus, Constantiensem,* etc.

He sold the bishoprics of Constance, Bamberg, Mainz, and divers other for money; those of Augsburg and Strassburg for a sword; that of Münster for sodomy; and the abbacy of Fulda for adultery. Heaven and earth witness and cry out of these; and for the same abominations he standeth excommunicated and deprived and therefore hath no power nor just title to reign over us Catholics.[70]

But to go forward: this same Gregory the Seventh did the like commendable justice upon the King of Poland, Boleslaus the Second; as well excommunicating as depriving him for murdering of his Bishop, St. Stanislaus, at the very altar. Against which sentence though he stood by force and contempt for a time, yet at length he was forsaken and resisted wholly by his subjects, fled, and in fine slew himself.[71]

For heresy also was George King of Boemland[72] excommunicated and thereupon by the forces of the King of Hungary at length actually deprived. As also John Albert had half his kingdom of Navarre taken from him by Ferdinandus surnamed Catholicus of Aragon, for that he gave aid to Lewis the Twelfth, being excommunicated by Julius the Second. For great injuries also done to Holy Church, and for persecution of bishops and religious, was John, one of our kings of England, with his whole land interdicted and brought (after long struggling against God and the See Apostolic) to yield his crown to the courtesy of the Pope's Legate and to make both his realms of England and Ire-

[69] [See Uspergen. lib. 5. Annal.] Reference, probably, to the *Chronicum Abbatis Urspergensis,* attributed to Burchard of Biberach (d. 1230), published several times in the sixteenth century. See text in *Monumenta Germaniae Historica, Scriptorum,* XXIII, 337–383, especially p. 339.

[70] [Trithem. in Chron.] By Johannes Trithemius, Abbot of Sponheim, author of several works whose titles begin with the word *Chronicon.*

[71] [Chrom. lib. hist. Polon. li. 4.] Martin Cromer, *De origine et rebus gestis Polonorum,* lib. 4; in the Basel, Oporinus ed. of 1568, pp. 61–62.

[72] Bohemia.

land tributaries. The authentical instrument whereof John Bodin saith he hath seen.[73]

For like causes, and namely for that he was vehemently suspected of the murder of the blessed Bishop, St. Thomas of Canterbury, was Henry the Second driven by Alexander the Third to order and penance. A number of the like examples more we might recite of our country and of the Christian world; whereby not only the practice of the Church in all ages may be seen, but also Catholic men warranted that they be no traitors nor hold assertions treasonable, false, or undutiful in answering or believing that for heresy or suchlike notorious wickedness a prince (otherwise lawful and anointed) may be excommunicated, deposed, forsaken, or resisted by the warrant of Holy Church's judgment and censure.

Whereunto we will add only the sentence of Gregory the Great and first of that name, whom the adversaries confess to have been both learned and holy, who being, as they know, many hundred years before Gregory the Seventh, and our special apostle, practiced the point we now stand on, and therefore likely to be believed of all reasonable men. He, therefore, in the form of his privilege granted to St. Medard's monastery, thus decreeth: *Si quis (inquit) regum, antistitum, judicum, vel quarumcunque personarum saecularium hujus apostolicae auctoritatis et nostrae praeceptionis decreta violaverit, cujuscunque dignitatis vel sublimitatis sit, honore suo privetur.*[74] "If any king, prelate, judge, or what other secular person soever, shall transgress this decree of our authority and commandment, of what pre-eminence or height soever he be, let him be deprived of his dignity."

This was the right and power of St. Gregory; and this hath been the faith of Christian men ever sith our country was con-

[73] [Lib. 1. de Repub. cap. 9.] Jean Bodin, *De republica libri sex,* lib. 1, cap. 9, several editions and translations.

[74] [In fine libri 12. epist.] Pope Gregory I, *Privilegium monasterio sancti Medardi concessum,* no. 4 in *Appendix ad Sancti Gregorii epistolas.*

verted, and never subject called in question, much less accused of treason for it, till this miserable time, and least of all made or found treason by the old laws in King Edward the Third's reign, as is pretended; howsoever by their new laws they may and do make what they list a crime capital.

And ever sith the said St. Gregory's time, or thereabout, all kings in Christendom, specially those of Spain, France, Poland, and England, take an oath upon the holy Evangelists at their coronation to keep and defend the Catholic faith; and ours of England expressly to maintain also the privileges and liberties of the Church and clergy given by King Edward the Confessor and other faithful kings their ancestors.[75]

Whereof St. Thomas of Canterbury putteth his sovereign, Henry the Second, in memory, both often in speech and expressly in an epistle written to him in these words: *Memores sitis confessionis quam fecistis et posuistis super altare apud Westmonasterium, de servanda Ecclesiae libertate, quando consecrati fuistis et uncti in Regem a praedecessore nostro Theobaldo.*[76] "Keep in memory the confession which you made and laid upon the altar at Westminster, touching the keeping of Holy Church's liberties, when you were consecrated and anointed King by my predecessor Theobald."

And the Patriarchs of Constantinople took an instrument of such as were to be crowned emperors (specially in the times of heresy), wherein they made the like promise and profession to keep and defend the faith and decrees of holy Councils. So did the Patriarch Euphemius in the coronation of Anastasius; Nicephorus, in the investing of Michael; and others in the creation of other Emperors of the East. And Zonaras writeth that the Patriarch of

[75] See above, Ch. III, p. 110 and n. 49.

[76] [In vita S. Thomae.] From letter of Thomas à Becket to Henry II, 1166, in J. C. Robertson and J. B. Sheppard, eds., *Materials for the History of Thomas Becket, Archbishop of Canterbury,* Rolls series (London, 1875–1885), V, 282.

Constantinople plainly told Isaac Comnenus the Emperor that as by his hands he received the empire, so, if he governed not well, by him it should be taken from him again.[77]

Likewise, when kings that before were infidels do enter by baptism into the Church, they submit their scepters to Christ and consequently make themselves subject and punishable if they revolt from their faith and promise.

Upon these conditions, therefore, and no other, kings be received of the bishop that in God's behalf anointeth them; which oath and promise being not observed, they break with God and their people; and their people may and, by order of Christ's supreme minister, their chief pastor in earth, must needs break with them; heresy and infidelity in the prince tending directly to the perdition of the commonwealth and the souls of their subjects and notoriously to the annoyance of the Church and true religion, for the defense of which kings by God are given.

By the fall of the king from the faith, the danger is so evident and inevitable that God had not sufficiently provided for our salvation and the preservation of His Church and holy laws if there were no way to deprive or restrain apostate princes.

We see how the whole world did run from Christ after Julian to plain paganism; after Valens, to Arianism; after Edward the Sixth, with us, into Zwinglianism; and would do into Turkism, if any powerable prince will lead his subjects that way.

If our faith or perdition should on this sort pass by the pleasure of every secular prince, and no remedy for it in the state of the New Testament but men must hold and obey him to what infidelity soever he fall, then we were in worse case than heathens and all other human commonwealths, which both before Christ and after have had means to deliver themselves from such tyrants

[77] [Zonor. tomo. 3 & Cuspinianus in Anastasio, & in zimiste.] Joannes Zonaras, *Annals,* lib. 18, cap. 3. Cf. lib. 14, cap. 3, and lib. 15, cap. 16, re the other coronations. Johannes Cuspinian, an Austrian Renaissance historian, was among the first to rediscover and use Zonaras.

as were intolerable and evidently pernicious to human society and the good of the people; for whose peace and preservation they were created by man or ordained by God.

The bond and obligation we have entered into for the service of Christ and the Church far exceedeth all other duty which we owe to any human creature. And therefore, where the obedience to the inferior hindereth the service of the other which is superior, we must by law and order discharge ourselves of the inferior.

The wife, if she cannot live with her own husband (being an infidel or an heretic) without injury and dishonor to God, she may depart from him, or contrariwise he from her for the like cause. Neither oweth the innocent party, nor the other can lawfully claim, any conjugal duty or debt in this case.

The very bondslave, which is in another kind no less bound to his lord and master than the subject to his sovereign, may also by the ancient imperial laws depart and refuse to obey or serve him if he become an heretic, yea, *ipso facto* he is made free.[78]

Finally, the parents that become heretics lose the superiority and dominion they have by law or nature over their own children.[79]

Therefore let no man marvel that in case of heresy the sovereign loseth his superiority and right over his people and kingdom, which cannot be a lawful Christian state or commonwealth without due obedience to Christ and to the Church's laws; but may well consist and not perish at all by the change of their prince or king, no any one person being simply necessary for the preservation of the same, as some one (being an heretic and enemy to religion) may [be], and lightly is (if he be suffered), the destruction thereof.

[78] [Theodos. 1. Manachaeos. c. de haereticis.] A possible construction of *Codex Theodosianus,* 16. 5. *(de haereticis)* 40. Cf. 16. 6. 4, providing for emancipation of slaves rebaptized by Donatist owners.

[79] [Cap. fin. extra de haereticis.] Cf. provisions for right of children to property of heretic parents in *Codex Theodosianus,* 16. 5. 7; 16. 5. 40; 16. 6. 4.

And thus much may (as we trust) suffice with all reasonable indifferent persons for defense of our brethren's answers touching the question of excommunication or deposition of princes by the Pope; whereof by occasion more shall be said in the next chapter and others following, the libeler's importunate insolency enforcing us thereunto; like as the civil magistrates' most captious and bloody conceits constrained some of our blessed brethren before their martyrdoms to speak more thereof than otherwise they desired; though nothing so much as by warrant of God's word and Holy Writ they might have done.

❦

Chapter VI

That it is much to the benefit and stability of commonwealths, and specially of kings' scepters, that the differences betwixt them and their people, for religion or any other cause for which they may seem to deserve deprivation, may rather be decided by the supreme pastor of the Church, as Catholics would have it, than by popular mutiny and fantasy of private men, as heretics desire and practice

THE libeler once or twice in his discourse seditiously calleth upon the monarchs and princes of the world, warning them of the doubtful and servile state they be in while the Popes may be suffered to make and unmake kings and princes at their pleasure and to license their subjects to resist them.

And the man perchance might have his tale heard if he spake to the simple sort, or to such kings as feared neither God nor man, nor sought otherwise, nor any longer, to uphold their estates but by desperate force and practice and for their own time, without regard of their posterity. But speaking to them whose wisdoms sustain the world; whose crowns are worn and swords are borne for Christ and His Spouse; whose glorious ancestors partly first rose, and partly were established, and themselves yet safely stand and happily flourish (which Our Lord God long continue) by the benediction of the See Apostolic and good intelligence and correspondence with the high bishops of the same; good audience hardly can they look for. The example of some other princes Protestants about them, forsaking the fellowship of the Catholic and Apostolic See, and specially of King Henry the Eighth first, and his son and daughter after him, in England—a man, a child, and a woman—not only severing themselves from the same but annexing to their regality by strange laws all apostolical and papal power spiritual, with infinite emoluments made by confiscation of all religious men's lands and goods in the whole realm (which was the beginning of that new ecclesiastical regiment); these things (being of greater temptation than the libeler's bare words) could yet never move the Emperor, nor either of the great monarchs, nor any other king of wise counsel in the world, to break with God's Church and the chief pastors thereof, knowing by the records of all ages sithence Christ that what princes or potentates soever have formally opposed themselves to Christ's Vicar and refused to communicate with him in the faith and fellowship of the Catholic Church were ever in themselves or their posterity confounded and their kingdoms overthrown or brought to miserable servitude of Turk or other heathen tyrant.

It is not the good fortune of a few years' felicity that moveth the grave and sage governors of the world (though the libeler, to make fools fain,[1] urgeth their good luck in England much, since their breach with God's Church). But they will look farther about them and see the events of these strange attempts in us and the judgments of God for the same not only till the end of King Henry the Eighth his race (who was *Radix peccati*[2]) but afterward, if Our Lord defer his sentence so long, to some new generations to come. Over which, as upon the prince and state pres-

[1] Happy, pleased.

[2] I Macc. 1:10: "A wicked root."

ent of our country, we humbly on our knees, with continual tears, desire God to have mercy and to avert His indignation from them and us, that the princes and people of the world may rather be edified by the example of our conversion and return to God's Church than be instructed by the sight of our punishment and confusion.

But now, for the conceit that this good man would drive into men's heads that no state should be in safety if the Pope might deprive the prince at his pleasure: it is a bug[3] fit only to fear babes. All wise men in the world that either see the present times or look back into the ages past know that the Pope neither challengeth nor usurpeth nor useth any such authority at his pleasure to depose or exalt whom he list. And all learned divines confess that he hath not any direct or immediate jurisdiction or superiority over the temporalities, civil states, or regalities of secular princes or magistrates and therefore cannot dispose of their kingdoms nor actions, alter nor abrogate their laws, as he daily doth and may do at his good pleasure of prelates, bishops, and priests' affairs, upon whom he hath direct power and jurisdiction; but that he may only intermeddle indirectly with temporal princes, as he is the chief officer under Christ, and hath charge of their souls, and thereby hath to look whether their regiments tend any way to the injury of the Church and true religion or to their own and their subjects' damnation, as in case of schism, heresy, apostasy, idolatry, sacrilege, and other intolerable defects in government; for which he, being their bishop, is bound to admonish them sundry times with all lenity; if that serve not, to excommunicate them; and if they contemn that and the Church's discipline and authority, then be they esteemed as heathens and unworthy of superiority over God's people.

This is not to depose kings at his pleasure; nor is cause sufficient why any just and Christian prince should stand in doubt of the Pope's censures; only such as be heretics or intend to shake off

[3] Bogey, bugbear.

the yoke of Christ and their faith in Him have cause in their conscience to doubt both the Church's discipline and the plagues of God; which will not fail them, howsoever by human force and violence they protect themselves for a time from His minister's sentence and sweet corrections.

All just and Catholic kings are so far from doubting or misliking God's ordinance and the practice of the See Apostolic herein that they perceive it most necessary for the stability of their kingdoms and the continuance of their posterity in the glory thereof that for their regiment in faith and life they stand in some reverent awe of their chief pastors; which is a necessary and honorable bridle of princes in their youth, and all the days of their life, to stay them from dangerous disorders and so to temper them in their government that they may reign long and happily over their people; where otherwise they might fall into infinite calamities and be either forsaken, deposed, or shamefully destroyed by their own subjects, whether they be deprived by Holy Church's censure or no.

Neither doth any godly Christian prince at this day (as we think) wish their empire, either in themselves, their children, or posterity to dure [4] any longer than they continue in the Catholic faith and the communion of the See and Church Apostolic, nor would suffer any of their name or blood to reign after them that were like to be heretics; but rather would disinherit or execute them with their own hands than fear or expect their deposition by the Pope.

Therefore though with such as feel their own fault it soundeth evil to hear of the authority and usage of God's Church in censuring kings, yet it troubleth not any just and lawful prince; especially when by their wisdom and experience they may perceive that princes, above all other, both good and evil, be subject to human casualties and may fall and lose their kingdoms by an hundred accidents of mutinies and rebellions of their subjects or

[4] Last, endure.

by external or domestical wars of competitors or enemies. To all which the Pope's high authority and interest giveth great stay and moderation, in deciding the controversies of titles and causes of civil or foreign wars, and by his manifold endeavors of pacification and composition, whereof all the kings and states Christian have at sundry times of their distresses received singular profit; as appeareth in the histories of the wars betwixt our nation, France, and Scotland, and in our own civil tumults, which have been often appeased by the mediation of the Pope, both parties deferring to him as to the high priest and general arbiter of Christian princes and people (being to all indifferent without all partiality) the decision of those things which otherwise could not by laws nor by arms, without lamentable destruction and much blood, be determined. Whereby princes of less power, injured by the greater and mightier, have ever found succor and redress, and just kings, distressed by their rebellious subjects, have had singular assistance.

As we may see in the stories both of our own country, where the Popes have sent divers legates to the barons, being up against their lawful sovereigns, to admonish them to lay down their arms, and when they would not, excommunicated them; by which means many a king with us hath kept his crown which otherwise had been deprived by tumultuous and popular sedition. And no less in the examples of other nations, and that in our own memories; having experience of divers blessed Popes' diligence in aiding the two great monarchs, as well by the powers temporal which God hath given them, as by ecclesiastical censures against their rebels and large spiritual graces and benedictions bestowed upon all that would faithfully adjoin to the repression of the seditious subjects and the preservation of the sovereign.

The Apostolic Bishop is not an enemy to superiority and domination, which he knoweth best to be of God, as his own high estate is, but a spiritual and most loving parent and common father of all Christians, and specially of princes. He seeketh not their depositions, nor maintaineth revolts from them, no, not then when, to his infinite grief, he is forced sometimes (though marvelous seldom) to give sentence for the people and subjects against the prince, but useth needful discipline toward them for their salvation.

Let the grave and wise men of all nations consider with us whether princes be in more danger of their state by the lawful pastors of their souls that judge by God's spirit, by counsel, deliberation, order, and authority, without malice, hatred, or partiality; or by heretics, seditious and rebellious persons that deal by erroneous conscience, fantasy, and fury.

The Protestants plainly hold in all their writings and schools, and so practice in the sight of all the world, that princes may for tyranny or religion be resisted and deprived. We and all Catholics likewise affirm that for heresy and some other great enormities they may be excommunicated and further censured. But the Protestants would have themselves and the subjects to rebel and throw down their superiors, on their own head and willfulness, and themselves to be judges of their sovereigns' deserts and religion. Now we demand of the libeler, that giveth princes so friendly warning of their dangerous estates, if Popes may use such authority over princes, whether the kings of Christendom (whom their own sect-masters confess may be deposed) stand not in far greater hazard of their dominions and persons by the brutish and seditious people, armed always with fury, and often also (as at this present) with heresy, than they are of Popes?

It was not the Pope that gave license or encouragement to the subjects of Scotland to take arms against their natural liege and Queen,[5] to imprison her, and to cause her by fear of death to resign her crown. It is not the Pope that emboldened them barbarously to restrain their noble young King,[6] and so often to rebel against him; though neither they for his religion have any

[5] Mary Stuart, Queen of Scots, forced to abdicate in 1567.

[6] James VI, King of Scotland (1567–1625), under regents until 1578.

reason to deprive him, nor the Pope's Holiness (otherwise than for the justice of his quarrel against his rebels) any cause to defend him. It was not the Pope that licensed the subjects of the King Catholic [7] to fight so long and obstinately against their lord and master, nor that encouraged them to deprive him of his sovereignty and ancient inheritance. It was not the Pope that hath hazarded three mighty kings, His Most Christian Majesty that now is, and his two crowned brethren before him,[8] of their states and bereaved them of many great parts and cities of their kingdom, or that went about to deprive them, even in the time of their innocency and young years. Popes use to defend innocents, not to destroy them in their nonage or to abuse their minority. And such is otherwise the manifold hazard of kings by rebellions that in our own country the child hath deposed his father, the uncle his nephew, the wife her own husband; [9] and most commonly the worse and more wicked, the more godly and innocent. And we marvel much this libeler, that would seem to be such a statesman and a counselor to foreign kings, could find no danger to them and their countries, saving of the Pope's power over them; which in very truth, by Christ's special providence, is the greatest protection, guard, and stay that innocent princes and their people can have, the awe and reverend respect of his holy authority keeping thousands from rebellion and intrusion and a number of just princes in their empires which else had been in divers countries overthrown.

The Protestants cannot prove by example of all nations and

[7] Philip II of Spain, against whose authority the Netherlands had been in revolt since 1566.

[8] Henry III (1574–1589), and his predecessors, Francis II (1559–1560) and Charles IX (1560–1574), minor kings of France, against whose governments the Huguenots had been fighting off and on since 1562, with several incidents before that.

[9] Edward II was forced by an army led by his wife Isabella to abdicate in favor of his son Edward III in 1327. Richard III seized power from his nephews, heirs to Edward IV, in 1483.

times since Christ that anyone hath been deposed that was not proved to be a notorious heretic or evil man. On the other side, rebels and, namely, heretics, by unlawful means deprive commonly none but innocent, just, and holy princes; unto whose barbarous cruelty this libeler would have Their Sacred Majesties rather thrall [10] and obnoxious than to submit themselves to the sweet yoke of Christ's kingdom and priesthood, or to concur in happy unity with such as Christ and the Holy Ghost have placed over the Church for the guiding of her people to salvation, and that also in worldly peace and tranquillity as much as in them lieth. Which is their chief honor and greatest guard that may be both to prince and people; as the contrary motion of wicked men to sow debate between princes and pastors is surely more unnatural than to put discord betwixt the body and the soul in the regiment of a man's person. Wherein, as the whole frame is best governed and preserved when the flesh can be contented to be ruled by the spirit, so, no doubt, the temporal power consisteth most safely, and endureth longest, when it hath good correspondence and subordination to the spiritual; which seeketh ever all advancement and safety to the secular powers appointed by God for the worldly weal of their subjects. Which terrene felicity (necessary for the clergy also in this life no less than for others) is always by the state ecclesiastical most zealously maintained against the disturbers of peace, concord, and due obedience to superiors.

And, therefore, as the Church of God and, namely, the See Apostolic, hath received (in respect of the honor due to Christ and His principal Apostle St. Peter) infinite exaltation by the Christian kings of all nations; so, on the other side, the Popes of all ages have sought by all means possible to advance to honor, glory, and increase Christian kings and states not only spiritually, which is their first and chief care, but also temporally; whereof every nation Christian hath had sufficient proof.

[10] Enslaved, subject.

But to say nothing of Catholic kings or countries which gladly acknowledge the benefit and will avouch the right and just title of any their dominions received of the See Apostolic or adjudged theirs by the same (for though the libeler would make them ween it were a base and perilous matter to stand at the Pope's courtesy in such things, yet he can persuade none of them that they hold any piece of their states by evil conscience which is fallen unto them that way by the Pope's warrant; nor is he so eloquent as to make them yield up the same to their old owners again), the states and princes Protestants must either acknowledge the benefit and just possession of divers high dignities, titles, and crowns received by the said See of St. Peter, or else they be neither kind nor wise.

Is not the imperial dignity the highest human pre-eminence that can be in this world? And can the German Protestants deny but that they hold or had that of the Pope? For where some wrangle that it came by election of the people of Rome, that is most false and contrary to all histories and reason. Dare they deny the Pope to have had lawful power to translate the empire out of Greece? Or will they say their Emperor that now is, and all other his predecessors since Charles the Great, were usurpers, as they should be if the order or disposition of the Holy See were not lawful? No Protestant nor other man in his wit will so say, and specially no Almain,[11] to the glory of whose nation this thing so much pertaineth. This nation, therefore, hath no cause to complain of the high spiritual authority by which itself hath been an hundred times more advanced than hindered or diminished.

As likewise, the order of the election and (which all men esteem for a title of most high dignity) the electorship itself was given to certain princes of Germany by Gregory the Fifth, who, as the Magdeburg historians themselves speak, being a German and desirous to adorn his native country with some excellent honor, devised that the election of the king (which after his

[11] German.

coronation by the Pope should also be called *Imperator* and *Augustus*) should only pertain to the Germans.[12]

Now let the heretics speak and yield their reason, who took the matter so much in dudgeon these last years past that the Pope should intermeddle with the displacing of the Elector of Cologne.[13] "What! A Pope to depose an Elector?" said they. As though a Pope might not deprive an unworthy apostate bishop of his see and electorship, who first created and gave unto that nation and to that see both elector and electoral dignity itself. Let them tell us why his authority is not as great in depriving for just cause as his power was sufficient to establish that honor in Germany.

And let the libeler that accounteth it so unworthy a thing that some Popes have given censure upon the princes of the Holy Empire be demanded who established that high state in that country. And whether he that had power to do that can want any warrant to deprive an evil or wicked person of the Empire. And in brief, let him be asked whether that noble nation have not received more dignity and profit temporal than hurt and hindrance by that papal power over kingdoms which this man in his seditious pride so much abhorreth.

But to come to that which we and the libeler best of all do know and toucheth us English more near at home, and may be an instruction and proof of the cause in hand to other strangers abroad. Surely if the people of our country knew their own good and were grateful as they were wont to be (for now this brutish

[12] Matthias Flacius Illyricus *et al., Ecclesiastica historia . . . secundum singulas centurias . . . per aliquot studiosos et pios viros in urbe Magdeburgica,* commonly called the Magdeburg Centuries (Basel, 1561–1574, and separate editions), [Cent. 10. cap. 10], Gregorius V, col. 546 in the 1567 Oporinus folio ed.

[13] Gebhard Truchsess of Waldburg had been deposed as Elector and Archbishop of Cologne by Pope Gregory XIII in 1583 for turning Protestant and was soon driven out of the see by the new papal appointee. Herman of Wied had similarly been deprived of the same see in 1546–1547.

heresy hath made them without affection, as St. Paul speaketh of such unnatural sectaries),[14] they would acknowledge that, as to the See Apostolic they owe their first faith and Christianity (not only for converting the Britons, who were the ancient inhabitants of the island, but also the English themselves afterward, and that in very memorable sort, reconciling them eftsoons again to Holy Church after their relapse and endowing their princes and prelates with such singular prerogatives as no particular church or commonwealth in the world, with the good grace of all other Christian states be it spoken, had greater or more honorable), so would they in like manner, besides these spiritual favors, confess themselves indebted for the temporal advancement of our princes, received from the same See Apostolic, seeing the regiment and lordship of Ireland was by the Pope's only gift bestowed upon our sovereigns in the time of Pope Adrian the Fourth and King Henry the Second, four hundred years agone, they having no other title thereunto in the world but by this grant of the See Apostolic.[15] Which title notwithstanding, we doubt not but that our English Protestants will account sufficient even unto this day. And King Henry the Eighth, being fallen from the Church and making himself of a member the head thereof in his realm, went forward upon this title and of his own new papal authority from the Lord of Ireland made and called himself the king thereof.[16] Which style was afterward (as we take it) by due authority of the Pope confirmed to Queen Mary.[17] So desirous hath been always the Holy See of Rome to increase our princes with all due honor and to enlarge their dominions. None of which titles, prerogatives, authorities, or dignities (though received only or principally by the Pope's favor or gift) any one of

[14] Reference, probably, either to Rom. 1:31, or II Tim. 3:3.

[15] By the bull *Laudabiliter,* ca. 1155, text in *Bullarum,* Turin ed., II (1858), 627–628.

[16] Statutes of Ireland, 33 Hen. VIII, c. 1.

[17] By the bull *Illius, per quem reges,* June 7, 1555, text in *Bullarum,* Turin ed., VI (1860), 489–490.

our kings, of what religion soever, was yet so willful to reject or let go, or yet so nice in faith as to make scruple of conscience to receive or retain as lawfully possessed, whatsoever they have obtained that way, though ungrateful persons acknowledge no benefit therein.

And not only large kingdoms so obtained princes are contented to keep without scruple, but hold also all other titles of honor annexed by His Holiness to their regal dignities upon what cause soever; as is to be seen in sundry great and mighty monarchs of Christendom upon whom divers high titles have been bestowed by the See Apostolic for their most Christian and heroical endeavors for the Church and their zeal against heretics and infidels: as "Catholic" in Spain,[18] "Most Christian" in France,[19] and suchlike elsewhere, and in our country a style no less honorable than the former, that is, "Defender of the Faith." Which style and title all the Protestants in the world do know that it was given by Pope Leo the Tenth to King Henry the Eighth for his defense of the Catholic Roman faith by writing, yet extant under his own hand, against Martin Luther.[20] And albeit the cause for which it was given be now quite altered and the Pope's authority from which it was received extremely impugned; yet the right thereof coming only from that authority now accounted so unlawful, none of our kings will leave or will renounce the same, as indeed we wish they should not, for that it notably putteth them in mind what church and faith it is that they are bound to defend and against what kind of men they bear the sword which God hath put into their hand.

We might add to this the singular and incomparable favors and daily benefits done by His Holiness that now is to our nation,

[18] Awarded to Ferdinand of Aragon by Pope Innocent VIII in 1492.

[19] Used sporadically since the early Middle Ages and regularly by the papal chancery after 1464.

[20] By the bull *Ex supernae dispositionis,* October 11, 1521, text in *Bullarum,* Turin ed., V (1860), 773–775. Henry VIII's work was titled *Assertio septem sacramentorum adversus M. Lutherum* (1521), STC 13078.

above all his predecessors assuredly, excepting St. Gregory the Great, our first apostle, whose divine grace and example of charity he so zealously doth imitate toward us, not only for the salvation of the whole deceived country, but for the particular relief of many hundreds of all sorts, ages, and sexes that are driven by violence of cruel persecution into divers Catholic provinces and are forced to leave their country and whatsoever is dear unto them to learn that faith in which all their forefathers so honorably lived and died. By which his rare benefits, his happy name (as Gregory's the First) must needs be in English memories immortal maugre [21] this ungrateful heresy, to which (we hope) he shall once be the bane.

Of the said Gregory the Great his more than common love of our souls we have (besides other apostolical charity) this grateful example: that His Holiness, receiving great sums of money in those days out of France, and having intelligence that there were dispersed through that province numbers of English children bought as bondslaves for doing of all drudgery for their masters' profit (as the state of servitude required), and that they lived there in thralldom both of body and soul, unbaptized; the blessed father taking deep compassion of their miserable case, specially because they were of that nation which was then newly gained by his travail unto Christ, he wrote letters to his receiver in those parts [22] that he should not make the French money (which was there to be received) over to Rome by exchange but employ it in France, where it was current, upon charitable uses; specially therewith to deliver English children from servitude and to bring them into Italy by troops, having good grave priests to oversee and instruct them in the faith; and if any dangerous sickness should fall to any of them in the way, to baptize them. So as he did not only procure our people's salvation at home by sending in

[21] In spite of.

[22] Candidus, a presbyter responsible for administering an estate belonging to the Roman Church in Gaul.

divers learned men to preach and teach the Gospel, under the conduction of holy St. Augustine [23] our apostle, but also by education abroad of great numbers of our nation, to his great charges temporal. So did this renowned Pope and doctor for our country to bring it from paganism to Christ, and through God prevailed and deserveth for the same immortal glory both in heaven and earth. And no less truly doth Gregory the Thirteenth for reconciling our country from heresy deserve, both bringing up abroad great numbers of the nation at his own charges in godly discipline and the same faith that the foresaid St. Gregory his patron and predecessor first caused to be taught to our forefathers, and also disposeth of many fit persons endued with zeal and spiritual power to return in peaceable, humble, and apostolic manner to their country, there to teach the deceived and to reconcile them by spiritual power and priestly function to the unity of God's Church again, out of which they are most sure to perish; and not by raising rebellion or tumults, as this libeler most falsely pretendeth.[24]

Which holy function for that they have done (by God's great grace and goodness) with far more fruit and increase of the Catholic religion and notorious damage of heresy than Protestants feared at the beginning, therefore have they subtly and falsely turned all these heroical endeavors of His Holiness and good offices of God's priests into matters of state and treason and would make all princes and people abroad believe (that are not acquainted, as necessity hath driven us to be, with the practice of the first apostles and Fathers of the primitive Church, achieving the conversion of many cities and countries in no other sort than our brethren most godlily and dutifully do attempt in our nation) that all our preaching, persuading, praying, offering sacrifice, hearing confessions, absolving, reconciling, having of beads, crosses, images, and the like, were seditious, rebellious, traitorous, and plain conspiracy against the Queen's Majesty and the realm.

[23] Of Canterbury, dispatched to England in 596.

[24] Cecil, p. 6.

Yea, they would so far (if they could) abuse the patience and simplicity of Christian people, both of their own country and others, that they would have them think our holy and high pastor to have erected the two seminaries,[25] and other commodities of learning and godly education for our countrymen, upon no other occasion but to move sedition and rebellion, and therefore are so far from giving him humble thanks, as they ought to do (and as our nation will once do, if ever it come to itself again), that they hate his person and office for this cause most deadly and do publish by this libel and otherwise that it is a work of high hostility against Her Majesty. But alas for pity, and woe be to our sins, that the state of our commonwealth is now so nearly joined unto heresy that neither Christ's Vicar by charity and discipline, nor God's priests by any office of their life and death, can seek to remedy the one but they shall be accounted enemies and traitors to the other! Which fond malice yet (through our infelicity) is more apparent in England than in any other people of the world besides, though in error and out of God's Church as ours. It is the peculiar glory of Gregory the Thirteenth above all his predecessors and other prelates of all ages that in so sweet and apostolic sort he provideth for the instruction of innumerable youths, for their own salvation and for the reduction of their native countries and entertaining the Catholic faith in most provinces of the world. Many are the people in the world abroad, especially in the east, south, and north parts thereof, which are in schism, heresy, or error no less than the English; and the incomparable care of this general pastor provideth for every one in the best manner that is possible, as well by corporal as spiritual relief. He hath at this day some of the fathers of the Society of Jesus in Constantinople, Alexandria, and elsewhere soever is any opportunity to gain souls in the dominions of the Turk; in Muscovia likewise, and other provinces addicted to the errors of the Grecians. He

[25] In Reims (moved from Douai in 1578, supported partly by a papal pension since 1575) and Rome (founded in 1579).

hath instituted seminaries for the Greeks, Armenians, and Sclavonians; he hath placed colleges of the Society and seminaries in Suetia,[26] Livonia, Polonia, Bohemia, Transylvania, for Scotland also, and specially for the noble province of Germany. Yea, his pastoral solicitude reacheth even to the East Indies, where in Japan he hath founded this last year past and maintaineth a goodly college, not without his great expenses.

Thus he doth in the cause of Christ, from one end of the world to another, whilst his and Holy Church's miserable adversaries waste their time in wrangling and wrestling against the truth. And there is none of all these nations, of what sect or sort soever, that can be so suspicious or malicious as to interpret His Holiness' meaning as the English do; or that conceive any fear of treasons, confederacies, invasions, or destructions of their countries, as our men dream of.

The Germans, though all be not Catholics but many much altered by their unadvised following of Martin[27] and other as mad sectaries; yet they all count it a singular honor and profit to their nation that they have so famous a college in Rome itself; as our nation did of old, when it had there a great school, about a thousand years ago, built by King Offa[28] and afterward an hospital. Where now we of England be come, by this wicked heresy, to be so careless of our public profit and honor that we contemn and maliciously condemn a gift far more excellent than ever was bestowed upon our country before in foreign places and most devilishly do hate the giver.

Wherein the heretics in this libel and otherwise show such ignorant and barbarous mockery touching the term of "seminaries" (as though they were estranged from all actions of the Christian world, throughout all which that term and calling is so common; namely, since the godly decree of the holy Council of Trent, giving order for the erection of such nurseries for the

[26] Sweden. [27] Luther. [28] Of Mercia, d. 796.

clergy)[29] as it is too-too ridiculous in our English heretics to make themselves sport at it; as they wisely do in this libel also at the name of the Pope's "bulls," by pretty allusion as they think (but indeed with small grace) resembling them to the bubbles of water;[30] with such scornful companions the Church of God hath now to deal. But, for defense of the Society, seminaries, and the sending of priests into England, the men of those orders and quality have age and ability to answer for themselves; and it is done to our hands plentifully in their *Apology*,[31] which the adversaries shall never answer with reason and credit. And therefore of that matter enough.

Chapter VII

Of the late wars in Ireland for religion; how the Pope may use the sword; and that the differences betwixt temporal princes and him, or their resisting him in some cases of their worldly interest, can be no warrant to the Protestants to contemn his censures or authority in matter of faith and religion

BUT the adversary objecteth that whatsoever the Pope doth or may do by his bulls, excommunications, institution of seminaries, or other suchlike spiritual endeavors may either be contemned or neglected by the example of Her Majesty, who regarded not his doings against her so long as he sat still in his chair; but when he rose up in anger and left *verbum*, the word, and took *ferrum*, the sword (against St. Bernard's direct advice to Eugenius, saith this

[29] Canons and decrees of the Council of Trent, 23rd session (1563), *Decretum de reformatione*, cap. 18, *Forma erigendi seminarium clericorum*.

[30] Cecil, p. 32.

[31] [William Allen] *An Apology and True Declaration of the Institution of the Two English Colleges* (1581), STC 369.

libeler);[1] yea, and when contrary to the Scriptures he drew forth the sword, which Christ commanded Peter to put up into the scabbard, and invaded by his forces Her Majesty's kingdom of Ireland, then (saith this good man) she could do no less but use such resistance by arms and otherwise as was requisite for her own defense.

Whereat we marvel less, indeed, for that before she had contemned the Pope's spiritual rod of excommunication and all ecclesiastical admonition and censure, which is the high priest's and Church's most proper weapon and is more to be feared of all faithful persons (as holy St. Augustine saith) "than to be hewed in pieces with the sword, burned with the fire, or torn in sunder of wild beasts"[2] and is a punishment so dreadful that even then when it is known to be executed without just cause by some error or wrong information it may not be contemned. Therefore, where that was not regarded we know there could be no scruple to withstand any other martial attempt against Pope or whomsoever, neither could it seem strange.

But at this all the world may wonder, and it is marvelous in our eyes, why the Pope's hostility in Ireland should condemn so many innocent priests and Catholics that never were in Ireland nor ever were acquainted with the action of that country or any other rebellion against the Queen in either of her kingdoms. Put down to the world (if you can) any one word, writing, or approved witness that any Jesuit, priest, or seminary man of all those whom you have executed these late years were either authors, persuaders, or dealers therein, and then you may have some shadow of defense for your justice. Prove only that His Holiness ever communicated his doings or intentions (whatsoever they were that way) to any one of them all, and we will confess that you have reason in the rest. If Pius the Fifth addressed Doctor

[1] Cecil, p. 33.

[2] St. Augustine, [lib. 1. cont. Faustum cap. 17.] Apparently an error; there is no cap. 17 in lib. 1 of *Contra Faustum Manichaeum.*

Nicholas Morton sixteen years since about the matter of the excommunication into England,[3] shall all priests and Jesuits be deemed traitors therefore? If Doctor Sanders, either upon his own zeal and opinion of the justness of the quarrel, or at the Pope's appointment, were in the wars of Ireland employed for defense of the Catholic religion against the Protestants,[4] may you by your laws or any other divine or human ordinance condemn therefore to death a number that never knew either the man or the matter? Some pretense you may have to be offended with the Pope, and perhaps lack no laws to punish the said two doctors that never were either of the Society or seminaries; but to make all the priests and Catholics at home or in banishment traitors thereby, it is too unreasonable; and to murder so cruelly one man for another's fault is too-too foul and intolerable iniquity.

And as for His Holiness' action in Ireland, we that are neither so wise as to be worthy nor so malapert as to challenge to know his intentions, counsel, and disposition of those matters can nor will neither defend nor condemn it. Only this is evident, that those small succors which were given by him to the Irish, or rather suffered at their own adventure to go into those wars, came upon the importunate suit of the sore afflicted Catholics and some of the chiefest nobility of that country. Of whose continual complaints, known calamities, and intolerable distresses of conscience and otherwise, it may be he was moved with compassion and did that in cause of religion (against one whom he took in his own judgment rightly by his predecessor's sentence to be deposed and in a quarrel in his sight most just and godly) which both Her Majesty and other temporal princes stick not to do very often toward their neighbors (with whom otherwise they pretend good amity and no breach of their league at all) in cases which either they esteem lawful or at least behooveful[5] for their own estate and affairs.

[3] Reference to Cecil, p. 14.

[4] Reference to Cecil, p. 13.

[5] Advantageous, needful.

And it is a strange case that these men should with such full mouth cry out against the high priest and pastor of God's Church for using the sword or giving his consent thereunto against a prince not any way his superior, if no way his subject; whereas the ministers and masters of their sects both in Flanders, Scotland, and other places do not only counsel and persuade subjects to take arms against their own lawful princes and sacred kings but also do practice and in person oppose themselves against them; yea, in Scotland against a prince of their own religion.

For tell me (Sir Libeler, if you please), were not the ministers of Scotland the principal fans and firebrands of the last conspiracy and open rebellion against His Majesty's person and the state of that country? Were not they in person at Stirling and elsewhere both in field and counsel with the Earls of Angus, Mar, and other rebels against his royal person? Were not all their pernicious machinations of betraying their country and their prince's blood detected by the Earl of Gowrie, before his late beheading for that conspiracy? [6] Are not Patrick Galloway, minister of St. Johnstoun,[7] Andrew Pollard, subdean of Glasgow; James Carmichael, minister of Haddington; Andrew Hay, parson of Renfrew; Andrew Melville, professor of divinity in St. Andrews; and divers other chief ministers of that country, fled into England for this traitorous fact and there received, cherished, and protected? [8]

And since that time, whereas in a Parliament holden in Edinburgh by His Majesty and all the three states of Scotland begun the nineteenth of May last past, certain laws were amongst others enacted for the restraint of these ministers' tumultuous authority

[6] The Earls of Angus and Mar had led troops which seized Stirling Castle in April, 1584, as part of an unsuccessful plot to seize the King. Gowrie was implicated and seized, confessed, and was executed shortly thereafter.

[7] Perth.

[8] Melville and other ministers had incurred the animosity of Arran, the King's chief adviser, and had fled to England, but were not very directly involved in the Stirling plot.

and to bring them under their own bishops' jurisdiction [9] (a thing so reasonable and consonant to God's word as nothing can be more, and practiced not only in England among their fellow sectaries but also throughout all Christendom, disorderly and seditious Geneva only excepted); and when these laws that were made by authority of the three estates and published, not only in the council house called Tolbooth but also at the Cross of Edinburgh by heralds-at-arms for the state, did not Robert Pont and Walter Balcanquhall (two most impudent and rebellious ministers of that town, by the consent and provocation of James Lawson, chief preacher there, as afterward appeared) oppose themselves in public against the King's authority (thereby to raise up some commotion) by their open protestation, made by instrument in the hands of George Wakeson, public notary and town clerk of that city;[10] and did not all these three named ministers by night fly presently into England after their insufferable insolency and are there received, harbored, and maintained?

Again, in the last Parliament before this, being about two years agone, did not these ministers (intending thereby some dangerous revolt and seditious defection) demand of their King in most impudent wise to be admitted into the Parliament as equal or above their bishops, whom they deny by God's word to have any supereminent authority? [11] Is not this one of their articles for which their Archbishop of St. Andrews [12] doth withstand them and hath been of late in England to confer with the Protestants of that country about the same? Is it not another of their articles that it is an heresy for any prince to call himself "Head of the

[9] *The Acts of the Parliaments of Scotland,* James VI, A.D. 1584, c. 2.

[10] Cf. the similar reports of this incident in *Calendar of State Papers, Scottish,* VII, 156, May 27, 1584; David Calderwood, *History of the Kirk of Scotland,* IV (Edinburgh, 1843), 65.

[11] *Acts and Proceedings of the General Assemblies of the Kirk of Scotland, II, 1578–1592* (Edinburgh, 1840), p. 527, report of the sixth session of the General Assembly convened on October 17, 1581.

[12] Patrick Adamson.

Church" within his own realm? [13] And that he may be excommunicated and deposed by the ministers? Have not they excommunicated and held out by violence these two years and more their Archbishop of Glasgow elected by the King, named Mr. Robert Montgomery,[14] until now that this last Parliament of May hath absolved and restored him unto his archbishopric again? [15]

You exclaim against the Pope, being the first and chief prelate of all Christendom (even by your own confession), for giving his consent that anything be done or attempted by arms and violence against any lawful or anointed prince whatsoever, be it for religion or any other never so rightful or just cause in his conceit; but what would these good fellows of your Gospel do if they had his authority, his power, and his pretense against foreign princes of a contrary religion, seeing, in quarrel of faction and favor of rank traitors, they deal thus against their own liege, and against their own anointed sworn King, of their own country, blood, education, and religion; who, as he never justly offended them in any sort, so hath he by infinite favors and graces bound them unto him in all most dutiful allegiance.

Again, as in the rebellions of Scotland, so likewise in Flanders and France, hath England these late years yielded no aid to the subjects against their lawful princes? Have not their banners been openly displayed upon their ancient friends' and confederates' walls? Have they not holden their towns from them by main force? Have they not many ways stirred and succored with men, money, and munition the rebellious subjects of all countries near about them? Yea, have they not in divers Parliaments, and namely in the Parliament holden in the fifth year of Her Majesty's reign, 1563,[16] as also in another Parliament in the thirteenth year of her reign, 1571,[17] published in print that the chief confedera-

[13] *Acts and Proceedings,* p. 489, cap. 1, section 12, of the "Book of Policy" adopted by the General Assembly on April 28, 1581.

[14] *Ibid.,* pp. 559–560, eighth session of the General Assembly convened on April 24, 1582.

[15] *The Acts of the Parliaments of Scotland,* James VI, A.D. 1584, c. 31.

[16] 5 Eliz. I, c. 29, c. 31.

[17] 13 Eliz. I, c. 26.

tions (moving the whole assembly of Calvinists both of the clergy and temporality gathered in those Parliaments to grant those two great "subsidies") were in respect of the "inestimable charges" (for such is their own phrase) sustained by the Queen in maintenance of the rebellious heretics, their dear brethren, against their liege lords and sovereigns of France, Scotland, and other places? Is it not now a special rule in government amongst the worldly Machiavellians to maintain their own repose by their neighbors' trouble? If this be usual in all other cases, and of many not much reprehended, for the advantage of the temporal state of any prince, is it only so great a marvel that the Pope should do that for zeal of true religion which other kings do for matters of far less importance? And if our conjecture may serve anything in this matter, perhaps he was the rather ready to do this for Ireland for that the See Apostolic hath an old claim unto the sovereignty of that country, and that before the covenants passed between King John and the same See. Which challenges princes commonly yield not up, by what ground soever they come. Though for this Pope present (whom God long preserve), we may be bold to say that he had rather have the two islands Catholic than the real possession of all the world, for the salvation of the people whereof, no doubt, he would spend in apostolic wise his own blood; so great an enemy he is to our nation.

But the libeler saith he should use the "word" and not the "sword" according to St. Bernard's admonition.[18] Well, let us then stand to that holy Father's judgment herein and the matter will be more easily tried; as also the fraud of this faithless libeler, by our faithful repeating the whole sentence, shall be discovered, and withal the Scriptures (alleged for the same purpose) expounded.

Propter hoc [saith he] *magis aggredere eos, sed verbo non ferro. Quid tu denuo usurpare gladium tentes, quem jussus es ponere in vaginam? Quem tamen qui tuum negat, non satis mihi videtur*

[18] Cecil, p. 33.

attendere verbum Domini dicentis sic: Converte gladium tuum in vaginam.[19] *Tuus ergo et ipse, tuo forsitan nutu, etsi non tua manu evaginandus. Alioquin si nullo modo ad te pertineret, et is, dicentibus apostolis, Ecce duo gladii hic, non respondisset Dominus, satis est, sed nimis est.*[20] *Uterque ergo Ecclesiae, et spiritualis scilicet gladius et materialis. Sed is quidem pro Ecclesia, ille vero ab Ecclesia exercendus est; ille Sacerdotis is militis manu; sed sane ad nutum sacerdotis et jussum Imperatoris.*[21]

That is in our tongue:

For that cause thou shouldst the rather set upon them, marry, with the word, not with the sword. Why seekest thou again to usurp the sword which thou wast commanded to put up into the scabbard? Which sword for all that, whosoever denieth to appertain to thee, seemeth to me not to mark the word of Our Lord thus speaking: "Return thy sword into his scabbard." Therefore even the sword is thine, at thy beck perhaps to be drawn, though not by thine own hand. For otherwise, if it should noway belong unto thee, when the apostles said to Christ, "Lo, two swords here," he would not have answered them that 'it was enough,' but that it had been too much. Therefore both the swords belong to the Church, the spiritual and material. But the material is to be used for the Church and the other by the Church; the spiritual by the hand of the priest, the other by the hand of the soldier and commandment of the Emperor, but at the priest's appointment.

So far this holy Father in the very place alleged by the adversary.

Whereby we see that though it be not always comely nor commendable for priests, which should be the authors and persuaders of peace to all princes and people, to be given to blood, wars, and destruction (especially by their own hands), or without great cause to use external force and violence against offenders, yet the sword may be drawn for their defense, and is to be drawn according to their counsel and direction.

[19] John 18:11. [20] Luke 22:38.
[21] St. Bernard of Clairvaux, *De consideratione ad Eugenium,* [li. 4. cap. 3.]

Whereunto we add further that though the apostles were taught and counseled evangelical meekness by that metaphor of putting up the swords, and had prescribed to them a sweeter form of governing their flock than the heathen or other temporal powers use toward their subjects, yet all temporal or corporal punishment was not thereby prohibited to the rulers of the Church. As we see by the example of St. Peter himself, who, after the said prohibition, did not only feed with the word but struck also corporally even to death Ananias and Sapphira.[22] Which as he might do lawfully by miracle, so his successors now may do the like by ordinary justice. Which example we use the rather for that the said St. Bernard useth it for proof of the very same matter when he saith: *Qui locum Petri tenet, potest uno ictu extinguere Ananiam; uno, Simonem Magum.*[23] "He that occupieth St. Peter's room may with a word destroy Ananias; and at one word extinguish Simon Magus."

And the next epistle before that, speaking also to Eugenius the Pope, he saith thus: *Ad hoc enim constitutus es super gentes et regna, ut evellas et destruas; ut aedifices et plantes.*[24] "For that end art thou constituted over nations and kingdoms; that thou mayest pluck up and build and plant," etc. Wherein, as in other execution of justice, though the Pope as a mortal man may sometimes do things out of season and without good success, even then when the cause he would advance is most godly and lawful (as we read in the first of the Maccabees of the priests' unfortunate fight against the heathen),[25] yet to make this a general rule (as this libeler doth), that the Pope may noways use the sword for defense of justice or religion, is most false and absurd.

The true way of defense for English Protestants in this case touching the wars of Ireland, and for impugnation of the Pope concerning his allowing or assisting the same, should be (in mine

[22] Acts 5:1–11.
[23] St. Bernard of Clairvaux, Letter 239, to Pope Eugenius III.
[24] *Idem* to *idem,* Letter 238.
[25] I Macc. 2 ff.

opinion) not to affirm absolutely (as our fond and most ignorant libeler doth) that the Pope may noway fight or take arms at all (for that is against a known truth, and not only we but all Catholics in the world will therein stand against him); but rather, for condemnation of His Holiness' actions, to prove that his cause was not just; Her Majesty not to stand rightly excommunicate, not any way to be an heretic, as Pius the Fifth declared; and consequently her subjects in no case to remain absolved from their oath and obedience. Of which points we may not at all dispute, seeing our defense is only general that the Pope may in some cases excommunicate, for some causes deprive, and in many respects fight and wage war for religion.

And it may be thought that the Protestants would never deny this but in regard of their own particular interest in some private case only. For they will not affirm, neither doth it displease them (as we think), that Pius the Fifth, the last Pope, was an author of the late league and wars against the Turk and had also his captains and banners displayed in that renowned battle [26] against him by the same. Against whose arms the Turk, notwithstanding, might as well have alleged the Scriptures, as now our Protestants do, to make him put up his sword. For in truth if it be lawful for him to occupy his forces which God hath given him against the heathen, that be noway under his jurisdiction, much more may he employ them against these whom he accounteth as rebels to the Church, which be properly under his correction, first, in respect of their souls, and then, secondarily, of their temporal goods so far as is requisite to their souls' good.

All which is most true, even in consideration of his priestly and apostolical function only; as is plain in Phinehas, whose priesthood was established upon his zealous pursuing the enemies of God to death with his own hand.[27] But further, marking that the

[26] Of Lepanto, October 7, 1571. The Christian fleet included a papal detachment commanded by Colonna.

[27] Num. 25:6–13.

high priests of God's people have been lightly in all ages temporal princes also and judges of the world, not only in spiritual but in worldly affairs too, there can no doubt remain but they may use their forces temporal to the maintenance of justice.

Melchisedek, the sampler[28] of our new priesthood, was both a priest and a king;[29] and always, in the law of nature, the eldest of the principal stocks were both kings and high priests; as St. Jerome witnesseth.[30] So is it plain that Noah, Abraham, Isaac, Jacob, and the like had the rule spiritual and temporal over their families and people. And so likewise in the law, Moses was both the high temporal officer and also a chief priest. Eli judged not only in temporal but spiritual causes forty years together. Finally, the Maccabees, Judas, Jonathan, Simon, and others were both godly high priests, wise judges in politic, and valiant captains in martial affairs. Even so, the chief bishops of Christ's Church, our supreme pastors in earth, by God's providence and by the grants of our first most Christian emperors and kings, and by the humble and zealous devotion of the faithful princes and people afterward, have their temporal states, dominions, and patrimonies whereby they most justly hold and possess the same, and are thereby lawful princes temporal and may most rightfully by their sovereignty make wars in their own or other men's just quarrel, as occasion shall urge them thereunto.

And whatsoever the enemies of God's Church and See Apostolic do bark or blaspheme against the Pope's high pre-eminence in these things (as they do no less indeed against all spiritual sovereignty), there is no king nor man in Christendom that hath better title to his state, or so many years of prescription for rightful possession, or so long and sure protection from God, in such infinite mutability of states and kingdoms, or such great likelihood of constancy and continuance, as hath the temporal state of

[28] Archetype, example.

[29] [Gen. 14]:18; [Heb. 7]:1–3.

[30] [In quaest. Hebrai.] St. Jerome, *Hebraicae quaestiones in libro Geneseos,* commenting on Gen. 14:18–19.

the See Apostolic. For, as for the spiritual function and power thereof, it shall not fail till the day of judgment, though (to use St. Augustine's words)[31] heretics never cease to bay and bark on every hand round about it.

And as these human succors of temporal things be often necessary for the Church's peaceable regiment and the double honor due to the chief pastors of our souls, so the free gift of such things by devout princes and people is marvelously commended in the example of Barnabas and others, who of devotion sold their lands and goods and dedicated the price thereof to God's Church by the disposition of the Apostles, humbly laying the same down at their feet.[32] As, on the other side, the profane persons that disdain such honors and livelihoods of the Church and seek to defraud her of the same may be warned by the terrible death of Ananias and Sapphira, which they suffered by St. Peter's word for their like sacrilegious fact and conceit. For if these were thought worthy to be thus excommunicated (seeing it was an excommunication according to St. Augustine's judgment)[33] and withal were so extremely punished corporally for withholding (upon pretense perhaps of a little better consideration of their necessity to come) a piece only of that which they promised to God before, in the Church's behalf, and yet was not actually bestowed; how much more do they deserve excommunication and death, or rather damnation perpetual, that endeavor to spoil the mother and mistress of all churches in the world of her prerogative and patrimony and sacrilegiously to rob her not of some part of their own gifts but of all that by the devotion of others, the first and most faithful princes, hath been for the honor of Christ and His chief apostle, with great alacrity and good will, bestowed that

[31] [Li. de util. credendi.] St. Augustine, *De utilitate credendi,* cap. 35.
[32] Acts 4:36–37.
[33] [Lib. 3. ca. 1. cont. Parmeni.] St. Augustine, *Contra epistolam Parmeniani,* lib. 3, cap. 1.

way? The which alms and patrimony dispensed by the godly prudence and charity of the Apostolic Bishops redoundeth more to the avail of God's Church and the poor thereof, to Christ's honor, and to the benefit of all Christianity (be it spoken without comparison and to the honor of God alone), than any temporal prince's patrimony living, though many of their worldly abilities be far greater than any Pope's are or ever have been. Which every indifferent man that beholdeth the immortal works of charity which this one blessed Pope hath done in the days of his high priesthood must of necessity confess.

Whereof we thought meet to make some mention in this place for that both other Protestants are not ashamed to accuse the Holy See of robbery and rapine in getting and holding the temporal state which now it hath so many ages occupied to the great honor of God, as also for that this libeler often glanceth at some injuries which he pretendeth to have been done by the Pope's tyrannous and excessive power, as he termeth it, to the princes of the world in this case; sometimes seditiously and subtly suggesting to the Emperor and other the greatest and best kings of Christendom to abridge his power; sometimes craftily commending them, upon a devilish and deceitful fiction of his own, that they only tolerate his title and jurisdiction for a time and of policy, so far as they see it is not prejudicial to their own states; otherwise neither caring for his curses, excommunications, canons, nor commandments no more than the Protestant princes do, who have withdrawn from him in their states all, both temporal emoluments and spiritual prerogatives.

Of which restraint, limitation, or plain contempt of the Pope's power and censures the writer allegeth certain examples of divers Catholic kings and countries, that the English may seem to have done no new thing in this their shameful revolt from the See Apostolic and contempt of the ecclesiastical curse and excommunication. Which this profane atheist affirmeth none but the simple people to fear or care for; wise men and princes to have no scruple or conscience at all in such matters, but to resist by arms all laws and ordinances as they list.

For proof whereof he bringeth (to no purpose) how divers kings of France have by their laws pragmatics restrained the Popes of divers claims, prerogatives, and profits; how they in England in old time limited and abridged his jurisdiction by the law specially called praemunire; how the noble Emperor Charles the Fifth feared not their curses when by his captains he besieged, took, and sacked Rome, imprisoned and ransomed the Pope himself; how his son, the King Catholic now reigning, nothing respected excommunication when his army was led before Rome walls by the conduction of the Duke of Alva; how King Henry the Seventh resisted the Pope in a matter of alum; and his niece Queen Mary herself (as much as she was devoted to the Roman religion) withstood him in favor of her cousin Cardinal Pole against Doctor Peto about a cardinal's hat; the bringer of which hat and the bulls for the said Peto she did forbid to enter the realm, commanding them to be stayed at Calais; and finally that Cardinal Pole himself, having the Queen for him in the cause, had no fear to disobey the Pope's commandments and his threatened excommunications or curses but continued legate and made the other poor Peto, being an Observant friar, to go a-begging still. Thus much in sense saith the libeler in defense of their resistance of the Pope and contempt of his censures.[34]

But look attentively into the particular reasons and examples of this his discourse, and you shall find nothing but fraud and falsehood. First, it is a most impious and godless conceit that the Emperor and other great kings and potentates of Christendom, either of old or at this present, have suffered or do yet endure the Pope to command or have jurisdiction in their countries only for some respects in policy and so far as they list, rather than upon conscience and for religion; when it is certain that his spiritual

[34] Cecil, pp. 26–28.

authority and high prelacy over all faithful princes and people (as instituted by Christ, clearly deduced out of the Scriptures, approved by decrees of ancient councils, testimonies of all the old doctors, and by both imperial and national laws of the Christian world) is acknowledged in conscience of all Catholic kings that have been or yet be within the happy unity of Holy Church. And it is a most shameless slander of Their Sacred Majesties that this atheist would make the world believe that, pretending conscience, devotion, religion, and sincerity in their obedience to the See Apostolic, they do all indeed of policy. As well might this Machiavellian bear men in hand that the Christian religion is no otherwise admitted in commonwealths but so far forth as it serveth for policy and the advancement of the prince or temporal state. And God grant this be not the mark that our Protestants and politiques shoot at; much it is to be feared that it is our English elne [35] and analogy of faith for measure of all actions. And certes [36] to no other end they use their pretended ministry and new clergy of their creation, occupying them to entertain and amaze the people "with the Word of the Lord," whilst they accomplish their worldly and wicked intentions; as apparent it is that the good author of this libel would not, if he were a prince (as such be too near princes' elbows these days), admit either Peter, Paul, or Christ Himself into any jurisdiction either spiritual or temporal within his realm, nor would be deprived or excommunicated by any of them more than now by the Pope, nor further deal with them than his advantage and policy requireth.

And indeed by the means of such Lycurgians [37] as this, we have in England new laws against all claim of jurisdiction spiritual or temporal that can be made by any person whosoever, born out of the realm. Which (no question) might exclude Christ and His apostles no less than their successors, being as well

[35] Comfort, grace. [36] Certainly.

[37] [The Machiavellian drift of this libeler.] Lycurgus was an early Spartan lawmaker.

foreigners as they. Wherein it seemeth singularly to be noted that this crafty politique putteth no difference betwixt spiritual regiment and temporal; yea, rather taketh away all ecclesiastical jurisdiction, calling, in this his pestiferous libel (which you shall not, as we think, read in any other of the heretics' writings of these days), the Queen's spiritual power, which she challengeth against the Pope's supremacy, her "regality"; seeking by all means possible wholly to extinguish the hierarchy and prelacy of Christ's Church, and concluding all in kingly authority. Whereby, as also by the Scriptures which they, foolishly in the sight of wise men, but to the simple persuasively, allege that "all men must obey the king as the chief or precellent,"[38] they exclude Peter from his high spiritual function, which he had in the time of Nero, and give unto the said Nero as his "regality" no less than now they yield both papal and all other bishoply and ecclesiastical authority in England to the Queen as a piece of her "regality."

As though there were no difference between a king and a priest. As though there were no distinction betwixt Christ's Body Mystical and a body politic or human commonwealth. As though Christ had given His said Body, Spouse, and spiritual Commonwealth to be governed either unto kings and emperors (who were then and some hundred years afterward persecutors of His Church and faith, and yet had as large, whole, and perfect "regality" as any faithful prince hath); or unto Christian kings afterward, who are, by receiving Christ's sweet yoke and faith, made children and members of the Church and not heads thereof. As though our Savior had not in His time appointed special officers for the regiment of His Church; or the Holy Ghost afterward not placed apostles, prelates, pastors, and doctors to govern the same even to the end of the world.

This devilish confusion of things and attributing all spiritual

[38] I Pet. 2:13: "Submit yourselves to every ordinance of man [Vulgate: *humanae creaturae*] for the Lord's sake, whether it be to the king as supreme [Vulgate: *praecellenti*]. . . ."

sovereignty to the temporal prince and power, which the Scripture calleth for distinction sake *humanam creaturam,*[39] or rather this turning all prelacy into "regality" (if it be permitted), will take away the very life and essence of the Church of God and of all religion, and will plane the way to Antichrist, who shall by the title of his only "regality" destroy (if it be possible) all power spiritual and temporal and set himself to be adored above whatsoever is named in heaven or earth.

Woe be to our nation and to the sins of our people, which God hath suffered to be the first example of this abominable converting of the spiritual power and regiment of our souls into our kings' "regality"! And fie on this godless libeler and his profane intention that by the defense of this special turpitude of our kings and country so foully slandereth also other most godly princes with his shameful surmise that they do but permit in their dominions the Pope's authority of policy, and no further than is for their advantage! Whose impudent calumniation may easily be refuted by Their Majesties' zealous devotion and most sincere obedience to His Holiness in all matters of faith and religion (wherein his superiority specially and properly consisteth); by their daily royal offices done against heretics for defense of the Roman See and faith and by open profession of the same both in their lives and deaths; by their continual resistance of the enemies thereof, to their infinite charge, yea, and often to the hazard of their persons, crowns, and dominions; by the due observation of the holy decrees of the See Apostolic as far as the great looseness of this time and the manifold importunity of heretics and atheists will permit; by exact justice done in many of their kingdoms upon the rebels of the Church and Holy See; and finally, by their continual intelligence with His Holiness in all their affairs of conscience and religion and the use of all his spiritual graces, indulgences, and benedictions with as great humility as the poorest Catholic man in the world.

[39] [I Pet. 2]:13. Cf. n. 38.

But the adversary telleth us for all this that divers princes and countries before named have abridged, limited, and resisted the Pope's doings and authority. To which we say that in such cases we should not stand always upon examples but rather on reason and law. For a man might say that Herod killed John Baptist; Philip made away Babylas; Theodosius banished St. Chrysostom; Constans persecuted Athanasius; King Henry of England caused to be murdered his primate and holy Metropolitan, Thomas of Canterbury; and many more have resisted the bishops and pastors of their own souls, whereof divers have been sorry and sore repented their iniquity afterward, as our said Henry the Second amongst other. Whose examples may not be made a rule how kings should behave themselves toward their prelates. God forbid! No more in this other kind we now speak of need we to allow all the pragmatics, praemunires, or other national decrees and provisions which every particular prince hath made or may make (though in conscience Catholic) by which the Pope's jurisdiction and pre-eminences in some sort and in some cases are abridged and limited.

As, on the other side again, we neither need nor will condemn the same because they be not of things mere spiritual but either plain temporal or mixed; such as had either by the prince's laws or custom of countries been granted of devotion to the See Apostolic before, and afterward, upon farther consideration by the difference of times or of less devotion, revoked, upon pretense of preservation of the temporal state and benefiting particular provinces, unto which the emoluments and large privileges yielded before to the chief bishop and other of the clergy might seem some hindrance; or else were of that nature that the supreme bishop might indeed of reason challenge as things incident to his high office and requisite for the better administration of the same but yet not such for all that as were necessarily or by divine laws appertaining directly to his spiritual regiment and jurisdiction and therefore might by his wisdom either be tolerated (as many things in this case be which he alloweth not) for avoiding of scandals or for other detriment of souls; or by composition (for the better retaining princes and provinces in ecclesiastical peace) be condescended and agreed unto; the limitation or imminution [40] of his accidental rights, honors, and pre-eminences nothing esteemed so material unto him as the salvation and preservation of kingdoms and countries in the unity of Christ's faith and Church.

There is no human prerogative, be it holden never so rightly or given never so justly for the honor of Christ and his high office, but he may either himself for just causes yield it up or by violence either of persecutors or carnal and worldly persons be bereaved thereof. Only his pre-eminence and prelacy over our souls and over all Christian countries and persons, be they public or private; and whatsoever our Savior granted to the Prince of the Apostles (upon whom He builded His whole Church, and to whom and to his successors He gave the keys of heaven with full commission to bind, loose,[41] punish, pardon, feed, confirm in faith, decide, and determine, etc.), this he cannot yield; this can no earthly power take from him; this doth no Catholic king or country restrain him of; neither ever were there any laws made in France, Spain, or in our own country (so long as it was Catholic) for abridging his apostolical and mere spiritual authority in the premises.

Though, otherwise, as it falleth out in a man's own person, wherein (as the Apostle writeth and as we all feel) the flesh resisteth the spirit and contrariwise the spirit the flesh,[42] each one of them seeking after a sort to enlarge his own limits and commodities by some hindrance of the other; which combat and conflict, notwithstanding, is either tolerable or not damnable so long as the inferior, which is the flesh, by over-greedy appetite of her own advancement destroyeth not the superior, which is the soul; so doubtless in a Christian commonwealth the spiritual and

[40] Diminution, lessening. [41] Matt. 16:18–19. [42] Gal. 5:17.

temporal state, being joined together as it were in one body, must needs keep some moderate strife and combat for maintenance of either of their limits in external regiment; which may be borne withal of each side, so long as neither part seeketh over-obstinately the destruction of the other but do agree and conjoin in preservation of the principal.

But where the body politic (as it is now in our miserable country) by intolerable disorder doth strive not so much with the See Apostolic and Body Mystical of Christ for things either indifferent or not merely necessary to the spiritual regiment, but by evident rape and violence against the laws of God and man bereaveth Christ's Vicar of his whole sovereignty, high priesthood, and prelacy and the Catholic Church of all the rights and dowries which our Master her Spouse endowed her withal and tyrannically draweth all to the prince's regality, altering by the authority thereof the whole faith and true worship of God into abominable apostasy, schism, and desolation; there the libeler can find no example in any Christian laws or countries throughout the world, in any age, to prove his purpose, though vainly and impertinently he alleges these concordats of France and other nations, as also the compositions of England with the Pope, or what orders and laws soever besides, either lawful or unlawful, concerning restraint of any papal or ecclesiastical power, which serve nothing at all for defense of the late English general and most impudent revolt from the unity of God's Catholic and Apostolic Church.

Many things might the worldlings of our country even in Catholic times attempt for their own advantage against the commodities of the Church. Our kings and other, in times of dissension with certain Popes of their days, might drive the weaker to unequal conditions and serve their own ambitious humors to the Church's disadvantage. Some laws might also pass by the powerableness of princes in their own dominions, the See Apostolic utterly reclaiming against them, which, though they were not directly against any point of faith or religion, yet might be very prejudicial to the state ecclesiastical and liberties of Holy Church. As the law of praemunire [43] was, which is mentioned by the adversary, against which divers Popes (specially Gregory the Eleventh and Martin the Fifth) opposed themselves earnestly and dealt with King Edward the Third and Henry the Sixth for abrogating the same, which they both promised to do but never did; and consequently it remaineth still in his first unconscionable force (if the makers had any such meaning as their followers have found out), for that it may by calumnious interpretation be used at the only pleasure of the prince, to the confiscation of all churchmen's goods, imprisonment of their persons, and destruction of the whole clergy. Whereof King Henry the Eighth, in the beginning of his schism, gave an horrible example. Which iniquity the libeler himself is not ashamed to commend and to propound to other princes for imitation.

These injustices and the like may be by some kings committed and are (as we have said) for peace and charity's sake borne by them who are taught by their Master and by the Apostolical Bishops of the primitive Church to set more by one soul than by all the honors, goods, and privileges in the world otherwise. So that God be honored, whether causes at the first instance, or by appeal only, be deferred to the court of Rome or no; whether the Pope, prince, clergy, or people appoint the pastors or no (a thing diversely used in divers ages); the Church can bear all and turn all to good so long as the true faith and substance of ecclesiastical jurisdiction be not destroyed.

Wherein yet this may be comfortable to all obedient children of the Church and worthy to be considered of discreet persons: that in all, or surely in most part of such limitations, restraints, diminishings, or alteration of the Pope's and Church's authority, things have afterward so fallen out that wise men heartily wish no change ever had been made. And for the evidence thereof we

[43] 38 Edw. III, st. 2. Cf. Cecil, p. 26.

refer all men to the pondering of this one point specially amongst many, concerning the nominations and elections of bishops, abbots, and other prelates: whether the world went not as well when such things passed by canonical election or the Pope's provision as it hath done since or hereafter ever is like to do. At the beginning of such alterations men pretended reasons for the particular Church's commodities of sundry nations, which a few years' experience and the event of things have in most matters controlled.

But, were it well or evil, it can neither be example nor warrant to our present country to destroy abbeys, kill the religious, murder God's priests, imprison all the sacred persons of bishops throughout the realm; to hate, blaspheme, abolish all authority and jurisdiction apostolical; yea, and to make a solemn public prayer in the litany that "God would deliver our country from the Pope," [44] instead of that which the whole Christian world devoutly singeth and sayeth daily, *Ut Dominum Apostolicum et omnes ecclesiasticos ordines in sancta religione conservare digneris.*[45] Would any man think that either they should fall to such barbarousness, or to such impudency, as to defend so gross impiety by the examples of other Catholic kings, countries, and times, in the cases afore said?

Or can it be possible they could imagine the difference between King Henry the Seventh and the Pope that then was, about a matter of alum, should warrant Her Majesty that now is or her counselors to stand against the high priest of God and to go to law with him for his spiritual prelacy? What a grosshead [46]

[44] The phrase, ". . . from the tyranny of the Bishop of Rome and all his detestable enormities . . . good Lord deliver us," was included in the litany in the Books of Common Prayer issued under Edward VI and in Elizabeth's 1558 prayer book but omitted in the Book of Common Prayer issued in 1559.

[45] "That it may please Thee to preserve our Apostolic Lord, and all orders of the Church in holy religion," in the Litany of the Saints.

[46] Thick-headed person, dullard.

is this libeler, or rather what a deceitful person (for he cannot be so rude as not to know the difference of things so far distant), that allegeth the wars sometimes fallen out betwixt certain Popes and princes about their temporal interests to prove that Catholic kings care not for the Pope or that themselves may resist him by arms and contemn his authority in matters of faith and religion!

Wherein his examples also are very evil chosen when he goeth about to make us believe that Charles the Fifth cared not for the Pope's excommunication and curse, because his soldiers under the conduction of Bourbon [47] committed horrible violence and villainy in the city of Rome against His Holiness, the cardinals, and all other whom they found there as their prey. Where indeed the said noble Emperor, though then very young, yet was neither consenting thereunto nor had any knowledge of the disorder till it was done, purging himself thereof afterward to the Pope very humbly; and the said Bourbon, author of that wicked enterprise, by God's mighty hand and judgment, and for a sign how highly that impious fact displeased His Divine Majesty, was slain suddenly, and, as it is thought, the first of all other, upon the wall of the suburbs. Let all those that take such examples take heed of the like ends.

As for the loyalty of the Most Catholic King that now is of Spain to the See Apostolic, notwithstanding what temporal differences soever have fallen, or may fall out between them, it were too much idleness to stand upon against this fond wrangler. And the Duke of Alva, His Majesty's general, behaved himself even at that time when he had his army before Rome (as well of his own singular devotion as by his King's commandment) most religiously and honorably, without any violence in the world or damage to the city, other than the waste of a few places of pleasure, vines, and orchards about the walls; for which this good

[47] Charles de Bourbon, former Constable of France, renegade commander of imperial troops for Charles V, was killed during the unauthorized assault of his army on Rome in 1527.

fellow with whom we deal maketh much moan (as it seemeth); where indeed he would rather have wished the whole city both sacked and sunk for devotion.

But these princes (saith he) cared not for the Pope's curses when they thus pursued their claims both by arms and laws. The truth is that the Pope excommunicateth not every one that either resisteth him in temporal quarrels or matter of emoluments of their peculiar churches or countries, whether it be by laws or arms. And therefore there is no cause why in such cases where no censures are usually published this libeler should say they "regard no curses nor anathematizings," etc. Neither then also when the injury done to Holy Church or Apostolic See seemeth so evident to the Pope that there may appear some reasonable cause of excommunicating the impugners, and the parties so censured in the contrary side, upon persuasion of their right, do persist notwithstanding in the defense thereof; not then (I say), do they contemn the censure (as is untruly conceived by the adversary), but rather, abstaining from the holy sacraments and company of such as to them by law are forbidden, do use humble means toward His Holiness for his better information in the cause, and do seek that the matter may be ended by good order of composition or arbitrament of other princes and godly persons. Or if (in such causes of strife for worldly commodities, where the temporal prince may sometimes either have the right on his side or seem to himself in conscience, or by the judgment of godly, learned, and indifferent men, to have it) we grant that he may without fear of censures by arms or otherwise pursue his just claim without impeachment of his obedience in spiritual affairs; may, therefore, sacrilegious persons, as heretics, apostates, and open obstinate offenders, contemn at their pleasures and violently resist the sentence of Holy Church? No, there is no match in these matters.

What if the late Queen Mary of England stayed the messenger of the Pope bringing a discharge of the late renowned Cardinal Pole from his authority legatine and a cardinal's hat for a person, though very godly, yet known to be unfit, till His Holiness might be better informed of the man and of the whole matter, as immediately he was, with all diligence and humility, by the said most devout princess. Should this be an example or encouragement to others of plain disobedience and revolt? Or wholly to abandon the Pope's authority and to invest a woman (which is against nature) in his supremacy and spiritual charge over all her subjects' souls? No, surely; no more than of reason it should have served Her Majesty's Council (sitting once in consultation together of the case) to deny entrance to the *Nuncio Apostolico* [48] sent by Pius the Fourth about the third year of Her Highness' reign to require and beseech her in God to send some of her learned men to the general Council of Trent then in hand, as most other great potentates of Christianity did, bringing with him a safe-conduct for their peaceable passage, audience, and entertainment, notwithstanding their contrary religion and faction.

So did the English Council then make their advantage of that unlike fact of the late noble Queen, at once both to maintain their unlike separation from the Christian world and the fellowship of other Catholic kings, as also (and that perhaps especially) to cover the ignorance, fear, and insufficiency of their superintendents; who, though Her Majesty and others of the nobility were well inclined to send some of them for the honor of the realm, yet for fear of burning (as they pretended), but indeed for fear of the Catholics' learning and their own shame, the good fellows made all the suit underhand they could that none might be enforced thither. And so at length it was agreed, and, moreover, that His Holiness' ambassador should not so much as be heard or

[48] Abbot Girolamo Martinengo, sent to Elizabeth by Pius IV with a request that she send ambassadors to the Council of Trent. After some delay, the Privy Council decided on May 1, 1561, to refuse him admission to the kingdom. For a full account, see C. G. Bayne, *Anglo-Roman Relations, 1558–1565* (Oxford, 1913), chs. 4 and 5.

suffered to come within the realm, upon the warrant (I say) of the foresaid unlike example of the former Queen Mary.

Which also serveth them further ever since, not only to renounce all the old authority, power, and interest of the See Apostolic over our country, and to make the chief bishop thereof a mere stranger, as other worldly princes of the provinces about us that have nothing to do with our affairs (whose messengers yet and ambassadors for needful intercourse and mutual intelligence by the law of nations they willingly admit, either in peace or wars as occasion serveth), but also to make him a devil, an Antichrist, and worse than the Turk himself, whose messengers (as the world seeth) may have audience with them and good correspondence, whereas the Pope can have none. Whereby is discovered the misery of wicked heresy and the extreme hatred that rebellious children do bear to their mother, whom they unhappily have forsaken and obstinately resist to their own perdition. And this shall be sufficient to show how wrongfully and unreasonably this libeler hath sought to defend their English general revolt from the Church of Rome, and their contempt of His Holiness' censures, by the examples of some Catholic princes' differences and worldly debates with certain Popes and prelates of the same upon matter of far different nature and quality from faith and religion.

Chapter VIII

That the separation of the prince and realm from the unity of the Church and See Apostolic and fall from Catholic religion is the only cause of all the present fears and dangers that the state seemeth to stand in. And that they unjustly attribute the same to the Pope's Holiness or Catholics and untruly call them enemies of the realm

JEROBOAM, for the better establishing of his sovereignty over the ten tribes, thought it an high policy to divide the temporal lot and partage, which by God's appointment was fallen unto him, from all communion and society with the other remaining in Jewry and serving their Lord in the temple at Jerusalem. And therefore instituted for himself and his people strange gods, new ways of worship, other unordered base priests, and several places to serve in; and all upon this human imagination, that if his people at their sundry appointed times should go up to the temple to do their sacrifice and other rites according to the law, as also converse with the priests and people of the other party and be subject to them in matters of conscience and religion as they were bound, that then they might easily be induced or much tempted to return to Solomon's successors in Jerusalem again; and that his people being subject to him only in temporal matters, and not in religion, he might seem to be but half a king.[1] Yea, as at this day our Protestants (for flattering the person whom hereby they will ruin) use often to say of our ancient kings of England and of other Catholic countries abroad that they were but half kings in their own realms, if we compare their authorities with the ample regality of Her Majesty now reigning, whose jurisdiction extendeth above the old wont, to all causes spiritual no less than temporal.

Well, so thought Jeroboam then, and so did he, and was (no doubt) most highly commended for the device by his politiques that were about him. But yet this thing which was esteemed so prudently done for preservation of his state was after as well by the mouth of God's prophet as by the miserable event of things proved within a very few years to be the only destruction of his whole house and perpetual calamity of his people.

The secular prudence of the children of this world, compared to the true wisdom of the godly, and resisting any way the course of virtue and salvation, is found, in fine, always deficient, and, in

[1] I Kings 12–14.

truth, folly. But it never appeareth so weak, deceitful, and pernicious as when it opposeth itself to the ordinance of God, to the force of His Spirit and truth, and to the Spouse, kingdom, and priesthood of Christ. In which case the giant's building of Babel prevailed not; the proposition of Ahitophel was dashed; [2] the purpose of Herod for murdering of Christ in His cradle, lest he should bereave him of his crown, and of the Jews afterward in prosecuting His death to save their state and country from the Romans, was turned to their own destruction. Saul found how hard it was to spurn against the spur. Julianus cried out, *Vicisti Galilee,*[3] that is, "Thou hast the victory of me, Man of Galilee" (so that apostate of contempt called Christ); and, finally, true it will ever prove that there is no counsel against God, nor no long peace to any that resist Him.

And therefore those princes and people only to be happy both in this world and in the next, and their states alone lawful and durable, that have learned faithfully to submit their scepters to Christ's sweet yoke and to join their terrene kingdoms with the priesthood and Spouse of Him by Whom all kings do reign; of Whose Church it is said long sithence by the prophet, and proved by the experience of all ages, that the nation and people that serveth her not shall perish; whosoever hear and obey her not must be accounted as ethnics; whosoever despise her and her governors despise Christ Himself; whosoever refuse her regiment and superiority, specially for matter of faith and religion, and would rather have a king over them to lead both their body and souls, do not so much refuse to be ruled by God's priests as they reject Christ Himself, being not contented that He should reign over them. Finally, whosoever do give to Caesar that which is due to God,[4] preposterously preferring the temporal prerogative of

[2] II Sam. 17, report of the rejection of Ahitophel's proposals for fighting David.

[3] This report of the Emperor Julian the Apostate's dying words, 363, can be found in Theodoret, *Ecclesiastical History,* lib. 3, cap. 20.

[4] Cf. Matt. 22:21; Mark 12:17; Luke 20:25.

worldly princes before the spiritual power of the priests of the New Testament, directly do repine against God's ordinance and shall at length prove (with what human prowess, power, or prudence soever they sustain their factions) that they have unevenly and unadvisedly matched their combat.

The house they impugn is founded upon an impregnable rock; there is no tempest of heathen, heretical, or domestical persecution, nor no storms of weather or water, that can overthrow it. Hell itself and the powers thereof cannot prevail against it. And to the end that the Nimrods [5] and other new evangelical giants of our country mistake us not, nor beguile themselves in their desperate contradiction against the City of God, St. Augustine telleth them, it is the See and succession of the Church of Rome which is so invincibly guarded. These be his words: "Count the priests from the very See of Peter, and in that order of Fathers who to whom hath succeeded; that same is the rock which the proud gates of hell do not overcome." [6]

The chosen cornerstone of this building is, by the prophets and by Christ's own declaration, such as whosoever falleth upon it shall be broken, and on whom it falleth it shall crush him in pieces. Not only the faith of Peter by Our Lord's promise and protection, being infallible, but the apostolic regiment, by the assistance of the Holy Ghost, shall endure to the end of the world. Which hath already borne down by her patience and constancy all the heathen emperors, against whom the high throne of Christ's priesthood in earth and tribunal of faith and religion was placed and preserved by the mighty arm of God in the very chief city and seat of their empire for divers hundred years together after Christ's ascension, notwithstanding all the human means of worldly policy or tyrannical cruelty that could be devised or exercised against them. Those great monarchs in that time more doubting and fearing the Popes in their poverty and persecution, and more loath to have them in their own city of

[5] Tyrants.

[6] St. Augustine [*Psalmus contra partem Donati.*]

Rome so near them (if they could have chosen) than any other powerable competitor or emulator of their empire; as St. Cyprian saith of Decius the Emperor in regard of Pope Cornelius,[7] who was therefore afterward (as all other his predecessors before him) martyred.

By the same promise and like assistance of the Holy Ghost the same See hath worn out all the old heretics, of far greater power, pride, and learning than these Protestants be; sustained not only by some particular princes of certain provinces but by divers most mighty Emperors, persecuting the Catholic bishops, priests, and other through the whole Roman world as heavily as now some smaller princes Protestants do within the bounds of their dominions only. The same See hath gone through all other distresses, foreign and domestical; standeth and flourisheth now (notwithstanding all the threats, molition,[8] and machination of her forsakers) in all virtue, strength, and glory. Never more loved, honored, and regarded of the Catholic kings in the world. Never more reverenced and obeyed of the Church's children. Never more feared of her forsakers. As we may see by the desperate and most obstinate course they take in our poor afflicted country: not so much thinking to defend themselves by the daily shedding of most innocent men's blood, as basely to wreak their unquenchable anger at the See of Rome, which they fear must be the instrument of Christ's rod of justice toward them in time for forsaking the fellowship thereof in Christian faith and religion. Themselves doubting that the stroke of this excommunication (so often revived by themselves) will never in the end fall void (as otherwhere we see it hath not), though by the flattery of a few years' good fortune our men at home cry peace, sport, and security to the poor people, persuading them that all is well and safe by the killing of a few priests, when there is no other way of

[7] St. Cyprian, Letter 52, cap. 9, to Antonianus, about Cornelius and Novitian.

[8] Contrivance, device.

saving our beloved country (assuredly) from perdition both temporal and eternal but by repentance and humble craving pardon of God's Church.

If they could kill all the clergy and true believers in the world, and had the Pope's own person to do their pleasure with him; or could make away as many Popes one after another as they have done priests and as the first persecutors of our faith did martyr; yet could they not prevail nor escape the hand of God, revenging always at length these contempts, schisms, heresies, and apostasies with memorable punishment. In warning whereof He giveth us a good admonition by His own writ, when He saith: *Ne dixeris peccavi, et quid mihi accidit triste? Altissimus enim est patiens redditor.* "Do not say, 'I have sinned and no misfortune hath fallen upon me for the same.' For that God is a patient restorer or payer." [9] So that God payeth home at length, albeit with great patience; and then taketh the saying of St. Austin's [10] place, that He recompenseth His slowness with the greatness of His punishment.

Into what desolation all Africa was finally brought by the schism and sect of the Donatists; how the heresy of the Arians, after the wearisome toil almost of the whole world for many years, discharged itself at length into Muhammadanism; how the division of the Oriental Church from the See of Peter hath been the loss of liberty and the eternal destruction of so many noble, most free, and flourishing provinces of that part, no man can be ignorant. As also not see into what hazard and extreme perils these devilish doctrines of our days and the seditious followers of the same have brought the glorious kingdom of France, with the states of Flanders, Germany, Poland, and most of the north parts of the world near unto us. Which consideration draweth us also into the doleful account of our English present fears and miseries; and much more to the foresight of our calamities to come: seeing clearly by the records of our country that no nation hath oftener

[9] [Ecclus. 5]:4.

[10] Variant spelling of Augustine.

sustained general alteration of the state and government than ours; nor yet ever any violent change or mutation but for some notable contempt of the house of God. As appeareth by the sundry invasions and conquests made on us and by the notes which Gildas the Wise, Venerable Bede, and other men of experience and foresight have in their monuments [11] set down, which were too long and needless to rehearse.

Only this is ever to be borne in mind: that when our kings of England had good intelligence with the Pope and mutual offices of love and honor passed betwixt them, and our body politic and civil magistrate had all godly and charitable correspondence with the spiritual commonwealth of Christ's Church and the prelates thereof, then had we a most happy and victorious country, blessed of God with all spiritual and temporal benediction. In such sort, surely, that to remember only what grace and glory our realm hath received by joining and submitting itself to the laws and regiment of Holy Church might make our hearts joyful, if the consideration of this our present infelicity, by severing ourselves from the same, did not eftsoons turn all to inconsolable sorrow.

Truly whatsoever is or hath been singular to our country's honor either in church, city, university, college, school, monastery, library, or any part of the commonwealth, not least renowned in the world, all came of the Catholic religion and the greatest part of the famous prelates of our nation. As likewise what piety, justice, fidelity, conscience, devotion, fear of God, peace, order, obedience, truth, and honesty was once in any state of men, it can be referred to no other but to the godly discipline, forcible doctrine, and manifold graces of the Church and her holy sacraments. As, on the contrary, the waste of all goodness is now by many years' experience found to proceed of the Protestants' not only fruitless but pernicious preachers and doctrine. Who by in-

[11] Gildas, *Liber querulus de excidio Britanniae,* 6th c.; Bede, *Historia ecclesiastica,* 731.

vading the old honorable rooms of most noble prelates (founded neither by them nor for them) have made pitiful spoil of the goodliest ecclesiastical states and monuments almost in all Christendom. And by taking away the daily dreadful sacrifice, confession, chastity, fidelity, obedience, humility, order, and all honesty of life and manners have given our people doleful experience of the deadly fruit of their schism and revolt from the See Apostolic and Catholic communion of the faithful world.

Which we are forced to treat of here more largely through the importunate and odious vaunting of this libeler concerning their felicity and unwonted prosperity in England since their breaking from the unity of the Church of Rome; specially sith the Queen (saith he) was cursed and excommunicated by the Pope, all matters have gone luckily. Not talking at all of the realm or people's increase in religion, devotion, conscience, fidelity, honor, and honesty; for therein the difference and decay from the old manners in all estates is too notorious and lamentable to behold: never so much injustice, never so much extortion, never so much theft, never so much pride, ebriety,[12] gluttony, riot, and all other sin and abomination. But only (as though he knew no other world or heaven but this) he profanely and proudly in sundry places of his little book maketh repetition of their good luck in this life, of their abundance in wealth, of their long peace, of the fruitfulness of their fields ever since the Pope's curses. Much like to the irreligious tyrant that never liked his luck better than after he had committed sacrilege and robbed sacred things. So this triumphant libeler braggeth that "the Queen hath reigned as long as three Popes; five times as long as Queen Mary her sister; in such felicity that any other prince of Christendom would be glad to have some piece of her good fortune." [13]

Which too-too profane and proud cogitations and comparisons of this writer we will not attribute to Her Majesty or to her prudent counselors, who have yet more feeling and sense in such things

[12] Drunkenness.

[13] Cf. Cecil, p. 25.

than to make so much of a few years' more or less reign and other terrene felicity; that either Her Majesty should pronounce of herself (as surely she will not) the words of that mystical woman of the Prophet Isaiah: "I sit a queen, and widow I am not, and mourning I shall never see,"[14] or that her wise counselors should admire her happiness for this thing and second her with such applause as the people used to Herod in the height of his arrogancy and proud proposition: *Voces dei, non hominis.*[15] They are all too wise (I say) and over-well experienced to do or say thus; for they know the judgments of God incontinently following. They are not ignorant that before ruin the heart is exalted.[16] They cannot forget the variableness and inconstancy of mortal things, with the sudden fall of very fortunate persons. They have read of Polycrates, King of Samos, whose prosperity being extraordinary, he was by his friends, and specially by the King of Egypt, advised to procure to himself some grief and alteration of fortune, lest some memorable calamity should in the end ensue, as indeed there did. Which example St. Gregory Nazianzen thinketh in this case worthy to be remembered.[17] They cannot but esteem St. Austin's judgment of good credit in this matter, who thinketh that nothing is more dangerous or unlucky to a Christian than to live long in continual prosperity.

Wherefore, all this vanity and triumphant flourish proceedeth only from the vein of our libeler, who is one of that popular stamp which in the psalm blessed the people that had their barns and butteries full, their sheep pregnant, their cattle fair and fat, all void of ruin, care, and clamor; where Christian men must measure their matters otherwise and say with the prophet: *Beatus populus cujus Dominus Deus ejus;* "That people is happy whose

[14] Isa. [47]:8.

[15] [Acts 12]:22: "It is the voice of a god and not of a man."

[16] [Prov. 16]:18: "Pride goeth before destruction, and an haughty spirit before a fall."

[17] St. Gregory Nazianzen, *Carminum,* lib. 2, sect. 1, cap. 24; sect. 2, cap. 3.

Lord and Master is God,"[18] without Whom, and out of Whose house (which is the Church) all human felicity is but matter of more damnation and, truly, where it is extraordinary, ever a very sore sign of everlasting perdition. Which we do not say for that we account not this terrene felicity a great benefit of God oftentimes, as well to private persons as specially to commonwealths; or that we reckon this few years' prosperity of our country anything comparable to the constant honor and felicity of our forefathers' days; but for that it maketh no certain, nor often no probable proof of God's favor toward them that enjoy the same, being lightly common to good and evil; though of the two more ordinary to the wicked and worser sort than to the better; because Lazarus often receiveth evil in his life, as the greedy glutton doth the contrary.[19] Yet our libeler thought it a good popular persuasion to the vulgar sort of men that have fastened their eyes and hearts only on these present delights and commodities, never thinking on the life to come.

But now we must go further with this vaunter and be bold to tell him that our country is in no such blessed state as he would make the sillier sort at home, or strangers abroad that feel not our miseries, to believe. For though a few persons in respect of the rest (not surely the third man in the realm, having given themselves to follow the present condition of things, and putting their conscience, reason, and religion to silence, to be partakers of the pleasures and commodities which there the world yieldeth by the spoil of infinite Catholics and honest innocent men of all sorts) are advanced to riches and degree and do reckon their present state a terrestrial paradise, feeling their own wealth and not regarding other men's woe; yet, indeed, knowing as we do that the far greater part of our country of all degrees are brought to ruin, misery, or extreme danger and desolation, as well themselves as their posterity, for the raising of others unto this pleasure, plenty, and felicity which they have now for some years

[18] [Ps.] 144:15.

[19] [Luke] 16:19–31.

enjoyed, we must needs confess and testify that the body of the realm generally was never in such extreme misery.

First and foremost, for the clergy (which was, and is in truth wheresoever it remain, and ought to be in all Christian commonwealths, the first and principal order of honor, and in ours, for number, learning, wisdom, and excellency of all kinds, inferior to none in Europe), it is wholly distained [20] and destroyed, as the world knoweth; the chief prelates, bishops, and others all spoiled of their dignities and livelihoods, thrust into prisons, forced into banishment, till by manifold and long miseries they be almost all wasted and worn away. These, then, so many, so notable, and so worthy, for whom both God, nature, and their place of birth do challenge a part of this so much praised prosperity, feel none of it; but for mere conscience and confession of that truth which their holy predecessors laid and left with them *in depositum* [21] have lost their terrene lot and either are dead or have passed so many years in misery as these other good fellows their intruders have lived in joy and felicity; who indeed are *Filii hominum, qui nubunt et nubuntur;* [22] that is, certain fleshly companions, unordered apostates, and contemptible ministers, who, entering into the right and rooms of others, provided not for them, do think all fair weather in England and have good cause to like of the luck of these later years, which maketh true men mourn while such thieves be merry.

Secondly, if we go from spirituality to temporality and do make our consideration of all orders and degrees of men and of the whole corps and commonalty of the land, we shall find by reason, experience, and substantial conjecture that, the whole being divided into three parts, two of them are inclined to Catholic religion in their hearts and consequently are discontented with the present condition of things. Of which Catholics, so many as fol-

[20] Defiled, sullied.

[21] In trust, deposited for safekeeping.

[22] Paraphrase of Luke 20:34: "The children of the world marry and are given in marriage."

low the world and dissemble their religion for fear of laws, as they be (notwithstanding their dissimulation) many ways known and discovered, mistrusted, doubted, and hated of the Protestants, and generally kept under, injured, disauthorized, and watchfully overlooked and thereby in continual misery and discontentment; so also in respect of their own consciences, being forced to swear to such articles of this new faith and Her Majesty's ecclesiastical "regality" as they assuredly believe to be most wicked, untrue, and impossible; as also to receive such falsified sacraments as they in their hearts condemn to the pit of hell and know to be poison to their own souls and to their friends' who for company's sake do receive with them; and finally, being constrained to hear and hire such ministers as daily read, speak, and preach nothing but blasphemy against Christ's Vicar, Church, sacraments, saints, and all holies; they are enforced to live, and, alas, often also to die, in infinite distress of mind and torments of conscience, passing all other human miseries. So as all these have little part of this goodly joy whereof this libeler speaketh but do live in perpetual anguish, wishing sometimes (which we have seen and heard) with many a sigh and groan that Her Majesty would be content with half their goods, so that she would grant them liberty but in secret sort to have the use but of the holy sacraments; and sometimes lamenting their manifold infirmities and impediments of wife and children, for whose only needful relief they continue in that damnable state of schism.

Now for the other zealous and sincere Catholics, being marvelous many throughout the whole realm, and the number by God's goodness daily increasing, such we mean as know it is not enough to salvation to believe with heart, except, when occasion is given, they confess with mouth; and that if they deny Christ before men, they shall be refused of Him before His Father; these, being no small part of the land—of the greatest calling, some; of honor, worship, wealth, and substance, many; the rest, of the honestest, orderliest, and best beloved of the whole country

—taste not of the pleasures of this libeler's paradise but have passed these years in greater griefs, fears, and miseries than any man's pen or tongue can express, not the tenth part of their calamities discovered by any of our brethren's books, epistles, pictures, or complaints.

If our fellows in the Catholic faith through Christendom could conceive that in heart which these confessors do indeed feel and we often with our eyes behold, they would with infinite tears bewail our case and with daily devout prayers procure God's mercy toward us, as we trust they do. If they might see all the prisons, dungeons, fetters, stocks, racks, that are through the realm occupied and filled with Catholics; if they might behold the manner of their arraignment, even among the vilest sort of malefactors; how many have been by famine, ordure, and pestiferous airs pined away; how many by most cruel death openly dispatched; how many have suffered proscription and condemnation to perpetual prison; how many have been spoiled and otherwise grievously punished by forfeiting to the Queen an hundred marks for every time they hear mass; [23] how many gentlemen and other persons of wealth are wholly undone by losing thirteenscore pounds by the year [24] for not coming unto the heretical service; how many have lost all their lands and goods during life for flying out of the country for their conscience sake; how many of the most substantial, profitablest, and persons of greatest hospitality in divers provinces are chased out of their own houses by spials, promoters, and catchpoles; [25] how many wander in place where they are not known, driven into woods, yea, surely, into waters,[26] to save themselves from the heretics'

[23] [Viz. in crowns 222 and odd.] The mark was a unit in an English money of account, representing a weight of bullion; the crown was the common English name for several Continental coins, notably the French écu. This was the fine specified by 23 Eliz. I, c. 1, section 3, enacted in 1581.

[24] [Viz. in crowns 866 and odd.]

[25] Petty officers of justice.

[26] [John Westby of Mowbreck, Esquire, was glad to stand for a whole winter's day almost, in a pit in water up to the ears, and often forced to duck under the water lest he should be espied of the persecutors.]

cruelty; how many godly and honest married couples most dear one to another, by the imprisonment, banishment, flight, of either party are pitifully sundered; how many families thereby dissolved; into what poverty, misery, and mishap their children are driven; what number thereby run over sea into most desperate wars and fortunes; or by better luck and fortune go to the seminaries or other service, to pass their time during their parents' calamity. And for such as be of the vulgar sort of honest husbandmen or artisans (of which condition innumerable be Catholics in our country); they being not able to pay that impious mass-mulct, much less the forfeiture for not coming to the Calvinists' preaches and service, are most cruelly and barbarously whipped in the open market places; as both elsewhere, and specially of late, a blessed number in the city of Winchester (most pitiful to behold) were so used. Others have their ears cut off; others burnt through the ear; and others otherwise (of both sexes) contumeliously and slavishly abused.

These, then, and a thousand more which we need not to rehearse, being the miseries of the better sort and bigger number of the realm, and they falling upon them for their fathers' faith and no other crime in the world committed either against prince or country, as the libeler himself confesseth for the principal clergy and for many good subjects of the laity, who therefore, he saith, are not punished by any capital pain, as though the loss of liberty, lands, dignities, grace, and goods, were no punishment. But these calamities (we say) being common to our whole state of the realm and to the greatest part of the rest, shall we say the state is blessed, this regiment fortunate, all is peaceable and plentiful in England? Where indeed only a few newly raised by other men's fall are made happy by other men's infelicity; and where a very small number, in comparison, have divided the wealth, honors, offices, and pleasures of the whole land among themselves and do manage the country by their favorites, to the discontentment, disgrace, and destruction of the justest gentlemen in the same.

Now this condition and present fortune of certain men, that have by Her Majesty's lenity and by alteration of the Catholic religion into heresy thus advanced their particular, is by these men called the state, and their abundance, peace, and prosperity the happiness of the whole realm. Where the happiness of a king and country is the weal of subjects no less than of the sovereign, and where wicked men (as thieves, murderers, heretics, and others like) be in misery and bear the pains of the laws; and not where God's priests, the Church's children, and true Catholics (for whose defense and protection both kings and all just laws are made) be in continual trouble and vexation. To conclude, then, the greatest and best part of our country being in the extremest worldly misery (besides the torments of conscience which pass all other pain) that ever men were in sith Christianity was founded, the adversary's brag of the English felicity is too vain, fond, and frivolous.

But going further with this politique, or atheist (whether you will), that measureth all by worldly felicity, deeming the Pope's anathema or curse to be void toward us, or rather turned into blessing by the good success the Protestants of our country have had in all their life and doings since the publishing of the same; we will set aside the misery of so great numbers of particular men named before and presume for the clearer proceeding in this cause that the present happiness of some Protestants were the peace and prosperity of the whole realm and state; and, that being admitted, yet we have to tell the man, and shall prove it now in the sight of all indifferent people, that our country and state is in the greatest misery, most dangerous terms, that ever it was sith or before the Conquest, and far in worse case than any country of Christendom, which notwithstanding (he saith) would wish any piece of the English felicity.

It were a hard matter to persuade this to a thriftless younker,[27] a vulgar reader, a common person, or such an one as brutishly

[27] Youngster, child.

beholdeth and esteemeth the present pleasures or profits that he enjoyeth with licentious liberty above all that may fall to him or his, be it wealth, be it woe, afterward forever. But to wise men, and specially to such as have charge of commonwealths, it is nothing difficile; who if they know not of themselves (as lightly they do by the law of nature) precepts of policy, and Holy Scriptures, yet they may easily be induced to consider that the present peace and pleasure of a common body or state, or the calm of a few years (if it be either procured or supported by unjust and dishonorable means, or be joined with evident perils, present or to come) is indeed no true prosperity, neither in common nor in particular, but rather a prognostication of God's great plagues to come and of the future miseries either to fall afterward in our own days or to our posterity.

No weal public is happy without justice, honor, and security. If our wealth be obtained by spoil or sacrilege, it is unjust. If our peace be maintained by our neighbors' wars, it is injurious and dishonorable. If no respect be had for the continuance, security, and stability of this good fortune we seem to be in, then either we or our posterity shall feel as much woe as we now do joy.

Of the revolt from the See Apostolic, alteration of religion, spoil of churches and clergy (by which they made their entry into this new blessedness), how just and lawful it was we will not now stand upon, nor show what ignominious practices and plaguey injustice they have used to sustain the same, far differing from the old royal dealings of our kings and country, who either by lawful open wars or honorable leagues and assured amity procure their rest and peace.

To make the subjects of Scotland first, then of France, and last of all of Flanders and divers other states to rebel against their lawful princes; to imprison some; to surprise the towns of others; to seize upon the money of others; to hazard the persons of others; to maintain horrible civil garboils [28] in all the countries

[28] Turmoils, disturbances.

near us and against all their next neighbor princes (with whom otherwise they pretend good amity and intelligence); to be confederate with all the infamous heretics and rebels of these days, yea, surely, with the Turk himself; finally, by sundry piracies, proditions,[29] spieries, and foul arts to afflict and cozen the world round about us: what conscience, honor, or equity can be in this course? None at all, surely. Neither can our peace and prosperity, by such dishonorable and sinful means maintained, ever be secure or durable, but always full of fear, danger, and doubtfulness, as well to the authors of so foul and unwonted proceedings as to the people; though the simplest of this latter sort, averted by the present peace and pleasure of a few years, cannot espy their future misery so easily as those which, having led both their sovereign and her subjects by strange paths into these perplexities, are now themselves come almost both to their wits' and to their world's end; having neither God to stand for them, Whom they have highly offended by forsaking Him and abolishing His holy service, honor, and sacraments, nor any prince or state sure unto them, every of which they have so notoriously annoyed in the times of their distresses that they can look for no office of true friendship at their hands.

In all which God hath so wonderfully overwrought their human counsels, that seemed to such as had no deep insight in things present nor much foresight or care of that was to come to be full wise and far to excel the compass of our old fathers or any foreigners at this day, and therefore our nation, by the passing prudence of certain counselors, to stand in peace and joy, when all their neighbors about us by their devices were in misery; God Himself (we say) hath so controlled these wise follies, by the contrary events of every of their sinful devices, that the world may see and wonder at God's ways and how different they be from man's cogitations, and how far the sound counsels of such as be truly wise differ from the present and pregnant wits or desper-

[29] Betrayals, treasons.

ate adventures of such as manage all matters for their own present and particular, without regard of the general end or their own posterity.

See you not how even God Himself hath defeated all their drifts in Scotland and brought the matter by marvelous means of His providence to the just contrary issue of that which they shot at? Were not their endeavors even so crossed in France, in every of the three brethren's kings' days, where they have been always frustrate of their purposes and lost both their unthankful labors and their money? To what end their intelligence with the rebellious states of Flanders, or with the Apostate of Cologne,[30] or other their correspondents will come, they partly perceive and may acknowledge therein (as all other wise men do) the mighty, just, and provident hand of God. When our Protestants consider of these things deeply, and attend the issue of all their extraordinary proceedings, and, as men out of all aim now and compass of their intended course, can go no farther without desperate overthrow and hazard of all, what misery they may be in let wise men judge, howsoever themselves cover their perplexed cogitations from the vulgar sort by telling them of fair weather and of their plenty of corn and cattle, long reign and prosperity of Her Majesty above all Popes and princes of her days. But the origin of all the former dishonorable and desperate plots, and of the extreme fears and miseries they many ways show themselves to be in (and indeed are, notwithstanding the pretense of their prosperity), is their first fall from the God of their forefathers and the alteration of Catholic religion into this Calvinism or atheism by which our realm hath so long perished. Though this libeler and other English new writers (no wiser nor better than children or bears, that are offended with the rods, stones, or staves wherewith they be beaten, neither looking at the cause nor chief author of their punishment) attribute their troubles or apprehended fears to the

[30] Gebhard Truchsess of Waldburg, deposed Archbishop of Cologne. See above Ch. VI, p. 182 and n. 13.

excommunication and to the godly endeavors of Catholic priests, instructing the people peaceably to their salvation.

And how much this forsaking of Holy Church, faith, and communion of all Christian people displeased God, and how unwisely it was done in respect of the temporal state and safety of our prince and country, the same Lord God hath in their own days that were the authors thereof revealed, as otherwise natural reason and experience, if they were never so void of conscience and religion, might have foretold them. But, alas, their own particular advancement and infinite ambition, which they thought should not have so free course if the old state of religion had continued, either brought them into error of judgment (as it commonly happeth), or else (which is no rare case neither) made them against their own knowledge follow that which was so pernicious both temporally and spiritually.

For who could not see, though his judgment, reason, or reading were never so small, that all great alterations in commonwealths are dangerous? Let but an attempt be made to change your temporal statutes and national laws into the civil laws; change but your customs that now you be guided by in many things; change your form of government, which is now a monarchy, into another kind of regiment: what infinite broils would it bring? But there is no alteration so perilous as of religion, and of that religion which was planted by our first apostles, received from the Mother Church of Christendom, confirmed by miracles, approved by all the laws, councils, customs, and tribunals of the Church for to be the only true worship of God and consonant to His sacred word and will. What counsel could be more dangerous in the world than this? They could not but think that the subjects of the realm, so many of them being Catholic, so lately reconciled to the Church and by public embassy, oath, and promise to His Holiness avowed never to fall again into schism, could not but be much discontented. They could not but see what heartsore it would be to all those that depended on the old honorable clergy to behold the deprivation and imprisonment almost of the whole order and another fleshly company intruded into their rooms, whom no man almost liked of and sith are more and more taken and proved to be the filth of the land.

They were not ignorant that the Pope and See Apostolic (now the second time so contemptuously forsaken) could either of conscience or duty to his flock or his own honor not use one time or other the rod of the Church's discipline, which is excommunication, against the offenders. Which howsoever they thought by error of religion they might contemn and by power withstand, yet they could not be so far overseen that such censures (by which many a man's conscience at home might be pierced, and of which any foreign prince abroad, as time and advantage served him, would perhaps make his profit) might not seem to them very like to breed more troubles than were to be wished.

They looked not well about them, if they foresaw not that their defection from the Pope, who is most dearly confederated with all the Catholic and mighty kings of Christendom, might not breed a great alienation of their hearts from us and an occasion of much inconvenience and danger to our country. Their wisdoms and experience of the divers bloody conflicts foughten in our fathers' days for religion in Switzerland [31] and in our country in King Henry the Eighth's [32] and King Edward the Sixth's [33] late days, and the doubtful event of such things, might have forewarned them of the like that might fall and sithence have fallen, as well in England as Ireland, where, all the country being in good will Catholic, they might easily perceive with what a general torment of conscience and danger of civil war the new religion were to be enforced upon them.

[31] Reference, probably, to the war of Kappel, 1531.
[32] Reference, probably, to the Pilgrimage of Grace, 1536.
[33] Reference to the revolts in Cornwall, Devon, and Norfolk, 1548–1549.

Fear is never a sure nor long keeper of his master. And because no prince ruleth his subjects so securely by force and fear as by love and liking, how could they not conceive that all Ireland, and a great piece of England, was ever to be entertained in subjection by power and plain awe and nothing by love and sweetness? And which is of more perilous sequel in this case, and ought most of all to have been by them foreseen, is that the diversity of religion, joined with the censure and sentence of the See Apostolic, may make such alteration in the opinions of many otherwise most loyal subjects that divers may seem to obey only of fear and nothing of conscience. Which conscience of the subjects, doubtless, is the only sure pillar of the sovereign's estate.

They should have foreseen how many persons of honor and quality, for freedom of conscience and other discontentment grounded on religion, were like to fly into foreign parts, who might by zeal or misery be so irritated against the causers of their banishment and occupiers of their livelihoods that their absence might prove dangerous to their enemies' state. Whom they cannot repress by calling them fugitives or suchlike names of vulgar reproach; for that terrified not the noble prince Henry the Seventh, grandfather to the Queen's Majesty, for pursuing the cruel tyrant and usurper Richard the Third, whom he honorably, notwithstanding he was an anointed king and in possession of the realm, deposed of the crown.

They should have made their account before alteration of religion, that there would rise thereby implacable division among the subjects and pernicious difference betwixt the dearest friends and nearest kinsfolks; no dissension nor hatred being so capital and deadly as that which cometh of contrariety in faith and worship of God; and, the unity of Christ's Church being once broken, that the Protestants themselves should be cumbered with infinity of sects and opinions pernicious to the state. Whereof no doubt they should have received good proof and lamentable issue ere this had not the heads, as well of the rulers as of the Puritans, Anabaptists, Brethren of Love,[34] and other sects, been so fully and fearfully attent[35] upon the Catholics and their endeavors.

But the adversary telleth us that they have gone through all these perils, and have had so many victories against what enemies soever, at home or abroad, and that therefore all was wisely done and luckily. To which we say, that if all prove well in the end, it is better for them. And that it is not so properly pertaining to prudence to escape dangers when they fall (which good luck, fond men also sometimes have by fortune) as to prevent and provide that no dangers fall and to fly from such things whereof evident perils must needs ensue.

But in this matter of religion, God Himself also hath checked their worldly purposes and conceits marvelously. For where they had thought by severity of such strange laws as were never made in any commonwealth heathen or Christian, by putting all the old prelates into prison and wearing them away, by yielding all churches, pulpits, schools, offices, honors, and commodities to men of their own sect and creation, and by what other extremity, policy, or diligence soever, to have in a few years extinguished the name and memory of faith Catholic; they now yearly and daily find the number, zeal, constancy, patience, and knowledge of the children of the Catholic Roman Church so to increase in all orders, sexes, and degrees of men that they may see and confess that *digitus Dei est hic;*[36] and that if they persist *Novissimus error ipsorum erit peior priori.*[37]

Once they show themselves to be so terrified by God in the blood and death of so many martyrs, which they, in a kind of extreme desperate obstinacy and obduration, do daily kill, and yet are so appalled by the truth and the common sense of all men that they dare not or are ashamed to execute them for religion,

[34] Reference, probably, to the Family of Love, a mystical sect founded by Hendrik Niclaes in the Netherlands, then spreading in eastern England.

[35] Intent, attentive.

[36] [Exod. 8:19]: "This is the finger of God."

[37] [Matt. 27:64]: "The last error shall be worse than the first."

whereby even now in the vaunt of their wealth, peace, and prosperity they show such extraordinary fears as is wonder to behold.

Wherein their misery is so lamentable (as we construe it), the perplexity which God hath driven them unto so terrible, that there is not a poor priest can enter to say mass but they imagine he bringeth their destruction. There cannot a ship appear in any coast, nor any prince's preparation for his own affairs, but it is for invasion of the realm. There can be no college founded to relieve men's banishments abroad, no entertainment given to any Catholic either in camp or court, but all is against their state; every man crying out: *Quod venient Romani, et tollent locum et gentem nostram.*[38]

So long as our realm was in the unity of the Catholic Church and lived either in just wars or honorable peace with our neighbors, was there any such extreme fears of present invasion? Was there such mustering? Such diligent watch and swearing against the Pope at every port? Such examination of passengers? Such ado generally, and such mistrust of the subjects' fidelity? Such jealousy over all men, as though the whole realm were a camp that feared and expected every hour some secret camisado? [39] Is this the felicity and security that the libeler so much glorieth of, whereof he saith other countries wish some part? Surely, a moderate fortune with security is without comparison much better than all the pleasures in the world with perplexity. And it seemeth by outward signs that there is no nation in Europe which standeth this day in so doubtful terms as ours doth. Woe be to our sins therefore!

Which we say not upon any likelihood of any such present dangers as seem there now so extremely to be feared; or for that the priests of God or other Catholic men can possibly be any

[38] [The speech of the Jews, John 11]:48: "The Romans shall come, and take away both our place and nation."

[39] Night attack.

cause thereof, which is indeed no more but this: *Deum non invocaverunt; illic trepidaverunt timore, ubi non erat timor.*[40] God only hath driven them unto it, to give them some sense of their misery and some remorse of their revolt from Him and motion of repentance.

But our consideration is specially of the dreadful and most desperate case our whole country, every order and each particular man thereof, is in by the uncertainty of the next heir to the crown; yea, by the certainty of most bloody civil and foreign wars among such a number of competitors, such diversity of religions, such ambitious spirits that already make their packs and complots [41] for the same; all our rest, peace, and felicity whatsoever depending upon a few uncertain days of one sole person's life, well grown in years, subject to casualties and under the hand of the omnipotent Lord, that taketh away when He listeth the spirits of princes and is terrible upon the kings of the earth. It were too miserable for any noble or gentleman, or other person either of possession, wealth, or issue in the whole land, not to know, or not to care, to whom his livelihood should descend after him but to provide for his own time only, and to let them go by the ears and scamble [42] for it afterward. Far more miserable, unnatural, and lamentable it is to see such a noble whole realm and public state driven to these straits and incomparable distresses that almost it looketh for no longer life and being, and no person subject thereunto, for longer peace, wealth, and use of their own goods, than Her Majesty liveth: that is to say, for ten, twenty, more or less years, as it pleaseth God to allot her. Which thing being an evident demonstration and palpable proof of our greatest calamity, the deceitful adversaries shame not to turn the same notwithstanding to the high commendation of their government; telling the people how happy they be by the same, and how needfully

[40] [Ps.] 53:4–5: "They have not called upon God. There were they in great fear, where no fear was."

[41] Plots, conspiracies.

[42] Struggle greedily or indecorously.

they have to pray and provide for the preservation of Her Majesty's person, by whose only life they enjoy so great felicity, afterward all to be in extremes.

Which the counselors themselves stick not to confess and publish; as you may read in an oration made by one of them [43] upon the accident that fell by the rashness of a certain servingman discharging his piece at random and striking one of the watermen in the Queen's barge, near Her Highness' person then present. In which oration he acknowledgeth nothing to be looked for after her death but confusion, persecution, blood, vengeance, wars, spoil, ravishments, and all other maledictions that the world can yield; and ten thousand more than (as he saith) can be by him foreseen. Not doubting to conclude that that day we shall be the most miserable men in the world, in the meantime only enjoying all felicities, heavenly and worldly, by her life.

Thus much hath that honorable person of our general calamity. In the meantime, the matters are so ruled that we must account ourselves happy if our commonwealth stand during the life of Her Majesty. This is (alas) the felicity of our country, praised and admired by them that esteem only the present uncertain pleasure of a very few years, without regard of the posterity, but of wise men deemed for the highest misery that can be; nothing in a common body being praisable that is not joined with security and durability.

Wherein our distress is more markable [44] that it is not only not prevented, in so many years of God's patience and general foresight of the miseries, by the grave counselors and all other wise men, but (which is more pitiful and unnatural) it is by special laws and capital penalties provided to the contrary, that none may know or name the next lawful heir and successor under pain of high treason; nor any make claim or challenge any future right

[43] [Sir Christopher Hatton's oration.] *A True Report of the Most Gracious and Merciful Message of Her Most Excellent Majesty, Sent by the Right Honorable Sir Christopher Hatton, Knight, Vice-Chamberlain* . . . (London, 1579), STC 7602, especially sig. B recto.

[44] Remarkable.

therein except Her Highness' natural issue. Whereby, under pretense of preserving their present state, they are contented to plunge their whole posterity into eternal or very long miseries. Yea, and (which passeth all dishonor to the realm and to Her Majesty's person) to insinuate that though the next in blood and lawful succession to Her Highness may not challenge or be named, yet only her natural may be advanced thereunto.[45] Which had been shameful enough, and to much injury to the next of lawful blood, if it were granted to the issue of a king gotten out of lawful matrimony; but to prefer the natural of a Queen (in whose person, by reason of her sex, fornication were fouler and the fruit thereof nothing so capable),[46] that passed all shame and honor; procured (no doubt) or set down in statute by some wicked forgeries of such as sought to dishonor Her Majesty contrary to the meaning of the whole Parliament, which (as we think) did never deliberate of that special article, though it be extant in the printed and published copies of the same.

Howsoever it be, our misery herein is notorious, and the old glory and felicity of our realm (the guides thereof wittingly and willingly beholding it and consenting thereunto) so fadeth and falleth to nothing in all men's sight that we cannot complain enough of our instant calamities, nor attribute them to any other cause than to God's judgments, whereby first (as the Italian saith) a man's brain is taken away when God intendeth to punish him,[47] lest he should by providence avert the intended plague.

This our country's scourge, proceeding wholly of our notorious forsaking the Catholic Church and See Apostolic, began first in King Henry the Eighth, being *radix peccati* of our days (as the

[45] 13 Eliz. I, c. 1, section 5, in 1571 had forbidden any publication affirming "that any one particular person, whosoever it be, is or ought to be the right heir and successor to the Queen's Majesty that now is (whom God long preserve) except the same be the natural issue of Her Majesty's body." Allen misinterprets the term "natural issue" to mean bastard.

[46] Qualified, entitled.

[47] A version of the Italian proverb, *Cui Dio vuol male, gli toglie il senno* (Orlando Pescetti, *Proverbi italiani e latini,* Venice, 1611), derived from the

Scripture speaketh of Antiochus),[48] upon that his most unjust title and challenge of the headship and supreme government of the Church, whence all these extremities are ensued sithence. Which king God plagued marvelously strait upon his revolt, both spiritually and temporally. For within a very short space (by his sufferance) he killed his own wife, mother to Her Majesty that now is; whom he loved so impotently a little before that for her sake he both divorced himself from his former wife (with whom he had lived so honorably twenty years together) and from the unity of the Church (which he and his predecessors had been in nine hundred years before), and shed the blood of the learnedest, worthiest, and to himself the best beloved of all his realm.[49]

After that he married and remarried, killed and dismissed, both wives and friends as often and as many as he thought good, in such intemperate sort as the like hath never been seen. He was in such torment of conscience and such perplexity for his revolt and other sacrileges that sometimes he went about to join with Protestant princes in religion, sometimes (thrice at least after his fall) to reconcile himself to the Pope again. Which thing Our Lord, for his greater punishment, suffered him not to bring to good effect, but to die in passing anguish of mind for the former offenses, and all the strange sacrileges committed by forcing into the world well near a hundred thousand professed persons, and by the destruction of ten thousand religious houses and churches in one year, as one testifieth of him in this epigram:

Milia dena unus templorum sustulit annus.
Quam timeo in poenas vix satis unus erit.[50]

Latin and Greek, best known to English readers in the version, "Whom the gods would destroy they first make mad." Cf. Bartlett's *Familiar Quotations*, under Euripides.

[48] [I Macc. 1]:10: "And there came out of them a wicked root, Antiochus, surnamed Epiphanes."

[49] [Fisher, More.]

[50] "One year destroys ten thousand temples.
How I fear that one in punishment will hardly be enough."

And he that without all fear of God brake so many thousand holy men's wills and foundations, had his own testament broken, falsified, and forged before his bones were thorough cold. And that Roman religion which he, by force of his own newly challenged supremacy, and by sharp laws and human devices and punishments maintained during his life, and was by him specially recommended unto such as he gave the government and education of his son, was immediately abolished and the whole realm altered into Zwinglianism, which of all other sects he most abhorred.

And for his issue, leaving behind him three goodly and towardly children: first, Edward, of marvelous expectation, whom God took away in his young years, even then when he was toward marriage; and after him his elder sister Mary, who, living long a virgin, married at length only for desire of issue and for the benefit of the realm, which Our Lord did not accomplish by her, but took her away within few years; and lastly the Queen's Majesty that now is, whom for her youth and great likelihood that way every man verily looked straight that she would have taken some noble prince, either stranger or subject, having proffer of the best in Christendom, and herself not seldom making semblance of good liking that way and of much love to many. Which yet the same Lord God, for the due punishment of the said King her father, would not suffer; but by little and little causing the realm to fall to this desolation that now we see it in and the whole stock and issue of the said King, contrary to all hope and expectation, to fail and be frustrate.

Wherein it is but a small comfort and remedy for these our public distresses that the libeler so often, by shameful flattery, and odious (we daresay) to the Queen's Majesty herself, telleth us she is "a Maiden Queen," [51] seeing that with the Protestants it is no great merit nor praise to be a virgin; who compare the state of married persons in all points of dignity unto virginity, prefer-

[51] Cecil, p. 23.

ring it also in some. And with us Catholics, in this case of the realm's extreme danger, even sacred and professed virgins have been justly taken out of their better life and by dispensation married. And would God instead of Her Majesty's virginity (so that it had stood with God's will and hers) we might rather have had, for the realm's safety, issue of her body in honorable wedlock. In which state there is godly continency also, and perhaps (as things stand) as meritorious and glorious to herself as her virginity.

But all are signs of God's ire toward our poor country; the evil luck whereof and of King Henry is so much more that, this noble line and issue now failing, they will not suffer us to go to the next of the same royal blood descending from the renowned prince, Henry the Seventh, grandfather to Her Majesty, by whose victorious entry, happy marriage, and issue all diversity of former claims of the crown and most cruel civil wars were ended and the conjunction of the two royal houses of Lancaster and York fortunately achieved, but by most shameful packing of certain Puritans and ambitious persons with the emulous house and contrary faction to the family of this said noble prince Henry the Seventh would bring all to scambling and, as they hope, gape after and work for to their own post. That so by God's just judgments our country should at once fall into two extreme miseries, both by forsaking God and the Catholic religion on the one side, as also by refusing and too-too shamefully abusing the only next true and lawful heir,[52] and consequently the whole blood of King Henry the Seventh, on the other side. Wherein our fears might be the less if they would or could prevent the said mischiefs by declaring at least now at length the heir apparent. But herein also our future calamities are showed to be inevitable, except God use mercy above human means. For the matter is so far past and overruled by certain that they can now scarce enter into any deliberation of the succession (as they imagine) without extreme peril, which they had rather put off to the end of the

[52] Mary Stuart, Queen of Scots, then in custody in England.

Queen's life and their own than have it to fall presently in their days. Our Lord God turn all to the best, and to that end that most shall tend to His glory, what deserved confusion soever fall unto us.

This yet we cannot but lament and marvel at in this cause: that the conjunction and uniting the two noble realms of England and Scotland into one monarchy, which we have sought for with so many cruel battles and so much blood of both nations, being now offered by God and nature in the sweetest and (doubtless) most indifferent sort that can be, and in two persons, mother and son —the one for approved prudence, virtue, patience, constancy, courage in adversity, and equal love of both the countries, the other for the rarest towardliness in all princely parts of any of his age in all Christendom,[53] both of our flesh and blood and the nearest of all the beloved race of Henry the Seventh, most proper for this purpose and even, as it were, provided by God Himself —cannot yet be accepted, but sought by unjust laws, shameful practices, imprisonment of the one, raising rebellion against the other, either utterly to be defeated or made uncertain of their certain right and forbidden to challenge or utter the same; while others, intending usurpation, upon the next lawful successor's uncertainty, make their profit and pack for achieving their ambitious purpose. Of whom as well the Queen as the whole state present stand in far more danger than they could ever do by the public acknowledging of the lawful heir; which yet is their pretense in concealing the same from the realm.

Into these straits, lo, on every hand, is our poor country brought by the judgments of God, whilst our libeler and other Protestants tell the simple people of their fair weather and present abundance of all things, to avert their minds from the foresaid endless miseries. Which, for our forsaking the faith of our fathers, all wise men extremely fear and certainly expect, if we return not to Our Lord God and unite ourselves again to the

[53] James VI of Scotland, son of Mary.

Catholic and Roman Church, which we have so unworthily left and cruelly persecuted. Out of whose company and obedience there is neither salvation in the next nor any true peace and security in this world. Which both Christian charity and natural love toward our dearest country, friends, flesh, and blood causeth us so often and earnestly to inculcate: *Ut gens absque consilio sapiat, et novissima provideat.*[54]

Alas, it is neither Pope nor priest (as the libeler untruly affirmeth and many deceived men simply may suppose) that desireth their destruction: the one as a most loving father and pastor, with unspeakable pains, solicitude, groans, tears, and expenses, and the other by voluntary death and shedding of their own blood, seeking their brethren's salvation and the reconcilement of their country to Christ and His Vicar. But they only are in truth (and so will in the end prove) most capital enemies to our Queen and country that first were authors to Her Majesty to forsake the Church and See Apostolic, and do still animate her and the realm, after so many signs of God's wrath toward them, to contemn the authority and censures of the same and violently to resist by force of arms and bloody laws the supreme pastor of God's faithful people; as though he used the rod of correction toward offenders upon malice, hatred, or partiality, and not of entire affection, love, and charity.

Moses and Aaron resisted Korah and his confederates, and executed God's sentence upon them, and were not their enemies. Samuel denounced and executed God's sentence against Saul, Elijah against Jezebel, and other prophets and priests against other kings without all malice and with much love. No otherwise than John *Roffensis,*[55] Sir Thomas More, and others did; who resisted upon great love and duty to their sovereign, dissuading both his divorce from the Church and from his wife. Which kind

[54] [Deut. 32]:28-[29]: "For they are a nation void of counsel . . . O that they . . . would consider their latter end!"

[55] John Fisher, Bishop of Rochester.

of men be neither traitors nor enemies to be resisted by sword or laws; but they are only such adversaries as our Savior commandeth the faithful to agree withal in the way, for divers dangers following.[56] And those men in such a case are only wise and godly counselors, Her Majesty's true subjects, and worthy members of the commonwealth that humbly exhort Her Highness not to be beguiled by her present fortune or to think obstinate and forcible resistance of the Pope or Church's sentence of excommunication to be her most security, but to see what Theodosius the Elder did when he was excommunicated by St. Ambrose; to remember how Theodosius the Younger behaved himself in the cause of St. Chrysostom, for whose unjust banishment the said Emperor's father and mother were excommunicated;[57] to consider well what the end of the controversy was betwixt King Henry the Second and the Pope and Bishop of Canterbury in his time, and afterward between King John and the See of Rome and clergy in those days; that all these, in fine (as mighty princes as they were), yielded and reconciled themselves to the See Apostolic. A thing that, after a little heat or headiness of young princes be past, was and ever shall be found, in fine, the only sure and honorable way before God and the world to keep themselves and their realms from perdition.

Which danger Her Majesty's father (in whom this revolt of our days and country began), both afore once or twice, and specially toward his death, saw and earnestly sought to avert from his posterity by the like reconciling himself to the Church. Which yet, through God's judgments, he had not time to accomplish in

[56] [Matt. 5]:25: "Agree with thine adversary quickly, whiles thou art in the way with him."

[57] [Lib. 10. trip. hist. cap. 18 & 26.] Cassiodorus, *Historia ecclesiastica tripartita*, lib. 10, caps. 18 and 26, regrets of Theodosius II for the treatment of St. John Chrysostom. Cf. lib. 9, cap. 30, for an account of the resolution of the conflict between Ambrose and Theodosius I. Both accounts are quoted from Theodoret, *Ecclesiastical History*, mostly from lib. 5, caps. 17 and 36.

himself, but was achieved afterward most honorably in his eldest daughter, not only for conscience sake otherwise, but especially for effectuating her said father's great desire therein, as some of her chief counselors (to whom he had communicated his mind in that matter) did publicly testify to the whole realm at Paul's Cross.[58] Would God our sins and the realm's could suffer Her Majesty's wise counselors to consider of the case with such sincerity as were requisite for themselves and us all; who by their better or worse election in this one matter are like either to be long happy or unhappy forever.

We trust the intolerable flattery of this libeler or other like (telling Her Majesty that she hath no superior but God, none above her but the Almighty, none that she need to fear or care for but Him, and therefore that she hath not to regard any sentence of Pope or others) cannot much move any of their wisdoms; this being a most shameful heresy and untruth, that a king hath no superior in matters of his soul and conscience. When not only the general pastor of the whole Church is his superior, if he be one of Christ's flock or fold (all the sheep whereof without exception by Our Master's express sentence were committed to Peter [59] and his successors' feeding and government); but also other prelates of his own kingdom that have charge of his soul, to whom likewise he oweth all Christian obedience in spiritual affairs, no less than the poorest man in the realm. For kings were not excepted from St. Paul's rule and admonition, given to all the faithful in these words: *Obedite praepositis vestris et subjacete eis,* "Obey your prelates and be subject unto them," whereof he yieldeth immediately the cause: "For that they watch as being to render account of your souls." [60]

If princes, then, have souls, they must needs be under the

[58] Reference, almost certainly, to the sermon by Bishop and Lord Chancellor Stephen Gardiner, on December 2, 1554, at St. Paul's in London. For relevant excerpts, see James Arthur Muller, *Stephen Gardiner and the Tudor Reaction* (London, 1926), p. 265.

[59] Cf. John 21:15–17.

[60] [Heb. 13]:17.

account and charge of prelates. If they have prelates, they must obey them and be subject unto them. If they be bound to obey them and be subject unto them, they must acknowledge them for their superiors. How then say these wicked flatterers that kings and queens have no superiors, none to be subject unto, but God? That they be the chief even in causes ecclesiastical and in matters of religion, soul, and conscience within their realms? That neither Pope nor prelate can excommunicate them, or use other discipline for correction of them, when they fall from their faith?

If Theodosius the Emperor had had such bolsterers of his pride about him, or so little grace and wisdom as to have given ear to them, he would little have esteemed St. Ambrose's authority, sentence, and censure against him. But he was more happy and Christian than to plead his superiority in such matters above his bishop, or to challenge exemption or impunity in this world for whatsoever he did or believed and only to be reserved to God. And it is a singular note of irreligiosity in our days that these profane heretics and godless persons do prefer human things before divine, the regiment temporal before spiritual, the body before the soul, earth before heaven, regality before priesthood, and this life before the next and all eternity. Which is an evident demonstration that all tendeth in this heresy to plain paganism and epicurism, esteeming and admiring none but such as be in worldly height, power, and dignity that can yield them these transitory honors, pleasures, and preferments.

But the truth of this matter may and ought to be learned, partly of the old, glorious, and most excellent doctors and bishops of the primitive Church, and partly by the behavior of the first great emperors and kings that were professors and defenders of the Catholic faith. "What is more honorable," saith St. Ambrose, "than that the emperor be called a child of the Church? For a good emperor is within the Church, and not above the Church." [61] And St. Chrysostom, admonishing priests of their duty in keep-

[61] St. Ambrose [Epist. 33]; actually *Sermo contra Auxentium*, cap. 36.

ing from the holy altar great offenders, expressly warneth them to use their authority therein, even toward kings, or whatsoever they be. "Whether," saith he, "he be duke, prefect, or crowned prince that would unworthily approach, forbid him; thy authority and power is greater than his." [62] So St. Gregory Nazianzen speaketh to his own emperor:

> The law of Christ hath made you subject to my power and to my tribunal, for we have our sovereignty, and that more excellent and perfect; unless the spirit should subdue itself to the flesh and heavenly things yield to the earthly. Which my liberty of speech I fear not, O Emperor, but thou wilt allow, seeing thou art an holy sheep of my sacred fold, and a pupil of the great pastor, and well instructed by the Holy Ghost from thine infancy.[63]

Also St. Athanasius plainly avoucheth and proveth the Emperor Constantius the Arian to be the precursor of Antichrist,[64] in that he made himself judge and superior in causes ecclesiastical over bishops; and that his arrogated pre-eminence and exercise of jurisdiction in such matters (which our gentle libeler calleth in our Queen, Her Majesty's "regality") is *abominatio desolationis* [65] foretold by Daniel. What would this holy Father have said if he had seen Cromwell made the Vicar General to King Henry *in spiritualibus,*[66] and sit among and before all the bishops and archbishops of the realm in their convocations? If he had heard tell of *Sigillum Reginae ad causas ecclesiaticas,*[67] of her commissioners

[62] St. John Chrysostom [Hom. 60 ad Popul. and 83 in Math.], Homily 21, *Ad populum Antiochenum de statuis;* Homily 82 or 83 (Migne uses both nos.) on Matthew, cap. 6, commenting on Matt. 26:26–28.

[63] St. Gregory Nazianzen [Orat. ad Cives], Oration no. 17, *Ad cives Nazianzenos,* cap. 8.

[64] [Epist. ad solit. vit. de gent.] St. Athanasius, *Epistola ad omnes, qui ubique monasticam vitam agunt et in fide Dei firmati sanctificatique in Christo sunt* (*Historia Arianorum ad monachos*), cap. 77, "Constantius the precursor of Antichrist."

[65] Dan. 9:27: "For the overspreading of abominations he shall make it desolate."

[66] In spiritual matters. [67] The Queen's seal for ecclesiastical matters.

and courts, of her deposing and creating bishops and determining of religion at her pleasure? Kings, neither Catholics neither heretics, ever went thus far, being much more capable than any woman can be. Of which sex St. Chrysostom saith thus: "When it cometh to the government of the Church and charge of souls, all womankind must needs wholly give place."[68]

That not only Athanasius the Great but the ancient Osius, Leontius, St. Hilary,[69] and other did so sharply reprehend it in that heretical king Constantius might have forewarned our country and Her Majesty's counselors to have taken heed, as well of the like absurdity, as of the suspicion of heresy that in men's heads might seem to be engendered thereby, seeing that such as first attempted it were notorious Arians. But to give the same and far more superiority to a woman (whereof, as you see by St. Chrysostom, she cannot possibly be capable), that passeth all the barbarous flattery and folly in the world and maketh our nation a very fable to all nations and to the posterity.

Which, in truth, is not to make her next to God in her realm (as the libeler saith) but to make her the god of her people. From which cogitation, though of herself having so many means to put her in mind of her mortality, we doubt not but she is very far; yet truly this abominable and blasphemous adulation of some about Her Highness may breed great temptations. As we see in certain of the old heathen emperors, who never rested till they were adored with divine honor. The next step unto which is (doubtless) to say and believe that a temporal king is above the priest in causes ecclesiastical; or that in a Christian commonwealth the next dignity to Christ or God is not the priest but the prince; and so arrogate the regiment of the Church to a queen, which St.

[68] [Lib. 2 de Sacerd.] St. John Chrysostom, *De sacerdotio,* lib. 3 (Migne), cap. 9.

[69] Hosius or Osius, Bishop of Cordova, and St. Hilary, Bishop of Poitiers, both joined Athanasius, for a time, in openly resisting the Arian policies of Emperor Constantius. Leontius, Bishop of Antioch, played a more ambiguous role in the controversy.

Paul expressly testifieth to be given to bishops, saying: "Take heed to yourselves and to the whole flock, wherein the Holy Ghost hath placed you bishops to rule the Church of God," etc.[70] Touching which our English singular absurdity, it is the greatest pity in the world to see them so many years, after so much holy blood protesting against that iniquity and so many learned men's admonitions, persist in the same and to allege still those Scriptures so impertinently for the prince's usurped spiritual sovereignty, by which Claudius or Nero (in whose days and of whom the Apostle spake specially) might as well challenge to be above Sts. Peter and Paul in the government of the Church and in causes ecclesiastical as any Christian king that now liveth. For when St. Peter admonished the Christians to whom he wrote, and all other in them, to "be subject to the king as excelling or pre-eminent"[71] (which place our adversary so confidently allegeth), first, can any man be so dull or obstinately blind as to think that he prescribeth any other duty toward the king than was common both to the pagan princes at that time persecuting the Church and to Christian kings afterward protecting the Church? Secondly, can any Protestant be so peevish to pretend hereby that the heathen emperors, by reason of this subjection to them that the Apostle prescribeth and by their imperial dignity, should be above St. Peter, Paul, or Christ Himself in the Church of God or in ecclesiastical regiment (for Christ behaved Himself to the Emperor in His days as the Apostle here commandeth Christians to do); and that the apostolical pre-eminence, or our Savior's own priesthood among the faithful, should not be esteemed so high in truth and afore God as the regality of Nero or any other either faithful or heathen temporal power?

Thirdly, can they be so ignorant as not to see the king to be called the chief or precelling[72] by the Apostle, not in comparison

[70] [Acts 20]:28.

[71] [I Pet. 2:13.]

[72] Pre-eminent, excellent. From *praecellenti* in the Vulgate text of I Pet. 2:13.

or respect of the spiritual dignity, but in regard of his dukes, presidents, and other lieutenants under him, as the text itself plainly giveth? Fourthly, cannot our adversaries discern the causes in which both Christian priests, religious, and all other men (as St. Chrysostom writeth) [73] do owe obedience to lawful kings, whether they be heathen or faithful, from those matters wherein neither pagan nor Christian prince may command the priest nor people, that is, in religion and affairs of the soul?

Fifthly, could they not espy, by the words of St. Peter next going before, that the occasion of his writing of this obedience to princes was to teach the faithful how they should behave themselves in company of the heathen without offense? Who among other things slandered and charged the Christians of treason, conspiracies, and disobedience to their prince (even as our Protestants do Catholics) because they would not leave their Christian faith and exercises at their commandment, nor obey them before God and their holy pastors in matter of faith and conscience. For stopping of all which false and slanderous tongues, St. Peter required them to obey their princes in all worldly, temporal, and civil matters; to pay their tribute, keep their civil laws, live peaceably and lowly amongst them; yea, and to pray for them, whether they tolerate the Christian religion or persecute the same.

Lastly, could our libeler and his fellows be in truth so gross as not to consider that though the apostles and holy bishops of those first times (when the emperors were yet heathen and strangers to Christ and His Church) could have no superiority over them nor use any discipline toward them, the other acknowledging no duty or subjection to the apostles or spiritual governors of the faithful people, yet now, when the princes of the world have submitted themselves and their people to the Gospel of Christ and to His sweet yoke, and are become members and children of the

[73] Reference, probably, to St. John Chrysostom, Homily 23 on Romans (13), ver. 1.

Church, as the spiritual power oweth in worldly things honor and obedience to his temporal sovereign, so likewise that the secular power must of reason yield honor and subjection to the spiritual in affairs of faith, soul, and religion; either of them having means in their kind of superiority to force by laws, penalty, and discipline the other to obedience and due subjection, if either should rebel against the other? Wherein, because the spiritual power consisteth in things *quae sunt ad Deum*[74] and that concern our souls and the conducting of them to life and peace everlasting, and the temporal pertaineth principally to the good and tranquillity of this transitory life, comparing them both together, it must needs be confessed that the spiritual is the higher, nearer, and liker to the sovereignty of God over His reasonable creatures than is the terrene power or "human creature"[75] as the Apostle here termeth the king and his presidents.

So as, every power both spiritual and temporal being of God (as St. Paul teacheth),[76] and obedience and subjection due to both in their kind, though in several subjects, causes, and respects, yet is it most clear that of the two the ecclesiastical power and regiment is more excellent. In respect whereof St. Ignatius giveth this order in honoring and respecting our superiors:

Honor God the Author and Lord of all, and the bishop as the prince of priests, being the image of God and holding his princedom of Him and his priesthood of Christ. And after him you must honor also the king. For none is to be preferred before God nor equal to Him, nor more honorable in the Church than the bishop, exercising the priesthood of God for the salvation of the world. Neither is any equal to the king in the host or camp, procuring peace and benevolence to the other princes under him. For he that honoreth the bishop shall be honored of God; and he that dishonoreth him shall of God be dishonored. For if any man rising against the king is worthy of damnation, how can he escape God's judgments that attempteth

[74] That are God's.

[75] From *humanae creaturae* in the Vulgate text of I Pet. 2:13; "of man" in the King James version.

[76] Notably in Romans 13; also elsewhere.

anything against or without the bishop? For priesthood is the chief and sum of all man's good; which whosoever disgraceth, dishonoreth God and Our Lord Jesus Christ, the chief priest of God, etc.[77]

And if any man list farther to see what the old Christian emperors thought and acknowledged in this matter, and how they behaved themselves toward God's priests in all causes of religion and spiritual affairs, and with what honor, privilege, and prerogative they respected their persons and holy calling even in temporal causes, let him read in Sozomenus how Constantine the Great behaved himself toward the bishops in the first Council of Nicaea,[78] and St. Augustine's 162nd epistle[79] of the same Emperor's contentment to ask pardon of the bishops for taking upon him to deal in the cause of Caecilian, properly pertaining to them, and St. Ambrose's epistle 32[80] of Valentinian the Elder's law, that in ecclesiastical causes none should judicially deal that were not of the same order. The like he writeth of the Emperor Gratian's behavior in the Council of Aquileia.[81] And to be brief, let him read the Emperor Justinian's sixth constitution, where he both putteth the true difference betwixt the priesthood and the empire and preferreth that before this, saying thus: "The greatest gifts of God among men is the priesthood and the empire; of which two the former having the administration of divine things, the other of human, both proceeding of one beginning, do adorn man's life," etc.[82]

[77] [Epist. ad Smirnen.] Reference, it would seem, to Ignatius of Antioch, *Epistola ad Smyrnaeos,* which contains an injunction to obey bishops, caps. 8 and 9, but says nothing of obedience due to kings.

[78] Cassiodorus, *Historia ecclesiastica tripartita* [Li. 2, ca. 2], quoted from the ecclesiastical history of Sozomen, lib. 1, cap. 17, containing quotation of Emperor Constantine's speech urging priests to submit complaints to the clergy in council rather than to him.

[79] St. Augustine, Letter to Glorius *et al.,* no. 43 in Migne.

[80] St. Ambrose, Letter to Emperor Valentinian II, no. 21 in Migne.

[81] St. Ambrose, Letters to Emperor Gratian, nos. 10, 11, 12.

[82] [Auth. Quomodo oport. Episcop. etc. in p.] Translated from the preface to *Novellae,* VI, *Quomodo Episcopi et Presbyteri et Diaconi masculi et feminae creandi sint,* in the *Corpus juris civilis.*

And thus it is, even in those countries where the Church and civil state concur in one commonwealth, and where, like as the prelates be in some respect and causes subject to the temporal prince, so again the prince and state reciprocally in spiritual matters are obedient to the Church and prelates, either of them deferring due honor to the other but the spiritual sovereignty ever preferred among the faithful, though for worldly power, force, and glory (most necessary to keep the people in awe and order) kings do lightly exceed the other. Which exterior show and splendor of princes the prelates of their several dominions do most humbly by all service and office maintain.

But now for the Pope (chief of all bishops and Christian people), being in respect of his temporal state subject to no prince nor potentate of the world, and for his spiritual dignity and jurisdiction far passing all the prelates of particular churches and provinces, his principality being in neither kind subject or subalternate to any other: he must needs be greater and more peerless without all exception and limitation. And though his state and authority temporal be not holden nor challenged by God's express law immediately of Him, as the spiritual supremacy is, which he hath and holdeth immediately and directly of Christ; yet it is God's great providence that sith the emperors and kings have been christened and submitted themselves to the obedience of Christ and His Church, that the chief bishop should for the honor of Christ and His high dignity be made free from all subjection by the princes' and emperors' own grants and be possessed of the capital city of all the world. Which could never have been brought to pass, nor so many worlds continued, in the revolutions, changes, and overturnings of so many kingdoms, states, and great monarchies round about him, had it not been done by God's special pleasure and ordinance; to the end that, being subject to none, he might with more liberty, less danger, and greater indifferency do justice to all and use discipline without fear or respect of persons, as well toward great as small.

Which, if he were subject to some secular princes, as most other bishops are, could hardly be done.

In which case, also, some of our ignorant heretics (as, among other, this libeler) be so insensible that they stick not to allege the saying of St. Paul that "every soul must be subject to superior power,"[83] to prove thereby (as it seemeth) that the Pope should be obedient to our Queen, or to some other particular king. As though every person should be subject to every power or to any other than to him that hath superiority over him, or in any other matters than wherein he hath superiority and may command. Or as though God had only ordained secular power and commanded all obedience thereunto, and not appointed spiritual power and prelacy with charge of subjection unto the same also. With such gross fellows the Church hath to do, that neither have sense, reason, nor religion, and which allege that for obedience to earthly powers only which either in express words or by necessary sequel much more commendeth subjection to spiritual powers.

As with like blindness the man also allegeth this our Savior's sentence: "The kings of the Gentiles have rule over them . . . but you not so,"[84] to prove that Popes should arrogate no temporal authority, but feed only, as he saith Peter did and many of the next Popes after him. Which he would never have cited if he had known that hereby only all tyrannical domination used among the heathen princes is forbid to all Christian magistrates both spiritual and temporal, and not any just rule, superiority, or regiment over others to either kind. Or if he had considered that feeding containeth not only preaching, but also all kind of just means and holy endeavors for the propagation of the Gospel and men's salvation, according to the difference of times, persons, and places, as excommunication and other ecclesiastical censures and corrections. Which things, at least, pertaining to the spiritual powers directly, our adversaries should admit and humbly obey;

[83] [Romans 13]:1. Cf. Cecil, p. 22.
[84] [Luke 22]:25–26. Cf. Cecil, p. 23.

and if they so would do, they should never need to fear either the Popes' or other men's swords, whereof they make so much impertinent brabble.

Marry, they pretend some zeal in the matter, affirming that the Popes of Rome, before they had these great temporal states and followed Christ and the apostles in humility, dilated the limits of Christ's Church and the faith more in one hundred years than the later Popes have done with their swords and curses in five hundred years. To which we say that they seem now not only desirous to have his temporal power and sword taken from him (as they pretended by their former speeches and allegations), but also his spiritual weapon and exercise of discipline toward offenders, called here by the libeler his curse. Which, no doubt, they used of old upon such as were subject to the Church and their regiment no less than the Popes do now, and somewhat more; though they could not then, before kings were converted to the faith, use any discipline or authority over them, much less any human forces, for that they had not then such worldly preeminence as was due to their high calling in Christ and as afterward God hath endued them withal, but were for some hundred years persecuted and put to death by the enemies of Christ's faith and glory. In which state it seemeth the adversaries would have them still, being miscontent that they have either forces to fight against the Turk or to pursue heretics that will not obey their spiritual sentence or rod of excommunication.

As for conversion of peoples or nations to the faith, whether there were more brought to Christ in those days and in the poorer worldly condition of Popes than afterward in the days of their wealth is not to the purpose to dispute; but whether this state of things be more agreeable to the time present and for the conservation of princes and people already converted, or rather the first poor apostolical condition, that is to be considered of wise men. Though the libeler shall hardly prove that more nations have been wholly converted in the time of the Popes' poverty and adversity than afterward in their greatness.

This is sure: that our own English people, the most part of Germans, Polackers, and other northern countries, besides the inhabitants of the East and West Indians and other extreme parts of the world, have specially been either first converted, or recovered since, by the holy travails of these later Popes. And further we may be bold to say that the Pope only, by the powers temporal and spiritual that God hath given him, doth more at this day for conversion and gaining of Paynims,[85] Turks, Jews, Moors, heretics, schismatics, and other infidels than all the Protestants put together in the world; besides other infinite immortal acts of charity which he doth in many parts of Christendom which he could never do if he had not such temporal abilities as thereunto, and to the upholding of his high and peerless dignity above all particular prelates and princes, were requisite.

But of the prerogative of the spiritual power, as well in this high priest, who is subject to none in earth, as in other prelates of particular provinces, who are often subject to other princes, we have said enough to repress the pernicious flattery of the libeler and the like that would exempt every secular person from all submission and obedience to their pastors. Only leaving to all the wise of our country these few lines of St. Ambrose, for a warning and a watchword in this cause and for the end in manner of all our dispute:

Mandatur [saith he], *Trade basilicam. Respondeo, Nec mihi fas est tradere; nec tibi accipere, Imperator, expedit. Domum privati, nullo potes jure temerare; domum Dei existimas auferendam? Allegatur; imperatori licere omnia, ipsius esse universa. Noli te gravare, Imperator, ut putes te in ea quae divina sunt, imperiale aliquod jus habere. Noli te extollere, sed si vis diutius imperare, esto Deo subditus: scriptum est, "Quae Dei Deo, quae Caesaris Caesari." Ad Imperatorem*

[85] Pagans, infidels.

palatia pertinent, ad sacerdotem ecclesiae; publicorum tibi moeniorum jus commissum est, non sacrorum.[86]

In English:

The commandment was this: "Give up the Church." I answer that it is neither lawful for me to deliver it nor expedient for thee, O Emperor, to receive it. Thou canst by no right violate any private man's house, and thinkest thou the house of God may be taken away? But they say the emperor may do what he list and that all are his. I answer, O Emperor, be not so much abused as to think that thou hast any imperial right in divine matters. Extol not thyself, but if thou list hold thine empire long, be subject to God; for it is written, "The things that are God's to God, and that are Caesar's to Caesar." [87] The palaces pertain to the emperor, the churches to the priest; the charge of the common walls of the city are committed to thee, and not the charge of sacred things.

So he spake to Valentinian the Emperor. And so we say to our princess and to all such as have charge under Her Highness of our country: that this libeler, and who else soever, by loathsome and base flattery extolling her regality and secular sovereignty above priesthood and the apostolic authority, thereby exempting her from all obedience and subjection to Christ's Church and to those whom the Holy Ghost hath placed over the same Church in earth, do shamefully abuse them, to their and the realm's destruction, except God be merciful above our merits.

We tell them plainly and sincerely, with the said glorious doctor and saint, and thereupon will pledge our lives in this world and our souls everlastingly, and that without detracting any obedience due to her temporal sovereignty in spiritual matters, that Her Majesty hath no charge, authority, or power over the Church or ecclesiastical affairs, no more than the poorest soul in her realm; nor so much neither till she be a member and

[86] St. Ambrose, [Epist. 33.] to Marcellina, no. 20 in Migne, cap. 19.
[87] [Mark] 12:[17]; [Luke] 20:[25].

obedient child of the Church and See Apostolic. With this only exception, that for the height of her dignity, and by her special oath and obligation, she is bound more to defend and protect the Church than her subjects be.

And finally, upon all the proofs, reasons, and authorities that have gone before, we avouch that besides God Almighty every temporal prince christened hath his pastor also, and specially the general governor of the whole Church, for his superior in earth in all causes of soul and conscience, to whose orders in matter of religion he is bound to obey under pain of damnation; and that God's just judgments are near the princes and countries whatsoever that will not obey Him but violently resist His ordinance and by Antichristian pride do challenge power not lawful to be yielded unto them.

Chapter IX

The conclusion, containing a charitable motion and a joinder with the libeler touching some means of toleration in religion and ceasing or mitigating this cruel persecution

AND now though in the deep conceiving of this our country's incomparable offense our hearts be wholly oppressed with fear and heaviness, yet either the force of our peculiar affection toward our flesh and blood driving us to hope for better than is deserved, or the largeness of God's immeasurable mercies yielding, contrary to man's demerits, pardon upon repentance, do cause us oftentimes to expect grace and mercy rather than extreme rigor and judgment.

In which cogitation it cometh often to our minds that if anything avert God's ire from our prince and country it is the abundance of holy blood shed these late years and ever sith the first revolt. Which though by justice it might cry rather to God for vengeance (and so it doth in respect of the impenitent, and the clamor thereof shall never be void), yet we trust it sueth for mercy, specially in respect of the infinite number of all estates that never consented to this iniquity. It is the heroical endeavor of a great many zealous priests and worthy gentlemen, that continually offer not only their prayers and other devout and religious offices but themselves in sacrifice for the salvation of their best beloved country. It is the ardent and incessant care of His Holiness, seeking our reconcilement with charity unspeakable. It is the general conjunction of all Christian minds in the whole world toward our recovery. No church, no company, monastery, or college of name in Christendom that with earnest devotion and public fasts and prayers laboreth not to God for mercy toward us. Finally, even those things and persons that the adversaries account to be the cause of all their troubles and fears are indeed the only hope of God's mercy, their own pardon, and our country's salvation.

In which case, to deal as freely for a farewell and as charitably with the libeler as he would seem to conclude with us: we wish no more for performance of that he proposeth and partly promiseth but that he were assured of Her Majesty's and the council's mind therein or were of such credit with them that he could bring that to good effect which in covert words he pretendeth toward us, which is, that he doubteth not but Her Majesty would shed no more the blood of her natural subjects, nor use any more bodily punishments at all, if they would desist from their practices abroad, from their writing of railing books, and from wandering in disguised apparel within the realm, and would employ their travail in the works of light and doctrine, according to the usage of their schools, and content themselves with their profession and devotion.[1] So the man speaketh, howsoever he meaneth. But, alas, if any mercy, just or tolerable treaty were

[1] Cecil, p. 40.

meant, or ever had been offered to Catholics upon any reasonable conditions whatsoever, our adversaries had never needed to have fallen to such extreme proceedings with their own flesh and blood; nor ever had any such troubles, fears, or dangers been thought upon whereof now they have so deep apprehension. If any pitiful ear had ever been given by the superiors to the incessant groans, cries, tears, and supplications of their Catholic subjects, desiring but relief of their infinitely distressed consciences, tormented by damnable oaths, articles, and exercises of Calvinism, that were forced upon them. If they might have had either by license or connivance, in never so few places of the realm, never so secretly, never so inoffensively, the exercise of that faith and religion which all their forefathers since our country was converted lived and died in, and in which themselves were baptized, and from which by no law of God nor man they can be compelled to any sect or rite of religion which they nor their forefathers ever voluntarily accepted or admitted. If, of all the noble churches, colleges, and other inestimable provisions of the realm, founded and made only by Catholics and for Catholics, and for no Protestants nor any their sacrilegious ministries at all, some few had been permitted to the true owners and to that true worship of God for which they were instituted. If they might have obtained any piece of that liberty which Catholics enjoy in Germany, Switzerland, or other places among Protestants, or half the freedom that the Huguenots have in France and other countries; yea, or but so much courtesy as the Christians find among the very Turks, or very Jews among Christians, upon any reasonable or unreasonable tribute, which hath been often in most humble and lamentable sort offered and urged. Or, to be short, if any respect, care, or compassion in the world had been had either of Catholic men's souls, bodies, or goods, our adversaries should never have been troubled nor put in jealousy of so many men's malcontentment at home, nor stand in doubt of departure and absence of so great a number of nobility and principal gentlemen abroad. They should never have had such colleges and seminaries in other princes' dominions erected and furnished with English youths, the issue whereof is now, and perhaps will be hereafter, more and more wonderful to the world. They should not have been controlled in their heresy so zealously and effectually by the priests created at home of old or lately ordained and sacred [2] abroad. There should have been no cause of writing so many books for defense of our innocency and the faith of our forefathers and for our just complaint to the Christian world of the intolerable rigor or cruelty used against us.

In all which books no Protestant in England is able to reprove the writers of any untruth or slander, railing, immodesty, or misbehavior toward our secular princess or persecutors, whatsoever the libeler without proof affirmeth here. Wherein I avow him to be so much destitute of truth as he is not able to allege one line or sentence or any one example out of our writings to the contrary; as, on the other side, neither he nor any else can clear our adversaries, the enemies of God's Church, of any one point of fact or doctrine wherewith they be by us charged.

Lastly, the said priests which pass into England, of whose covert working, disguising, and close keeping they so much complain, as though that were enough to prove them traitors, would have appeared openly in their own priestly habit and have done their holy functions in the sight of all men, if in any sort whatsoever they had been permitted. As also at this present, not only upon Her Majesty's grant and desire (insinuated here by the libeler) for them to use openly their devotion, doctrine, and profession according to the manner of their schools, but upon any sufficient warrant of safety, they are further also than that most ready and willing to give an account of all their doctrine publicly in the universities of England or before Her Highness and council wheresoever. A thing which by many books, petitions, and

[2] Consecrated.

supplications our brethren have often humbly and instantly asked and could never yet obtain.

The libeler putteth us in hope that if the priests and seminary men would deal openly the persecution and blood should cease. And we assure him that, the persecution first ceasing and Her Majesty's pleasure herein understood, which is the natural order, and not contrariwise, all priests, religious, and Catholics will appear and present themselves, and will do all such Christian exercises, duties, and functions, as now by persecution they are forced to do in secret, in the face of the whole realm; no man, thanks be to God, being ashamed of his order, faith, profession, or Master; though everyone be bound otherwise by the law of our religion to save himself, so long as it shall please Christ, from the persecutor. And it is a great sign of our priests' and Catholics' innocency, and of our adversaries' ignorance and malice, that, seeking to appeach [3] a Christian man or priest of treason, they have no more to lay against him than that he showeth not himself openly but dealeth secretly and weareth another habit than is belonging to his degree.

The holy king and prophet David, in place of danger, did not only otherwise cover his person often and fled from his enemies but feigned himself a plain madman before Achish King of Gath in all his behavior, to escape peril.[4] How often do we read in the Evangelists that our Savior fled,[5] that He did hide Himself, that He walked not openly, that He went up to Jerusalem on the feast day not openly but in covert? Who can be ignorant that it was no offense for Nicodemus that he came to Jesus in the night for fear of the Jews? [6] Who knoweth not that the apostles, as well before as after the coming of the Holy Ghost, kept themselves often secret in private parlors and chambers, as the first holy Bishops of Rome (for fear of their persecutors) kept their meetings, mys-

[3] Accuse. [4] [I Sam. 21]:10–15. [5] [John 10]:39.
[6] John 3:1 ff.

teries, and councils in caves and grottoes under the ground? How can they forget what holy Athanasius did in the days of his persecution? Or not be mindful how holy Barlaam feigned himself in apparel and all other behavior a merchant, to gain Prince Josaphat to the Christian faith? [7] Or of the notable example of the holy martyr and bishop, Eusebius Samosatenus, who in the time of Constantius the Arian Emperor, seeing many churches occupied by the heretics and void of true pastors, went like a soldier through Syria, Phoenicia, and Palestine, making priests and deacons and ministering the sacraments to the Catholic people, destitute of their holy rights then by the Arians [8] as they be now in England by Calvinists?

The case is ruled in all divinity that any religious, priest, or Christian, to avoid danger of his person, may in the places of infidels leave the habit of their profession or usage and cover themselves from the enemy by any disguise. And if we knew not the art and cunning of heresy, we might wonder to see our Protestants so religious now as to require of our priests to go priest-like, with open and present danger of their lives, when their own clergy at home make scruple to use distinct attire from the vulgar and account it plain superstition to wear any religious or clerkly apparel at all. But yet I must confess that they have good reason to wish every one of our priests would show himself openly; for so they might soon make an end of all (as they think) and attain the victory that they desire. But our Master, admonishing His disciples that He would send them as sheep amongst wolves, warneth them, and us in them, that men should not only

[7] [Apud S. Damase.] The story of how the hermit Barlaam had surreptitiously converted the Indian prince Josaphat to Christianity was often included in the works of St. John Damascene but seems to be a legend from some other source.

[8] St. Eusebius, Bishop of Samosata, d. 379 or 380, resisted the Arian policies of both the Emperor Constantius and the Emperor Valens. The trips in military disguise to which Allen refers seem to have taken place mostly in the reign of Valens.

be simple as the dove but wise as the serpent,[9] specially among wolves, that is heretics, which are of all creatures most cruel and subtle.

But to return to our purpose and to the libeler's proffer of mitigation or ceasing this persecution upon condition we would deal no more in secret, but openly. We protest before God and all His saints that we will, upon any reasonable security of our persons, liberty of conscience, permission to exercise Christian Catholic offices to the salvation of our own souls and our brethren, do the same things publicly which we now do secretly, in all peaceable and priestly sort as hitherto we have accustomed; and that so those things which now you suspect to be done against the state (for that they be done in covert) may plainly appear unto you nothing else indeed but mere matter of conscience and religion, as in verity they are.

Therefore, if such as govern our state under Her Majesty at this day cannot be induced to revoke themselves and the whole realm (which were absolutely the best) to the former Catholic state and condition wherein their ancestors left it and themselves found it, in respect perhaps of some little check or dishonor which they may conceive would ensue by acknowledging their former error, though in sincere truth it must needs prove finally more dishonorable and dangerous to persevere; yet at the least, let their wisdoms consider that their principal worldly error was that in the beginning, or long since, they gave not liberty of conscience to Catholics (being far the greater and more respective part of the realm) as other of their religion and profession have done, to their own great advantage, in Germany and other provinces adjoining. Which error, no doubt, might yet in great part or wholly be redressed if they would but now at length have some pity of their people; the greater part whereof languisheth away in body and soul most lamentably, only upon an obstinate punto[10] and formality (as is thought) of some few particular ad-

[9] [Matt. 10]:16; [Luke 10]:3.

[10] Small point, detail.

versaries, who will not seem to yield in any one jot or circumstance, though never so much commodity might ensue thereof.

Which matter of liberty of conscience we move not perchance for our own benefit so much as for our adversaries' weal and worldly security, whereof they will seem to have both mistrust and solicitude. And perhaps the wisdom of God will sound otherwise and say to us, *Nescitis quid petatis,*[11] judging it to be far more to His honor and glory, and the briefer way to salvation of our whole nation and of more souls in particular, that we should pass through this persecution and win our own and our brethren's salvation by our blood. And indeed if the German Catholics had been so restrained, persecuted, and put to death as the English have been these years, and had not gone by halves with the Protestants as in some places they have done, they had had, perhaps, far more Catholics at this day and them more zealous, and their whole nation, perchance, reduced ere this; which now, for the Protestants, standeth not so much on their religion or conscience in heresy as upon their mutual peace, concord, and concurrence with Catholics.

Well, what were best for us in this case God only knoweth. *Nos humanum dicimus propter infirmitatem nostram,* as the Apostle speaketh.[12] But sure we are that the first best for our English nation, as well prince as people, were both in respect of God and the world, of themselves and other men, to restore the state again to the obedience of God's Church and to the happy fellowship of all their forefathers and other faithful people and princes now living. The next best were, in respect of their own security and perpetuity (if the first may not take place), to desist from persecuting their Catholic subjects and brethren and to grant some liberty for exercise of their consciences, divine offices, and holy devotions; that so they may pray for Her Majesty and counselors

[11] [Matt. 20:22]: "Ye know not what ye ask."

[12] [Rom. 6:19]: "I speak after the manner of men because of the infirmity of your flesh."

as their patrons, whom now they pray for only as their persecutors.

If to none of these conditions they can be brought, but will have our bodies, goods, life, and souls; then let Our Lord God, the just arbiter of all things and judge of princes as well as poor men, and the only comforter of the afflicted, discern our cause. In Whose holy name, word, and promise, we confidently tell them, and humbly even in Christ's blood pray them, to consider of it, that by no human force or wisdom they shall ever extinguish the Catholic party, overcome the Holy Church, or prevail against God. There can no Herod kill Christ in His cradle; [13] nor any Pharaoh drown our male sex and destroy God's people; [14] nor any Haman extirpate the stock of Jacob.[15] Let them seek with all desperation to diminish, bridle, spoil, impoverish, disgrace, and extinguish the whole generation of Catholics at home and in banishment. Let them by artificial libels (as this against which we have written), and otherwise by most impudent lies and fictions slander us, charge us with treasons and other trespasses, *Mentientes, propter Christum,*[16] belying us for Christ's sake. Let them confederate themselves against us with all the Protestants, Turks, sectaries, and atheists in the world. Yet the Catholics (that is, the seed of God) will increase in number, power, and zeal; the priests will not leave off to follow their dutiful trade with more spirit, diligence, devotion, patience, and constancy than ever before; remembering the advertisement of their Master that he shall be saved that persevereth to the end; [17] as also that worthy record left in Scripture of Isaiah the great and faithful prophet: *qui spiritu magno vidit ultima,*[18] as the Holy Ghost saith of him, for that his courage never failed him in God's service to the end. The

[13] [Matt.]2:13–16. [14] [Exod. 1]:22. [15] [Esther 7.]

[16] Paraphrase of Matt. 5:11: *Mentientes, propter me;* "falsely, for my sake."

[17] [Matt. 10:22.]

[18] [Ecclus. 48]:24: "He saw by an excellent spirit what should come to pass at the last."

persecutors be now no stronger than they were of old. The Church is no weaker than she had wont to be. Her assistant and defender is as near her as ever He was. We are no better than our forefathers. We less fear death and less set by our lives than ever before. Our counts are cast and allowed. It is better to die in this apostolical fight and combat *quam videre mala gentis nostrae et sanctorum;*[19] assuring ourselves that to be undoubted which St. Leo writeth, *Nullo crudelitatis genere destrui potest Sacramento Crucis fundata religio. Non minuitur persecutionibus Ecclesia, sed augetur,* that "the religion founded in the sacrament of Christ's Cross can be destroyed by no kind of cruelty. The Church is not diminished by persecutions but increased." And that St. Augustine saith: *Nemo delet de coelo constitutionem Dei; Nemo delet de terra Ecclesiam Dei.*[20]

Laus Deo

[19] [I Macc. 3:59]: "than to behold the calamities of our people and our sanctuary."

[20] "No one destroys in heaven the order of God; no one destroys on earth the Church of God."

BIBLIOGRAPHY AND INDEXES

SELECT BIBLIOGRAPHY

Common Abbreviations:

CSP *Calendar of State Papers . . . preserved in the Public Record Office* [*Great Britain*].

Migne Migne, J. P., ed., *Patrologiae cursus completus . . . series graeca.* 167 vols. Paris: 1886–1912. *series latina.* 221 vols. Paris: 1879–1890.

STC Pollard, A. W., and Redgrave, G. R. *A Short-Title Catalogue of Books Printed in England, Scotland, & Ireland, and of English Books Printed Abroad, 1475–1640.* London: 1926.

Sixteenth-century Books:

[Allen, William.] *An Apology and True Declaration of the Institution and Endeavors of the Two English Colleges.* 1581. STC 369.

———. *A True, Sincere, and Modest Defense of English Catholics.* [1584.] STC 373.

Bilson, Thomas. *The True Difference between Christian Subjection and Unchristian Rebellion.* [1585.] STC 3071.2.

[Cecil, William.] *The Execution of Justice in England.* London: 1583. STC 4902.

———. *The Execution of Justice in England.* London: January, 1583 (O.S.). STC 4903.

———. *Justitia Britannica.* London: 1584. STC 4904.

Martin, Gregory. *A Discovery of the Manifold Corruptions of the Holy Scriptures by the Heretics of Our Days.* Reims: 1582. STC 17503.

[Parsons, Robert.] *A Christian Directory Guiding Men to Their Salvation.* 1585. STC 19362.

———. *A Defense of the Censure Given upon Two Books . . . against M. Edmund Campion.* 1582. STC 19401.

Bibliography

Editions of Sources:

[Allen, William.] *The Letters and Memorials of William Cardinal Allen (1532–1594)*. Ed. by Fathers of the Congregation of the London Oratory, with intro. by T. F. Knox. London: 1882.

Arber, Edward, ed. *A Transcript of the Registers of the Company of Stationers of London, 1554–1640 A.D.* 5 vols. London and Birmingham: 1875–1894.

Bullarum, diplomatum, et privilegiorum sanctorum romanorum pontificum. Ed. by Francisco Gaude *et al.* 24 vols. Turin: 1857–1872.

Calendar of State Papers . . . preserved in the Public Record Office [*Great Britain*].

Cobbett's Complete Collection of State Trials and Proceedings for High Treason and Other Crimes and Misdemeanors, from the Earliest Period to the Present Time. Vol. I, 1163–1600. London: 1809.

Gee, Henry, and Hardy, William John, eds. *Documents Illustrative of English Church History.* London: 1896.

Migne, J. P., ed. *Patrologiae cursus completus . . . series graeca.* 167 vols. Paris: 1886–1912.

———. *Patrologiae cursus completus . . . series latina.* 221 vols. Paris: 1879–1890.

[Parsons, Robert.] *Letters and Memorials of Father Robert Persons, S.J.* Vol. I (to 1588). "Publications of the Catholic Record Society," Vol. XXXIX. Ed. by L. Hicks. London: 1942.

Pollen, John Hungerford, ed. *Unpublished Documents Relating to the English Martyrs.* Vol. I (1584–1603). "Publications of the Catholic Record Society," Vol. V. London: 1908.

The Prayer-Book of Queen Elizabeth, 1559; to Which Are Appended Some Occasional Forms of Prayers Issued in Her Reign. With intro. by Edward Benham. Edinburgh: 1909.

[Ragazzoni, Girolamo.] *Girolamo Ragazzoni, évêque de Bergame, nonce en France: Correspondance de sa Nonciature, 1583–1586. "Acta Nuntiaturae Gallicae,"* Vol. II. Ed. by Pierre Blet. Rome and Paris: 1962.

The Statutes of the Realm. 9 vols. in 10, plus index vols. London: 1810–1824.

Strype, John. *Annals of the Reformation and Establishment of Religion, and Other Various Occurrences in the Church of England, during Queen Elizabeth's Happy Reign.* 4 vols. in 7. Oxford: 1824.

Secondary Studies and Reference Works:

Allison, A. F., and Rogers, D. M. "A Catalogue of Catholic Books in English Printed Abroad or Secretly in England, 1558–1640," in *Biographical Studies* (now *Recusant History*), Vol. III, Nos. 3 and 4. Bognor Regis: 1956.

Bayne, C. G. *Anglo-Roman Relations, 1558–1565.* "Oxford Historical and Literary Studies," Vol. II. Oxford: 1913.

Brodrick, James. *The Life and Work of Blessed Robert Francis Cardinal Bellarmine, S.J., 1542–1621.* 2 vols. London: 1928.

Challoner, Richard. *Memoirs of Missionary Priests . . . 1577 to 1684.* Ed. by John Hungerford Pollen. New York: 1924.

Clancy, Thomas H. *Papist Pamphleteers: The Allen-Persons Party and the Political Thought of the Counter-Reformation in England, 1572–1615.* "Jesuit Studies." Chicago: 1964.

Froude, James Anthony. *History of England from the Fall of Wolsey to the Defeat of the Spanish Armada.* 12 vols. London: 1856–1870.

Gillow, Joseph. *A Literary and Biographical History, or Bibliographical Dictionary of the English Catholics.* 5 vols. London and New York: 1885–[1902].

Guilday, Peter. *The English Catholic Refugees on the Continent, 1558–1795.* Vol. I, *The English Colleges and Convents in the Catholic Low Countries, 1558–1795.* London: 1914.

Haile, Martin. *An Elizabethan Cardinal: William Allen.* London: 1914.

Hughes, Philip. *The Reformation in England.* Vol. III. London: 1954.

Kretzschmar, Johannes. *Die Invasionsprojekte der Katholischen Mächte gegen England zur Zeit Elisabeths.* Leipzig: 1892.

Loomie, Albert J. *The Spanish Elizabethans: The English Exiles at the Court of Philip II.* New York: 1963.

Mattingly, Garrett. *The Armada.* Boston: 1959.

———. "William Allen and Catholic Propaganda in England," in *Aspects de la propagande religieuse. "Travaux d'Humanisme et Renaissance,"* Vol. XXVIII. Ed. by E. Droz. Geneva: 1957. Pp. 325–339.

Meyer, Arnold Oskar. *England and the Catholic Church under Queen Elizabeth.* London: 1916.

Muller, James Arthur. *Stephen Gardiner and the Tudor Reaction.* London: 1926.

Neale, J. E. *Elizabeth I and Her Parliaments, 1559–1581.* London: 1953.

———. *Elizabeth I and Her Parliaments, 1584–1601.* London: 1957.

Pastor, Ludwig von. *Geschichte der Päpste seit dem Ausgang des Mittelalters.* 12th ed. 16 vols. in 22. Freiburg and Rome: 1955–1961. There is also a complete English translation of an earlier edition.

Pollard, A. W., and Redgrave, G. R. *A Short-Title Catalogue of Books Printed in England, Scotland, & Ireland, and of English Books Printed Abroad, 1475–1640.* London: 1926.

Pollen, John Hungerford. *The English Catholics in the Reign of Queen Elizabeth . . . 1558–1580.* London: 1920.

Read, Conyers. *Lord Burghley and Queen Elizabeth.* London: 1960.

———. *Mr. Secretary Walsingham and the Policy of Queen Elizabeth.* 3 vols. Oxford: 1925.

———. "William Cecil and Elizabethan Public Relations," in *Elizabethan Government and Society: Essays Presented to Sir John Neale.* Ed. by S. T. Bindoff, J. Hurstfield, C. H. Williams. London: 1961. Pp. 21–55.

Simpson, Richard. *Edmund Campion; a Biography.* London and Edinburgh: 1867.

Southern, A. C. *Elizabethan Recusant Prose, 1559–1582.* London and Glasgow: [1950].

Tierney, M. A., ed. *Dodd's Church History of England.* 3 vols. London: 1839–1840.

Törne, P. O. de. *Don Juan d'Autriche et les projets de conquête de l'Angleterre, 1568–1578.* Vol. II. Åbo: 1928.

———. *Ptolémée Gallio, Cardinal de Côme.* Helsingfors: 1907.

Trimble, William Raleigh. *The Catholic Laity in Elizabethan England, 1558–1603.* Cambridge, Mass.: 1964.

Veech, Thomas McNevin. *Dr. Nicholas Sanders and the English Reformation, 1530–1581.* Louvain: 1935.

GENERAL INDEX

General Index

General Index

General Index

INDEX OF BIBLICAL REFERENCES

Index of Biblical References

ROBERT M. KINGDON, an authority on the Reformation period, has been Professor of History at the State University of Iowa and is currently a Fellow of the Institute for Advanced Study at Princeton University.